CHRISTOPHER MARLOWE'S
DOCTOR FAUSTUS
Text and Major Criticism

Christopher Marlowe's
DOCTOR FAUSTUS

Text and Major Criticism

Edited by

IRVING RIBNER

THE ODYSSEY PRESS
Bobbs-Merrill Educational Publishing
Indianapolis

Copyright © 1966 by The Bobbs-Merrill Company, Inc.

Printed in the United States of America
All rights reserved. No part of this book shall be reproduced or transmitted
in any form or by any means, electronic or mechanical, including photo-
copying, recording, or by any information or retrieval system, without
written permission from the Publisher:

The Bobbs-Merrill Company, Inc.
4300 West 62nd Street
Indianapolis, Indiana 46268

First Edition
Tenth Printing—1983

Library of Congress Catalog Card Number 65-26778
ISBN   0-672-63058-3

ACKNOWLEDGMENTS

BARNES & NOBLE, INC. For pp. 147–54 of *English Tragedy Before Shakespeare* by
Wolfgang Clemen, 1961. Reprinted by permission of the publisher.

THE CLARENDON PRESS. For "Marlowe's Faustus: A Reconsideration" by Leo Kirschbaum, from *Review of English Studies*, XIX (1943), 225–41. Reprinted by permission of The Clarendon Press, Oxford.

THE CRITICAL QUARTERLY SOCIETY. For "Magic and Poetry in 'Doctor Faustus' " by
D. J. Palmer, from *Critical Quarterly*, VI (1964), 56–67. Repinted by permission of
the author and the publisher.

HARVARD UNIVERSITY PRESS. For "Science Without Conscience," from Harry Levin's
The Overreacher, Cambridge, Mass.: Harvard University Press, copyright 1952, by
the President and Fellows of Harvard College. Reprinted by permission of the
author and the publisher.

THE JOHNS HOPKINS PRESS. For "The Comic Synthesis in 'Doctor Faustus' " by Robert
Ornstein, from *ELH*, XXII (1955), 165–72. Reprinted by permission of the author
and the publisher.

JONATHAN CAPE, LTD. For pp. 64–74 of "Marlowe's Heroes," from *Poetry and
Humanism* by M. M. Mahood, 1950. Reprinted by permission of the publisher.

METHUEN & COMPANY, LTD. For pp. 61–87 of *Christopher Marlowe* by Una M. Ellis-
Fermor, 1927; and pp. 147–154 of *English Tragedy Before Shakespeare* by Wolfgang
Clemen, 1961. Reprinted by permission of the publisher.

TULANE DRAMA REVIEW. For "The Form of Faustus' Fortunes Good or Bad" by C. L.
Barber, first printed in the *Tulane Drama Review*, VIII, No. 4 (Summer 1964),
copyright © 1964. Reprinted by permission of the author and the publisher.

YALE UNIVERSITY PRESS. For pp. 57–67 and 159–60 of *The Vision of Tragedy* by Richard Benson Sewall. Reprinted by permission of the author and the publisher.

Contents

Preface

While it is generally agreed that *Doctor Faustus* is both the greatest achievement of Christopher Marlowe (1564–1593) and the finest example of English tragedy up to its time, there is little else that may be said about this play with equal certainty. We are not sure of just when it was written, of when it was staged, of how much of the two versions which have come down to us is really from the pen of Marlowe, or of what the precise relation of these two versions to one another may be. Nor has there been much agreement as to what the play means, for different critics, all of perception and intelligence, have viewed it in ways so diametrically opposed that it has been difficult at times to believe that all were writing about the same play. *Faustus* has been viewed as an agnostic protest against the limitations imposed by Christianity upon the normal aspirations of the human spirit, with Marlowe the apostle of an aspiring Renaissance humanism, as a pious moral exposition of the human potential for damnation in conventional Christian terms, and as a play whose moral ambiguity defies analysis.

Although controversies about all of these matters continue to rage in the pages of the learned journals, considerable progress has, in fact, been made in recent years. The present volume is designed to offer the modern student a text which in the consensus of recent scholarship is as close a proximation to what Marlowe actually wrote as we are capable of attaining, and to provide a representative sampling of the more important critical approaches to the play. New critical analyses, of course, continue every day to appear, and the essays here included can provide only a small indication of the wealth of commentary that is available, and which is listed in detail in the bibliography. These essays have been chosen because each, in the editor's judgment, is among the best examples of a specific method of approach which has been historically important. They cover a wide range, from Una M. Ellis-Fermor's celebration of the free-thinking but despairing Marlowe, through Leo Kirschbaum's view of a Marlowe capable of reflecting an orthodox Christian vision of human damnation from which we need draw no conclusions about his own belief or lack of it. Here also are the Marlowes of Mahood and Levin, each an expression of a different concept of Renaissance humanism, and here is the uncommitted Marlowe of Richard B. Sewall and C. L. Barber capable of holding contrary moral positions in a tragic tension, as well as the skillful manipulator of dramatic illusion which is D. J. Palmer's conception of the artist. Many of these essays have already established themselves as classics of interpretation.

While the date of *Doctor Faustus* has long been and still continues to be debated, more and more scholars are coming to the conclusion that the play must have been written at the very end of Marlowe's career, in 1592 or shortly before his death early in 1593. Part of the argument for this late date rests upon the assumption that Marlowe relied for his source upon an English book which was not printed until 1592. This book was *The Historie of the damnable life, and deserued death of Doctor Iohn Faustus,* translated by an unidentified "P. F. Gent." from the German *Historia von D. Johan Fausten,* or "Faustbuch" first published at Frankfurt-am-Main in 1589, although it records a legend which goes back to the early Middle Ages. Students may find Marlowe's English source reprinted in *The Sources of the Faust Tradition from Simon Magus to Lessing* (New York, Oxford University Press, 1936), by Philip Mason Palmer and Robert Pattison More. This volume contains also a comprehensive account of the historical and legendary origins of the Faust story.

Most commentators are today agreed that Marlowe had a collaborator of some kind in *Faustus,* but the precise nature of this collaboration has been difficult to determine, and the problem is further complicated by the play's textual history, discussed more fully in the Textual Notes (pp. 59–62). Philip Henslowe in his *Diary* recorded a payment on November 2, 1602, of four pounds to William Birde and Samuel Rowley for "their adicyones in doctor Fostes." It used to be assumed that these additions are preserved in the B-Text of 1616, and that therefore the A-Text of 1604, which is considerably shorter, must represent Marlowe's own play without the additions. Most early editors accordingly based their texts upon the 1604 quarto. Thanks to the labors of F. S. Boas, Leo Kirschbaum, W. W. Greg and others, however, we are now fairly certain that the "additions" for which Birde and Rowley were paid are already preserved in the 1604 text, which is in fact a debased version of the text printed in 1616. The present text accordingly is based upon the B-text as preserved in the quarto of 1616.

We must not think, however, that the textual problems in Marlowe's *Faustus* have all been resolved, for controversy continues. C. L. Barber, for instance, has based his important essay on the A-text of the play, as his footnote explains, because in spite of Greg and the others, he is convinced that it represents a superior text of the play, and M. M. Mahood appears to endorse a similar point of view. Whether they be right or wrong in this fortunately has little effect upon the value of their essays. The essay by Una M. Ellis-Fermor was written at a time when almost all scholars accepted the authenticity of the A-text, and it is here reprinted as written. The essays by Levin and Ornstein when first written used the A-text for citation but, with the consent of the authors, B-text readings have been substituted in the present edition. All of the other essays in this volume use the B-text for quotation, and all reference numbers in brackets indicate line numbers of the present edition.

The comic prose scenes of the play usually have been attributed to Marlowe's collaborator, who is generally considered to have been Samuel Rowley. This may well be so, but it is important to remember that whether Marlowe wrote the comic prose scenes or not, they follow the source closely and as Robert Ornstein has well argued, they are an integral part of the total design of the play and thus cannot be ignored in any estimate of Marlowe's achievement.

The text of *Doctor Faustus* and the Textual Notes are reprinted from *The Complete Plays of Christopher Marlowe*, published by the Odyssey Press in 1963.

IRVING RIBNER

The Tragicall History of the Life and Death

of *Doctor Faustus*.

Written by *Ch. Marklin*.

LONDON,
Printed for *Iohn Wright*, and are to be sold at his shop
without Newgate, at the s: .... the
Bib' 1616.

THE TRAGICAL HISTORY OF THE LIFE AND DEATH OF DOCTOR FAUSTUS

THE PLAYERS

The Chorus
Doctor Faustus
Wagner, his student
   and servant
Valdes
Cornelius
Three Scholars
An Old Man.

Pope Adrian
Raymond, King of
   Hungary
Bruno, the rival Pope
Two Cardinals
The Archbishop of Rheims
Charles V, Emperor of Germany
Martino ⎫
Frederick ⎬ Gentlemen of the
Benvolio ⎭ Emperor's court
Beëlzebub
Duke of Saxony
Duke of Anholt
Duchess of Anholt

Robin, the clown, an hostler
Dick
A Vintner
A Horse-Courser
A Carter
Hostess

Good Angel
Bad Angel
Lucifer
Mephistophilis
Pride ⎫
Covetousness ⎪
Envy ⎪
Wrath ⎬ The Seven
Gluttony ⎪ Deadly Sins
Sloth ⎪
Lechery ⎭
Alexander, the Great
His Paramour
Darius, King of Persia
Helen of Troy
Two Cupids
Devils, Bishops, Monks,
Friars, Soldiers

THE SCENE

Wittenberg, Rome, The Emperor's court at Innsbruck, court
of the Duke of Anholt, and the neighboring countryside.

Enter Chorus.   Prologue.

Chorus.   Not marching in the fields of Trasimene
   Where Mars did mate the warlike Carthagens,
   Nor sporting in the dalliance of love
   In courts of kings where state is overturned,

Prologue.

   1–2 *Trasimene . . . Carthagens* (modern spelling—Carthaginians) This may
be an allusion to a lost play on the subject of the Carthaginian, Hannibal, who

achieved one of his greatest victories at
Lake Trasimene in 217 B.C. *mate* rival
(in military prowess).
   4 *state* government.

3

Nor in the pomp of proud audacious deeds   5
Intends our muse to vaunt his heavenly verse.
Only this, gentles: we must now perform
The form of Faustus' fortunes, good or bad.
And now to patient judgments we appeal,
And speak for Faustus in his infancy.   10
Now is he born, of parents base of stock,
In Germany, within a town called Rhode.
At riper years to Wittenberg he went,
Whereas his kinsmen chiefly brought him up.
So much he profits in divinity,   15
The fruitful plot of scholarism graced,
That shortly he was graced with doctor's name,
Excelling all whose sweet delight disputes
In th'heavenly matters of theology,
Till swoll'n with cunning of a self-conceit,   20
His waxen wings did mount above his reach,
And melting, heavens conspired his overthrow;
For, falling to a devilish exercise
And glutted now with learning's golden gifts,
He surfeits upon cursèd necromancy.   25
Nothing so sweet as magic is to him,
Which he prefers before his chiefest bliss;
And this the man that in his study sits.

                                                           I,i.

Faustus in his study.
Faustus.   Settle thy studies, Faustus, and begin
To sound the depth of that thou wilt profess.
Having commenced, be a divine in show;
Yet level at the end of every art,
And live and die in Aristotle's works.   5
Sweet Analytics, 'tis thou hast ravished me!
Bene disserere est finis logices.
Is to dispute well logic's chiefest end?

12 *Rhode* or Roda, a town in the
Duchy of Saxe-Altenburg, Germany.
   16. *fruitful plot . . . graced* i.e., he
adorned the university.
   18 *whose . . . disputes* whose sweet
delight it was to dispute.
   21 *waxen wings* See note to *Dido,* V,
i,243.

I,i.
   SD *Faustus . . . study* The chorus-
speaker probably draws the curtains of
the inner stage to reveal Faustus in his
study at Wittenberg.
   3 *commenced* taken a degree.
   4 *level* aim.
   7 *Bene . . . logices* The end of logic
is to dispute well. This notion is part
of the anti-Aristotelian system of Petrus
Ramus, introduced at Cambridge while
Marlowe was a student there. See note
to *Massacre at Paris,* viii, SD.

Affords this art no greater miracle?
Then read no more; thou hast attained that end.   10
A greater subject fitteth Faustus' wit!
Bid *On cay mae on* farewell; Galen come.
Seeing *ubi desinit philosophus ibi incipit medicus,*
Be a physician, Faustus; heap up gold,
And be eternized for some wondrous cure.   15
Summum bonum medicinae sanitas.
The end of physic is our body's health.
Why, Faustus, hast thou not attained that end?
Is not thy common talk sound aphorisms?
Are not thy bills hung up as monuments,   20
Whereby whole cities have escaped the plague,
And divers desperate maladies been cured?
Yet art thou still but Faustus and a man.
Couldst thou make men to live eternally,
Or, being dead, raise them to life again,   25
Then this profession were to be esteemed.
Physic, farewell! Where is Justinian?
Si una eademque res legatus duobus,   [*He reads.*]
Alter rem, alter valorem rei, etc.
A petty case of paltry legacies!   30
Exhæreditare filium non potest pater nisi—   [*He reads.*]
Such is the subject of the Institute
And universal body of the law.
This study fits a mercenary drudge
Who aims at nothing but external trash,   35
Too servile and illiberal for me.
When all is done, divinity is best.
Jeromè's Bible, Faustus, view it well:
Stipendium peccati mors est. Ha! *Stipendium, etc.* [*He reads.*]
The reward of sin is death. That's hard.   40
Si peccasse negamus, fallimur   [*He reads.*]
Et nulla est in nobis veritas.
If we say that we have no sin,
We deceive ourselves, and there's no truth in us.
Why then belike we must sin,   45

12 *On cay mae on* Aristotle's being or
not being (as Bullen seems to be the
first to have perceived). *Galen* a Greek
physician regarded throughout the Middle
Ages as a medical authority.

13 *ubi . . . medicus* Where the philosopher stops the doctor begins.

20 *bills* medical prescriptions.

27 *Justinian* Roman emperor of Constantinople (527–565) responsible for as-
sembling the Roman law; he was famous
throughout the Middle Ages as a jurist.

28–29 *Si . . . rei, etc.* If the same object is willed to two persons, let one have
the thing itself and the other its value,
etc. This is an incorrect version of one of
the rules in Justinian's *Institutes.*

31 *Exhæreditare . . . nisi* The father
cannot disinherit the son except (another
of Justinian's rules, roughly paraphrased).

38 *Jeromè's Bible* the Vulgate, translated by St. Jerome.

39 *Stipendium . . . est* Romans, VI,23.

41–42 *Si . . . veritas* St. John, I,8.

And so consequently die.
Ay, we must die an everlasting death.
What doctrine call you this? *Che serà, serà:*
What will be, shall be! Divinity, adieu!
These metaphysics of magicians   50
And necromantic books are heavenly.
Lines, circles, signs, letters, and characters—
Ay, these are those that Faustus most desires.
O, what a world of profit and delight,
Of power, of honor, of omnipotence   55
Is promised to the studious artisan!
All things that move between the quiet poles
Shall be at my command. Emperors and kings
Are but obeyed in their several provinces,
Nor can they raise the wind or rend the clouds,   60
But his dominion that exceeds in this
Stretcheth as far as doth the mind of man.
A sound magician is a demi-god.
Here try thy brains to get a deity!
Wagner!

Enter Wagner.

       Commend me to my dearest friends,   65
The German Valdes and Cornelius;
Request them earnestly to visit me.
Wagner. I will sir.

                                                Exit.

Faustus. Their conference will be a greater help to me
    Than all my labors, plod I ne'er so fast.   70
        Enter the Good Angel and the Evil Angel.
Good Angel. O, Faustus, lay that damnèd book aside,
    And gaze not on it, lest it tempt thy soul
    And heap God's heavy wrath upon thy head.
    Read, read the Scriptures. That is blasphemy.
Bad Angel. Go forward, Faustus, in that famous art   75
    Wherein all nature's treasury is contained.
    Be thou on earth as Jove is in the sky,
    Lord and commander of these elements.
                        Exeunt Angels.

Faustus. How am I glutted with conceit of this!
    Shall I make spirits fetch me what I please,   80
    Resolve me of all ambiguities,
    Perform what desperate enterprise I will?
    I'll have them fly to India for gold,
    Ransack the ocean for orient pearl,
    And search all corners of the new-found world   85
    For pleasant fruits and princely delicates.

79 *conceit* the conception of attaining.   81 *Resolve me of* explain to me.

I'll have them read me strange philosophy
And tell the secrets of all foreign kings;
I'll have them wall all Germany with brass
And make swift Rhine circle fair Wittenberg.   90
I'll have them fill the public schools with silk
Wherewith the students shall be bravely clad.
I'll levy soldiers with the coin they bring
And chase the Prince of Parma from our land
And reign sole king of all the provinces.   95
Yea, stranger engines for the brunt of war
Than was the fiery keel at Antwerp's bridge
I'll make my servile spirits to invent.
Come, German Valdes and Cornelius,   [*He calls within.*]
And make me blessed with your sage conference!   100
              Enter Valdes and Cornelius.
Valdes, sweet Valdes, and Cornelius,
Know that your words have won me at the last
To practice magic and concealèd arts;
Yet not your words only, but mine own fantasy
That will receive no object, for my head   105
But ruminates on necromantic skill.
Philosophy is odious and obscure;
Both law and physic are for petty wits;
Divinity is basest of the three,
Unpleasant, harsh, contemptible and vile.   110
'Tis magic, magic, that hath ravished me.
Then, gentle friends, aid me in this attempt,
And I, that have with subtle syllogisms
Gravelled the pastors of the German church,
And made the flowering pride of Wittenberg   115
Swarm to my problems as th'infernal spirits
On sweet Musæus when he came to hell,
Will be as cunning as Agrippa was,
Whose shadows made all Europe honor him.
Valdes.   Faustus, these books, thy wit, and our experience 120
Shall make all nations to canonize us.

90 *Rhine . . . Wittenberg* Wittenberg
is actually on the Elbe river, not the
Rhine.
94 *Prince of Parma* See note to *Massacre at Paris*, xx,83.
95 *provinces* i.e., of the Netherlands.
97 *fiery . . . bridge* In April, 1584, the
Dutch used a fire-ship to destroy a bridge
built across the Scheldt river by the
Prince of Parma in an attempt to block-
ade Antwerp.
114 *Gravelled* puzzled and amazed.
116 *problems* public disputations.

117 *Musæus* a semi-mythical Greek
poet whose name appears on a Greek
poem about the love of Hero and
Leander, but which actually was written
after his time. Marlowe, following Virgil,
has him visit hell like the mythical
Orpheus.
118-119 *Agrippa . . . shadows* Cornelius Agrippa (1486?-1535) a German physician and student of the occult, was
said to have had power to raise spirits
(shadows) from the dead.

As Indian Moors obey their Spanish lords,
So shall the spirits of every element
Be always serviceable to us three.
Like lions shall they guard us when we please,   125
Like Almain rutters with their horsemen's staves
Or Lapland giants trotting by our sides,
Sometimes like women or unwedded maids,
Shadowing more beauty in their airy brows
Than in the white breasts of the queen of love.   130
From Venice shall they drag huge argosies,
And from America the golden fleece
That yearly stuffs old Philip's treasury,
If learnèd Faustus will be resolute.
Faustus.   Valdes, as resolute am I in this   135
As thou to live; therefore object it not.
Cornelius.   The miracles that magic will perform
Will make thee vow to study nothing else.
He that is grounded in astrology,
Enriched with tongues, well seen in minerals,   140
Hath all the principles magic doth require.
Then doubt not, Faustus, but to be renowned
And more frequented for this mystery
Than heretofore the Delphian oracle.
The spirits tell me they can dry the sea   145
And fetch the treasure of all foreign wracks,
Yea, all the wealth that our forefathers hid
Within the massy entrails of the earth.
Then tell me, Faustus, what shall we three want?
Faustus.   Nothing, Cornelius. O, this cheers my soul!   150
Come, show me some demonstrations magical,
That I may conjure in some lusty grove
And have these joys in full possession.
Valdes.   Then haste thee to some solitary grove,
And bear wise Bacon's and Abanus' works,   155
The Hebrew Psalter, and New Testament;
And whatsoever else is requisite
We will inform thee ere our conference cease.
Cornelius.   Valdes, first let him know the words of art,
And then, all other ceremonies learned,   160
Faustus may try his cunning by himself.
Valdes.   First I'll instruct thee in the rudiments,

122 *Indian Moors* American Indians.
126 *Almain rutters* German cavalrymen.
129 *Shadowing* harboring, sheltering.
140 *Enriched . . . tongues* learned in Latin (the language traditionally used for communicating with spirits).
144 *Delphian oracle* the high priest to Apollo at Delphos who had power to foretell the future.
155 *Bacon's . . . works* Roger Bacon (1214?–1294) and Pietro D'Abano (1250–1316) were famous in the Middle Ages for their feats of magic.

And then wilt thou be perfecter than I.
Faustus.　Then come and dine with me, and after meat
　We'll canvass every quiddity thereof,　　　　　165
　For ere I sleep I'll try what I can do.
　This night I'll conjure, though I die therefore.

　　　　　　　　　　　　　　　　　Exeunt.

　　　　　　　Enter two Scholars.　　　　　I,ii.
First Scholar.　I wonder what's become of Faustus, that was wont to
　make our schools ring with *sic probo.*
　　　　　　　　Enter Wagner.
Second Scholar.　That shall we presently know; here comes his boy.
First Scholar.　How now sirrah! Where's thy master?
Wagner.　God in heaven knows.　　　　　5
Second Scholar.　Why, dost not thou know then?
Wagner.　Yes, I know, but that follows not.
First Scholar.　Go to, sirrah! Leave your jesting and tell us where he is.
Wagner.　That follows not by force of argument, which you, being
　licentiates, should stand upon; therefore acknowledge your error　[10
　and be attentive.
Second Scholar.　Then you will not tell us?
Wagner.　You are deceived, for I will tell you. Yet if you were not
　dunces, you would never ask me such a question. For is he not
　corpus naturale, and is not that *mobile?* Then wherefore should　[15
　you ask me such a question? But that I am by nature phlegmatic, slow
　to wrath, and prone to lechery—to love, I would say—it were not
　for you to come within forty foot of the place of execution, although
　I do not doubt but to see you both hanged the next sessions. Thus
　having triumphed over you, I will set my countenance like a　[20
　precisian and begin to speak thus: Truly, my dear brethren, my mas-
　ter is within at dinner with Valdes and Cornelius, as this wine, if it
　could speak, would inform your worships. And so, the Lord bless you,
　preserve you, and keep you, my dear brethren.

　　　　　　　　　　　　　　　　　Exit.
First Scholar.　O Faustus, then I fear that which I have long sus-
　　pected.　　　　　25
　That thou art fall'n into that damnèd art
　For which they two are infamous through the world.
Second Scholar.　Were he a stranger, not allied to me,

---

165 *quiddity* essential element (a term from scholastic logic).

I,ii.

2 *sic probo* thus I prove (a form used in scholastic argument).

15 *corpus naturale* The subject matter of physics, in scholastic terms, was *Corpus naturale seu mobile.*
21 *precisian* puritan.

The danger of his soul would make me mourn.
But come, let us go and inform the rector.   30
It may be his grave counsel may reclaim him.
First Scholar.   I fear me nothing will reclaim him now.
Second Scholar.   Yet let us see what we can do.

                                                 Exeunt.

          Thunder. Enter [above] Lucifer and four Devils.   I,iii.
                 Enter Faustus to conjure.
Faustus.   Now that the gloomy shadow of the night,
     Longing to view Orion's drizzling look,
     Leaps from th'Antarctic world unto the sky
     And dims the welkin with her pitchy breath,
     Faustus begin thine incantations,   5
     And try if devils will obey thy hest,
     Seeing thou hast prayed and sacrificed to them.
     Within this circle is Jehovah's name,
     Forward and backward anagrammatized,
     Th'abbreviated names of holy saints,   10
     Figures of every adjunct to the heavens,
     And characters of signs and erring stars,
     By which the spirits are enforced to rise.
     Then fear not, Faustus, to be resolute,
     And try the utmost magic can perform.   *Thunder.*   15
Sint mihi Dei Acherontis propitii! Valeat numen triplex Jehovae.
Ignei, aerii, aquatani spiritus, salvete! Orientis princeps, Beëlzebub,
inferni ardentis monarcha, et Demogorgon, propitiamus vos, ut
appareat et surgat Mephistophilis. Quid tu moraris? Per Jehovam
Gehennam, et consecratam aquam quam nunc spargo, signum- [20
que crucis quod nunc facio, et per vota nostra, ipse nunc surgat
nobis dicatus Mephistophilis.
             Enter [Mephistophilis,] a Devil.
     I charge thee to return and change thy shape;

30 *rector* head of the university.

I,iii.

4 *welkin* world.
12 *erring* wandering.
16–22 *Sint . . . Mephistophilis*   May
the gods of Acheron be propitious to
me. Let the triple name of Jehova (the
trinity) be gone. Hail spirits of fire, air,
and water. Prince of the East, Beëlzebub,
monarch of burning hell, and Demogorgon, we petition you that Mephistophilis may appear and rise. Why do you

linger? By Jehova, Gehenna and the holy
water which I now sprinkle and the
sign of the cross which I now make and
by our vows, let Mephistophilis himself
now rise to serve us.

Boas has held that the word *Dragon*
(here omitted) which appears before
quod tumeraris in the 1616 text may be
the fragment of a stage direction, indicating that at this point a dragon appears in the air. The suggestion, followed
by Greg, is very plausible.

Thou art too ugly to attend on me.
Go, and return an old Franciscan friar;   25
That holy shape becomes a devil best.

                                                    Exit Devil.

I see there's virtue in my heavenly words.
Who would not be proficient in this art?
How pliant is this Mephistophilis,
Full of obedience and humility.   30
Such is the force of magic and my spells.
Now Faustus, thou art conjuror laureate,
That canst command great Mephistophilis.
Quin redis Mephistophilis fratris imagine.
        Enter Mephistophilis [dressed like a Franciscan friar].
Mephistophilis.   Now Faustus, what wouldst thou have me do?   35
Faustus.   I charge thee wait upon me whilst I live,
    To do whatever Faustus shall command,
    Be it to make the moon drop from her sphere
    Or the ocean to overwhelm the world.
Mephistophilis.   I am a servant to great Lucifer   40
    And may not follow thee without his leave.
    No more than he commands must we perform.
Faustus.   Did not he charge thee to appear to me?
Mephistophilis.   No, I came hither of mine own accord.
Faustus.   Did not my conjuring speeches raise thee? Speak.   45
Mephistophilis.   That was the cause, but yet *per accidens,*
    For when we hear one rack the name of God,
    Abjure the Scriptures and his Savior Christ,
    We fly in hope to get his glorious soul;
    Nor will we come unless he use such means   50
    Whereby he is in danger to be damned.
    Therefore the shortest cut for conjuring
    Is stoutly to abjure the Trinity
    And pray devoutly to the prince of hell.
Faustus.   So Faustus hath   55
    Already done, and holds this principle:
    There is no chief but only Beëlzebub,
    To whom Faustus doth dedicate himself.
    This word 'damnation' terrifies not me,
    For I confound hell in Elysium.   60
    My ghost be with the old philosophers!
    But leaving these vain trifles of men's souls,
    Tell me what is that Lucifer thy lord?
Mephistophilis.   Arch-regent and commander of all spirits.
Faustus.   Was not that Lucifer an angel once?   65

34 *Quin . . . imagine* Return, Meph-   46 *cause . . . per accidens* The terms
istophilis, in the shape of a friar.   are from scholastic logic.
                                          61 *ghost* spirit.

Mephistophilis.   Yes Faustus, and most dearly loved of God.
Faustus.   How comes it then that he is prince of devils?
Mephistophilis.   O, by aspiring pride and insolence,
  For which God threw him from the face of heaven.
Faustus.   And what are you that live with Lucifer? 70
Mephistophilis.   Unhappy spirits that fell with Lucifer,
  Conspired against our God with Lucifer,
  And are for ever damned with Lucifer.
Faustus.   Where are you damned?
Mephistophilis.   In hell.
Faustus.   How comes it then that thou art out of hell? 75
Mephistophilis.   Why this is hell, nor am I out of it.
  Think'st thou that I who saw the face of God
  And tasted the eternal joys of heaven
  Am not tormented with ten thousand hells
  In being deprived of everlasting bliss? 80
  O Faustus, leave these frivolous demands
  Which strike a terror to my fainting soul.
Faustus.   What, is great Mephistophilis so passionate
  For being deprivèd of the joys of heaven?
  Learn thou of Faustus manly fortitude, 85
  And scorn those joys thou never shalt possess.
  Go bear these tidings to great Lucifer:
  Seeing Faustus hath incurred eternal death
  By desperate thoughts against Jove's deity,
  Say he surrenders up to him his soul, 90
  So he will spare him four and twenty years,
  Letting him live in all voluptuousness,
  Having thee ever to attend on me,
  To give me whatsoever I shall ask,
  To tell me whatsoever I demand, 95
  To slay mine enemies, and aid my friends,
  And always be obedient to my will.
  Go, and return to mighty Lucifer,
  And meet me in my study at midnight,
  And then resolve me of thy master's mind. 100
Mephistophilis.   I will, Faustus.

                      Exit.

Faustus.   Had I as many souls as there be stars,
  I'd give them all for Mephistophilis.
  By him I'll be great emperor of the world,
  And make a bridge thorough the moving air, 105
  To pass the ocean with a band of men.
  I'll join the hills that bind the Afric shore,
  And make that country continent to Spain,
  And both contributory to my crown.

107 *bind* enclose.

The Emperor shall not live but by my leave, 110
Nor any potentate of Germany.
Now that I have obtained what I desire,
I'll live in speculation of this art
Till Mephistophilis return again.

Exit.

Enter Wagner and [Robin,] the Clown. I,iv.

Wagner. Come hither, sirrah boy.

Robin. Boy! O disgrace to my person. Zounds, boy in your face! You have seen many boys with such pickedevants, I am sure.

Wagner. Sirrah, hast thou no comings in?

Robin. Yes, and goings out too, you may see, sir. 5

Wagner. Alas, poor slave! See how poverty jests in his nakedness. I know the villain's out of service, and so hungry that I know he would give his soul to the devil for a shoulder of mutton, though it were blood-raw.

Robin. Not so neither. I had need to have it well roasted, and [10 good sauce to it, if I pay so dear, I can tell you.

Wagner. Sirrah, wilt thou be my man and wait on me, and I will make thee go like *Qui mihi discipulus?*

Robin. What, in verse?

Wagner. No slave; in beaten silk and staves-acre. 15

Robin. Staves-acre? That's good to kill vermin. Then, belike, if I serve you I shall be lousy.

Wagner. Why, so thou shalt be, whether thou dost it or no; for, sirrah, if thou dost not presently bind thyself to me for seven years, I'll turn all the lice about thee into familiars and make them [20 tear thee in pieces.

Robin. Nay sir, you may save yourself a labor, for they are as familiar with me as if they paid for their meat and drink, I can tell you.

Wagner. Well, sirrah, leave your jesting and take these guilders.

Robin. Yes, marry sir, and I thank you too. 25

Wagner. So, now thou art to be at an hour's warning, whensoever and wheresoever the devil shall fetch thee.

Robin. Here, take your guilders again. I'll none of 'em.

Wagner. Not I. Thou art pressed. Prepare thyself, for I will presently

I,iv.

3 *pickedevants* pointed beards.
4 *comings in* earnings.
13 *Qui . . . discipulus* who is my disciple (the opening words of a Latin poem by William Lyly, well known to Elizabethan schoolboys).

15 *beaten* embroidered with metal.
staves-acre a plant used for killing vermin.
20 *familiars* attendant evil spirits.
29 *pressed* enlisted into service in exchange for money.

raise up two devils to carry thee away. Banio! Belcher!   30
Robin.   Belcher? And Belcher come here, I'll belch him. I am not
afraid of a devil.
Enter two Devils.
Wagner.   How now, sir? Will you serve me now?
Robin.   Ay, good Wagner; take away the devil then.
Wagner.   Spirits away! Now, sirrah, follow me.   35
[*Exeunt Devils.*]
Robin.   I will sir. But hark you, master, will you teach me this conjur-
ing occupation?
Wagner.   Ay, sirrah. I'll teach thee to turn thyself to a dog, or a cat,
or a mouse, or a rat, or any thing.
Robin.   A dog, or a cat, or a mouse, or a rat! O brave Wagner!   40
Wagner.   Villain, call me Master Wagner, and see that you walk at-
tentively, and let your right eye be always diametrally fixed upon my
left heel, that thou may'st *quasi vestigias nostras insistere.*
Robin.   Well, sir, I warrant you.
Exeunt.

✳

Enter Faustus in his Study.   II,i.

Faustus.   Now Faustus must thou needs be damned,
  And canst thou not be saved.
  What boots it then to think on God or heaven?
  Away with such vain fancies, and despair;
  Despair in God, and trust in Beëlzebub.   5
  Now go not backward; Faustus, be resolute.
  Why waver'st thou? O, something soundeth in mine ear:
  'Abjure this magic; turn to God again.'
  Ay, and Faustus will turn to God again!
  To God? He loves thee not.
  The God thou serv'st is thine own appetite,
  Wherein is fixed the love of Beëlzebub.
  To him I'll build an altar and a church,
  And offer lukewarm blood of new-born babes.
Enter the two Angels.
Bad Angel.   Go forward, Faustus, in that famous art.   15
Good Angel.   Sweet Faustus, leave that execrable art.
Faustus.   Contrition, prayer, repentance—what of these?
Good Angel.   O, they are means to bring thee unto heaven.
Bad Angel.   Rather illusions, fruits of lunacy,

II,i.

42 *diametrally* in a straight line.   3 *boots* avails.
43 *quasi . . . insistere* as if to walk
in our tracks.

That make men foolish that do use them most.   20
Good Angel.   Sweet Faustus, think of heaven and heavenly things.
Bad Angel.   No Faustus; think of honor and wealth.

Exeunt Angels.

Faustus.   Wealth? Why, the signory of Emden shall be mine.
When Mephistophilis shall stand by me,
What power can hurt me? Faustus thou art safe.   25
Cast no more doubts. Mephistophilis, come
And bring glad tidings from great Lucifer.
Is't not midnight? Come, Mephistophilis.
Veni, veni, Mephistophile.

Enter Mephistophilis.

Now tell me what saith Lucifer, thy lord?   30
Mephistophilis.   That I shall wait on Faustus whilst he lives,
So he will buy my service with his soul.
Faustus.   Already Faustus hath hazarded that for thee.
Mephistophilis.   But now thou must bequeath it solemnly
And write a deed of gift with thine own blood,   35
For that security craves great Lucifer.
If thou deny it, I must back to hell.
Faustus.   Stay, Mephistophilis! Tell me what good
Will my soul do thy lord.
Mephistophilis.   Enlarge his kingdom.
Faustus.   Is that the reason why he tempts us thus?   40
Mephistophilis.   *Solamen miseris socios habuisse doloris.*
Faustus.   Why, have you any pain that torture others?
Mephistophilis.   As great as have the human souls of men.
But tell me, Faustus, shall I have thy soul?
And I will be thy slave and wait on thee   45
And give thee more than thou hast wit to ask.
Faustus.   Ay, Mephistophilis, I'll give it him.
Mephistophilis.   Then Faustus, stab thy arm courageously,
And bind thy soul that at some certain day
Great Lucifer may claim it as his own,   50
And then be thou as great as Lucifer.
Faustus. [*stabbing his arm*]   Lo, Mephistophilis, for love of thee,
I cut mine arm, and with my proper blood
Assure my soul to be great Lucifer's,
Chief lord and regent of perpetual night.   55
View here this blood that trickles from mine arm,
And let it be propitious for my wish.
Mephistophilis.   But Faustus,
Write it in manner of a deed of gift.

---

23 *Emden* the chief city of East Fries-
land, near the mouth of the river Ems,
which had considerable trade relations
with Elizabethan England.

41 *Solamen . . . doloris* It is a consolation in misery to have a fellow
sufferer.

53 *proper* own.

Faustus.   Ay, so I do. [*He writes.*] But Mephistophilis,   60
  My blood congeals, and I can write no more.
Mephistophilis.   I'll fetch thee fire to dissolve it straight.

                                                   Exit.

Faustus.   What might the staying of my blood portend?
  Is it unwilling I should write this bill?
  Why streams it not that I may write afresh?   65
  'Faustus gives to thee his soul.' Ah, there it stayed.
  Why shouldst thou not? Is not thy soul thine own?
  Then write again: 'Faustus gives to thee his soul.'
        Enter Mephistophilis with the chafer of fire.
Mephistophilis.   See Faustus, here is fire. Set it on.
Faustus.   So. Now the blood begins to clear again.   70
  Now will I make an end immediately.   [*He writes.*]
Mephistophilis.   What will not I do to obtain his soul?   [*Aside.*]
Faustus.   *Consummatum est;* this bill is ended,
  And Faustus hath bequeathed his soul to Lucifer.
  But what is this inscription on mine arm?   75
  Homo fuge! Whither should I fly?
  If unto God, he'll throw me down to hell.
  My senses are deceived; here's nothing writ.
  O yes, I see it plain. Even here is writ
  Homo fuge! Yet shall not Faustus fly.   80
Mephistophilis.   I'll fetch him somewhat to delight his mind.
                                               [*Aside.*]
                                               Exit.

      Enter Devils, giving crowns and rich apparel to Faustus. They
            dance and then depart. Enter Mephistophilis.
Faustus.   What means this show? Speak Mephistophilis.
Mephistophilis.   Nothing, Faustus, but to delight thy mind
  And let thee see what magic can perform.
Faustus.   But may I raise such spirits when I please?   85
Mephistophilis.   Ay Faustus, and do greater things than these.
Faustus.   Then, Mephistophilis, receive this scroll,
  A deed of gift of body and of soul,
  But yet conditionally that thou perform
  All covenants and articles between us both.   90
Mephistophilis.   Faustus, I swear by hell and Lucifer
  To effect all promises between us made.
Faustus.   Then hear me read it Mephistophilis.
  On these conditions following:
  First, that Faustus may be a spirit in form and substance;   95
  Secondly, that Mephistophilis shall be his servant and be at his com-
  mand;

69 *Set it on* i.e., set the dish of blood   73 *Consummatum est* It is completed
on the fire.   (St. John, XIX,30).
                                  76 *Homo fuge* Man fly.

Thirdly, that Mephistophilis shall do for him and bring him what-
soever;
Fourthly, that he shall be in his chamber or house invisible; 100
Lastly, that he shall appear to the said John Faustus at all times, in
what form or shape soever he please:
I, John Faustus, of Wittenberg, doctor, by these presents, do give
both body and soul to Lucifer, Prince of the East, and his minister,
Mephistophilis; and furthermore grant unto them that four [105
and twenty years being expired, the articles above written inviolate,
full power to fetch or carry the said John Faustus, body and soul,
flesh, blood, or goods, into their habitation wheresoever.
                                                By me, John Faustus.

Mephistophilis. Speak Faustus. Do you deliver this as your deed? [110
Faustus. Ay, take it, and the devil give thee good of it.
Mephistophilis. So now, Faustus, ask me what thou wilt.
Faustus. First will I question with thee about hell.
 Tell me, where is the place that men call hell?
Mephistophilis. Under the heavens. 115
Faustus. Ay, so are all things else. But whereabouts?
Mephistophilis. Within the bowels of these elements,
 Where we are tortured and remain for ever.
 Hell hath no limits, nor is circumscribed
 In one self place, but where we are is hell, 120
 And where hell is, there must we ever be.
 And, to be short, when all the world dissolves
 And every creature shall be purified,
 All places shall be hell that is not heaven.
Faustus. I think hell's a fable. 125
Mephistophilis. Ay, think so still, till experience change thy mind.
Faustus. Why, dost thou think that Faustus shall be damned?
Mephistophilis. Ay, of necessity, for here's the scroll
 In which thou hast given thy soul to Lucifer.
Faustus. Ay, and body too. But what of that? 130
 Think'st thou that Faustus is so fond to imagine
 That after this life there is any pain?
 No, these are trifles and mere old wives' tales.
Mephistophilis. But I am an instance to prove the contrary,
 For I tell thee I am damned and now in hell. 135
Faustus. Nay, and this be hell, I'll willingly be damned.
 What? Sleeping, eating, walking and disputing?
 But, leaving off this, let me have a wife,
 The fairest maid in Germany,
 For I am wanton and lascivious, 140
 And cannot live without a wife.
Mephistophilis. I prithee, Faustus, talk not of a wife.
Faustus. Nay, sweet Mephistophilis, fetch me one, for I will have one.
 131 *fond* foolish.

Mephistophilis.   Well, Faustus, thou shalt have a wife.
   Sit there till I come.   [*Exit.*]   145
      *Enter [Mephistophilis] with a Devil dressed like a woman,
                      with fireworks.*
Faustus.   What sight is this?
Mephistophilis.   Now Faustus, how dost thou like thy wife?
Faustus.   Here's a hot whore indeed! No, I'll no wife.
Mephistophilis.   Marriage is but a ceremonial toy,
   And if thou lovest me, think no more of it.   150
   I'll cull thee out the fairest courtesans
   And bring them every morning to thy bed.
   She whom thine eye shall like, thy heart shall have,
   Were she as chaste as was Penelope,
   As wise as Saba, or as beautiful   155
   As was bright Lucifer before his fall.
   Hold; take this book; peruse it thoroughly.
   The iterating of these lines brings gold;
   The framing of this circle on the ground
   Brings thunder, whirlwinds, storm and lightning.   160
   Pronounce this thrice devoutly to thyself,
   And men in harness shall appear to thee,
   Ready to execute what thou command'st.
Faustus.   Thanks, Mephistophilis, for this sweet book.
   This will I keep as chary as my life.   165

                                     Exeunt.

      Enter Faustus in his study and Mephistophilis.   II,ii.
Faustus.   When I behold the heavens, then I repent
   And curse thee, wicked Mephistophilis,
   Because thou hast deprived me of those joys.
Mephistophilis.   'Twas thine own seeking, Faustus; thank thyself.
   But think'st thou heaven is such a glorious thing?   5
   I tell thee, Faustus, 'tis not half so fair
   As thou, or any man that breathes on earth.
Faustus.   How prov'st thou that?
Mephistophilis.   'Twas made for man; then he's more excellent.
Faustus.   If heaven was made for man, 'twas made for me.   10
   I will renounce this magic and repent.
         Enter the two Angels.
Good Angel.   Faustus repent; yet God will pity thee.
Bad Angel.   Thou art a spirit; God cannot pity thee.

                    II,ii.

154 *Penelope* the faithful wife of   13 *spirit* devil (indicating that Faustus
Ulysses in Homer's *Odyssey*.   by his apostasy is already a damned soul
155 *Saba* the Queen of Sheba.   in hell).
162 *harness* armor.

Faustus.   Who buzzeth in mine ears I am a spirit?
  Be I a devil, yet God may pity me;   15
  Yea, God will pity me if I repent.
Bad Angel.   Ay, but Faustus never shall repent.

                                         Exeunt Angels.

Faustus.   My heart is hardened; I cannot repent.
  Scarce can I name salvation, faith, or heaven,
  But fearful echoes thunder in mine ears: 20
  'Faustus, thou art damned!' Then swords and knives,
  Poison, guns, halters, and envenomed steel
  Are laid before me to dispatch myself;
  And long ere this I should have done the deed,
  Had not sweet pleasure conquered deep despair.   25
  Have not I made blind Homer sing to me
  Of Alexander's love and Oenon's death?
  And hath not he, that built the walls of Thebes
  With ravishing sound of his melodious harp,
  Made music with my Mephistophilis?   30
  Why should I die then, or basely despair?
  I am resolved; Faustus shall not repent.
  Come, Mephistophilis, let us dispute again
  And reason of divine astrology.
  Speak; are there many spheres above the moon?   35
  Are all celestial bodies but one globe,
  As is the substance of this centric earth?
Mephistophilis.   As are the elements, such are the heavens,
  Even from the moon unto the empyreal orb,
  Mutually folded in each others' spheres,   40
  And jointly move upon one axle-tree,
  Whose terminè is termed the world's wide pole;
  Nor are the names of Saturn, Mars, or Jupiter
  Feigned, but are erring stars.
Faustus.   But have they all
  One motion, both *situ et tempore?*   45
Mephistophilis.   All move from east to west in four and twenty hours
  upon the poles of the world, but differ in their motions upon the
  poles of the zodiac.
Faustus.   These slender questions Wagner can decide.
  Hath Mephistophilis no greater skill?   50

---

27 *Alexander . . . death* Paris, or
Alexander as he was sometimes called,
loved the nymph Oenone when he lived
as a shepherd on Mt. Ida. She died of
a broken heart when he left her.

28–29 *he . . . harp* Amphion, son of
Zeus and Antiope, caused stones to move
and build the walls of Thebes simply by

playing upon the lyre given to him by
Hermes.

42 *terminè* limit.

44 *erring stars* planets.

45 *situ et tempore* in position (the
direction of their movements) and in the
time they take to revolve about the earth.

Who knows not the double motion of the planets?
That the first is finished in a natural day?
The second thus? Saturn in thirty years?
Jupiter in twelve; Mars in four; the sun, Venus and Mercury in a
year; the moon in twenty eight days? These are freshmen's sup-   [55
positions. But tell me, hath every sphere a dominion or *intelligentia?*
Mephistophilis. Ay.
Faustus. How many heavens or spheres are there?
Mephistophilis. Nine—the seven planets, the firmament, and the em-
pyreal heaven.   60
Faustus. But is there not *coelum igneum, et crystallinum?*
Mephistophilis. No, Faustus, they be but fables.
Faustus. Resolve me then in this one question: why are not conjunc-
tions, oppositions, aspects, eclipses all at one time, but in some years
we have more, in some less?   65
Mephistophilis. *Per inaequalem motum respectu totius.*
Faustus. Well, I am answered. Now tell me who made the world.
Mephistophilis. I will not.
Faustus. Sweet Mephistophilis, tell me.
Mephistophilis. Move me not, Faustus.   70
Faustus. Villain, have not I bound thee to tell me any thing?
Mephistophilis. Ay, that is not against our kingdom.
This is. Thou art damned. Think thou of hell.
Faustus. Think, Faustus, upon God that made the world.
Mephistophilis. Remember this.   75

                                                        Exit.

Faustus. Ay, go accursèd spirit to ugly hell.
'Tis thou hast damned distressèd Faustus' soul.
Is't not too late?
                        Enter the two Angels.
Bad Angel. Too late.
Good Angel. Never too late, if Faustus will repent.   80
Bad Angel. If thou repent, devils will tear thee in pieces.
Good Angel. Repent, and they shall never raze thy skin.

                                            Exeunt Angels.

Faustus. O Christ, my Savior, my Savior,
Help to save distressèd Faustus' soul.
            Enter Lucifer, Beëlzebub, and Mephistophilis.
Lucifer. Christ cannot save thy soul, for he is just.   85
There's none but I have interest in the same.

---

56 *dominion or intelligentia* govern-
ing angel.

61 *coelum . . . crystallinum* the fiery
and the crystaline spheres of Ptolemaic
astronomy.

63–64 *conjunctions* seeming proximities
of heavenly bodies. *oppositions* diver-
gences of heavenly bodies. *aspects* any
other relations of such bodies to one
another. *eclipses* the blottings out of
one heavenly body by another.

66 *Per . . . totius* By their unequal
movements in respect to the whole (i.e.,
the different speeds of the various planets
within the total cosmos).

Faustus.   O, what art thou that look'st so terribly?

Lucifer.   I am Lucifer,
   And this is my companion prince in hell.

Faustus.   O, Faustus, they are come to fetch thy soul.   90

Beëlzebub.   We are come to tell thee thou dost injure us.

Lucifer.   Thou call'st on Christ, contrary to thy promise.

Beëlzebub.   Thou shouldst not think on God.

Lucifer.   Think on the devil.

Beëlzebub.   And his dam too.   95

Faustus.   Nor will I henceforth. Pardon me in this,
   And Faustus vows never to look to heaven,
   Never to name God, or to pray to him,
   To burn his Scriptures, slay his ministers,
   And make my spirits pull his churches down.   100

Lucifer.   So shalt thou show thyself an obedient servant,
   And we will highly gratify thee for it.

Beëlzebub.   Faustus, we are come from hell in person to show thee
   some pastime. Sit down, and thou shalt behold the Seven Deadly Sins
   appear to thee in their own proper shapes and likeness.   105

Faustus.   That sight will be as pleasant to me as Paradise was to Adam
   the first day of his creation.

Lucifer.   Talk not of Paradise or creation, but mark the show. Go,
   Mephistophilis, fetch them in.

                                        [*Exit Mephistophilis.*]

         Enter the Seven Deadly Sins, [with Mephistophilis,
                     led by a Piper].

Beëlzebub.   Now Faustus, question them of their names and dis-   [110
   positions.

Faustus.   That shall I soon. What art thou, the first?

Pride.   I am Pride. I disdain to have any parents. I am like to Ovid's
   flea: I can creep into every corner of a wench. Sometimes, like a peri-
   wig, I sit upon her brow. Next, like a necklace, I hang about   [115
   her neck. Then, like a fan of feathers, I kiss her lips, and then, turning myself to a wrought smock, do what I list. But fie, what a smell
   is here! I'll not speak another word unless the ground be perfumed
   and covered with cloth of Arras.

Faustus.   Thou art a proud knave indeed. What art thou, the   [120
   second?

Covetousness.   I am Covetousness, begotten of an old churl in a leather
   bag, and might I now obtain my wish, this house, you and all, should
   turn to gold, that I might lock you safe into my chest. O my sweet
   gold!   125

Faustus.   And what art thou, the third?

113–114 *Ovid's flea* The medieval
poem, *Carmine de Pulice* was generally
attributed to Ovid.

119 *cloth of Arras* Flemish cloth used
generally for tapestries.

Envy. I am Envy, begotten of a chimney-sweeper and an oyster-wife.
I cannot read and therefore wish all books burned. I am lean with
seeing others eat. O, that there would come a famine over all the
world, that all might die, and I live alone; then thou shouldst [130
see how fat I'd be. But must thou sit and I stand? Come down, with
a vengeance.

Faustus. Out envious wretch! But what are thou, the fourth?

Wrath. I am Wrath. I had neither father nor mother. I leaped out of
a lion's mouth when I was scarce an hour old, and ever since [135
have run up and down the world with this case of rapiers, wounding
myself when I could get none to fight withal. I was born in hell, and
look to it, for some of you shall be my father.

Faustus. And what are you, the fifth?

Gluttony. I am Gluttony. My parents are all dead, and the devil [140
a penny they have left me but a small pension, and that buys me
thirty meals a day and ten bevers—a small trifle to suffice nature. I
come of a royal pedigree. My father was a gammon of bacon, and my
mother was a hogshead of claret wine. My godfathers were these:
Peter Pickled-herring and Martin Martlemas-beef. But my god- [145
mother, O, she was a jolly gentlewoman, and well beloved in every
good town and city; her name was Mistress Margery March-beer. Now
Faustus, thou hast heard all my progeny; wilt thou bid me to a supper.

Faustus. Not I. Thou wilt eat up all my victuals.   150

Gluttony. Then the devil choke thee.

Faustus. Choke thyself, glutton. What art thou, the sixth?

Sloth. Heigh ho! I am Sloth. I was begotten on a sunny bank, where
I have lain ever since, and you have done me great injury to bring
me from thence. Let me be carried thither again by Gluttony [155
and Lechery. Heigh ho! I'll not speak a word more for a king's ran-
som.

Faustus. And what are you Mistress Minx, the seventh and last?

Lechery. Who, I, sir? I am one that loves an inch of raw mutton better
than an ell of fried stockfish, and the first letter of my name [160
begins with lechery.

Lucifer. Away to hell! Away! On piper!

Exeunt the seven Sins [and the Piper].

Faustus. O, how this sight doth delight my soul!

Lucifer. But Faustus, in hell is all manner of delight.

Faustus. O, might I see hell and return again safe, how happy [165
were I then!

---

142 *bevers* light snacks taken between regular meals.

145 *Martlemas-beef* salted meat hung for the winter on Martinmas, November 11.

147 *March-beer* a fine ale, made in the springtime and not drunk until it has been aged for two years.

159 *raw mutton* common slang for whore.

160 *stockfish* dried codfish.

Lucifer. Faustus, thou shalt. At midnight I will send for thee. Meanwhile peruse this book and view it thoroughly, and thou shalt turn thyself into what shape thou wilt.

Faustus. Thanks, mighty Lucifer.   170
This will I keep as chary as my life.

Lucifer. Now Faustus, farewell.

Faustus. Farewell, great Lucifer. Come, Mephistophilis.

                           Exeunt, several ways.

           Enter the clown, [*Robin, holding a book*].   II,iii.

Robin. What, Dick, look to the horses there till I come again. I have gotten one of Doctor Faustus' conjuring books, and now we'll have such knavery as't passes.

                       Enter Dick.

Dick. What, Robin, you must come away and walk the horses.

Robin. I walk the horses? I scorn't, 'faith. I have other matters in [5 hand. Let the horses walk themselves and they will. [*He reads.*] *A per se a; t, h, e, the; o per se o; deny orgon, gorgon.* Keep further from me, O thou illiterate and unlearned hostler.

Dick. 'Snails, what hast thou got there? A book? Why, thou canst not tell ne'er a word on't.   10

Robin. That thou shalt see presently. Keep out of the circle, I say, lest I send you into the hostry with a vengeance.

Dick. That's like, 'faith. You had best leave your foolery, for an my master come, he'll conjure you, 'faith.

Robin. My master conjure me? I'll tell thee what: an my master [15 come here, I'll clap as fair a pair of horns on's head as e'er thou sawest in thy life.

Dick. Thou needst not do that, for my mistress hath done it.

Robin. Ay, there be of us here that have waded as deep into matters as other men, if they were disposed to talk.   20

Dick. A plague take you! I thought you did not sneak up and down after her for nothing. But I prithee, tell me in good sadness, Robin, is that a conjuring book?

Robin. Do but speak what thou'lt have me to do, and I'll do't. If thou'lt dance naked, put off thy clothes, and I'll conjure thee [25 about presently. Or if thou'lt go but to the tavern with me, I'll give thee white wine, red wine, claret wine, sack, muscadine, malmesey and whippincrust. Hold belly, hold, and we'll not pay one penny for it.

II,iii.

9 *'Snails* by God's nails.
16 *horns* the common sign of the cuckold.
22 *sadness* seriousness.

28 *whippincrust* possibly a corruption of 'hippocras,' a highly spiced and sugared wine.

Dick. O brave! Prithee let's to it presently, for I am as dry as a dog.
Robin. Come then, let's away. 30

       Exeunt.

    Enter the Chorus.   III,Prologue.
Chorus. Learnèd Faustus,
 To find the secrets of astronomy
 Graven in the book of Jove's high firmament,
 Did mount him up to scale Olympus' top,
 Where, sitting in a chariot burning bright   5
 Drawn by the strength of yokèd dragons' necks,
 He views the clouds, the planets, and the stars,
 The tropics, zones, and quarters of the sky,
 From the bright circle of the hornèd moon
 Even to the height of *Primum Mobile.*   10
 And whirling round with this circumference,
 Within the concave compass of the pole,
 From east to west his dragons swiftly glide
 And in eight days did bring him home again.
 Not long he stayed within his quiet house   15
 To rest his bones after his weary toil.
 But new exploits do hale him out again,
 And mounted then upon a dragon's back,
 That with his wings did part the subtle air,
 He now is gone to prove cosmography,   20
 That measures coasts and kingdoms of the earth,
 And, as I guess, will first arrive at Rome
 To see the Pope and manner of his court
 And take some part of holy Peter's feast,
 The which this day is highly solemnized.   25

       Exit.

   Enter Faustus and Mephistophilis.   III,i.
Faustus. Having now, my good Mephistophilis,
 Passed with delight the stately town of Trier,

III, Prologue.
10 *Primum Mobile* in Ptolemaic astronomy the outermost sphere of creation which moves the other nine spheres.

20 *prove cosmography* i.e., explore the universe.
III,i.
 2 *Trier* or Treves, a German city on the Moselle river.

Environed round with airy mountain tops,
With walls of flint, and deep entrenchèd lakes,
Not to be won by any conquering prince;   5
From Paris next, coasting the realm of France,
We saw the river Main fall into Rhine,
Whose banks are set with groves of fruitful vines;
Then up to Naples, rich Campania,
Whose buildings fair and gorgeous to the eye,   10
The streets straight forth and paved with finest brick,
Quarters the town in four equivalents.
There saw we learnèd Maro's golden tomb,
The way he cut, an English mile in length,
Through a rock of stone in one night's space.   15
From thence to Venice, Padua, and the rest,
In midst of which a sumptuous temple stands,
That threats the stars with her aspiring top,
Whose frame is paved with sundry colored stones,
And roofed aloft with curious work in gold.   20
Thus hitherto hath Faustus spent his time.
But tell me now, what resting-place is this?
Hast thou, as erst I did command,
Conducted me within the walls of Rome?

Mephistophilis.   I have, my Faustus, and for proof thereof   25
This is the goodly palace of the Pope;
And 'cause we are no common guests,
I choose his privy chamber for our use.
Faustus.   I hope his holiness will bid us welcome.
Mephistophilis.   All's one, for we'll be bold with his venison.   30
But now, my Faustus, that thou may'st perceive
What Rome contains for to delight thine eyes,
Know that this city stands upon seven hills
That underprop the groundwork of the same.
Just through the midst runs flowing Tiber's stream,   35
With winding banks that cut it in two parts,
Over the which four stately bridges lean,
That make safe passage to each part of Rome.
Upon the bridge called Ponte Angelo
Erected is a castle passing strong,   40
Where thou shalt see such store of ordinance
As that the double cannons, forged of brass,
Do match the number of the days contained
Within the compass of one complete year;

---

4 *entrenchèd lakes* castle moats.
13 *Maro* Virgil.
14-15 *way . . . space* A tunnel between the bays of Naples and Baiae,
through Mt. Posilipo, was said to have

been cut by Virgil (regarded as a magician in the Middle Ages) by supernatural
art.

17-20 *In midst . . . gold* St. Mark's
cathedral in Venice.

Beside the gates and high pyramidès   45
That Julius Caesar brought from Africa
Faustus.   Now, by the kingdoms of infernal rule,
Of Styx, of Acheron, and the fiery lake
Of ever-burning Phlegethon, I swear
That I do long to see the monuments   50
And situation of bright-splendent Rome.
Come, therefore, let's away.
Mephistophilis.   Nay, stay my Faustus. I know you'd see the Pope
And take some part of holy Peter's feast,
The which, in state and high solemnity,   55
This day is held through Rome and Italy
In honor of the Pope's triumphant victory.
Faustus.   Sweet Mephistophilis, thou pleasest me.
Whilst I am here on earth, let me be cloyed
With all things that delight the heart of man.   60
My four and twenty years of liberty
I'll spend in pleasure and in dalliance,
That Faustus' name, whilst this bright frame doth stand,
May be admirèd through the furthest land.
Mephistophilis.   'Tis well said, Faustus. Come then, stand by me   65
And thou shalt see them come immediately.
Faustus.   Nay, stay, my gentle Mephistophilis,
And grant me my request, and then I go.
Thou know'st within the compass of eight days
We viewed the face of heaven, of earth, and hell.   70
So high our dragons soared into the air,
That looking down, the earth appeared to me
No bigger than my hand in quantity.
There did we view the kingdoms of the world,
And what might please mine eye I there beheld.   75
Then in this show let me an actor be,
That this proud Pope may Faustus' cunning see.
Mephistophilis.   Let it be so, my Faustus. But, first stay
And view their triumphs as they pass this way,
And then devise what best contents thy mind   80
By cunning in thine art to cross the Pope
Or dash the pride of this solemnity,
To make his monks and abbots stand like apes
And point like antics at his triple crown,
To beat the beads about the friars' pates   85
Or clap huge horns upon the cardinals' heads,
Or any villainy thou canst devise,
And I'll perform it, Faustus. Hark, they come.
This day shall make thee be admired in Rome.

45-46 *gates . . . Africa* Before the
gates of St. Peter's there still stands the
obelisk which was brought to Rome from
Heliopolis by the Emperor Caligula in
the first century A.D.

79 *triumphs* spectacular displays.

*Enter the Cardinals and Bishops, some bearing crosiers, some
the pillars; Monks and Friars singing their procession. Then
the Pope, and Raymond, King of Hungary, with Bruno, led
in chains.*

Pope.   Cast down our footstool.

Raymond.   Saxon Bruno, stoop,   90
Whilst on thy back his holiness ascends
Saint Peter's chair and state pontifical.

Bruno.   Proud Lucifer, that state belongs to me,
But thus I fall to Peter, not to thee.

Pope.   To me and Peter shalt thou grovelling lie   95
And crouch before the papal dignity.
Sound trumpets then, for thus Saint Peter's heir
From Bruno's back ascends Saint Peter's chair.

                                 A flourish while he ascends.

Thus, as the gods creep on with feet of wool
Long ere with iron hands they punish men,   100
So shall our sleeping vengeance now arise
And smite with death thy hated enterprise.
Lord Cardinals of France and Padua,
Go forthwith to our holy consistory,
And read amongst the Statutes Decretal   105
What, by the holy council held at Trent,
The sacred synod hath decreed for him
That doth assume the papal government
Without election and a true consent.
Away, and bring us word with speed.   110

First Cardinal.   We go my Lord.

                                 Exeunt Cardinals.

Pope.   Lord Raymond.   [*They talk apart.*]

Faustus.   Go, haste thee, gentle Mephistophilis,
Follow the cardinals to the consistory,
And as they turn their superstitious books,   115
Strike them with sloth and drowsy idleness,
And make them sleep so sound that in their shapes
Thyself and I may parley with this Pope,
This proud confronter of the Emperor,
And in despite of all his holiness   120
Restore this Bruno to his liberty
And bear him to the states of Germany.

Mephistophilis.   Faustus, I go.

Faustus.   Dispatch it soon.
The Pope shall curse that Faustus came to Rome.   125

                                 Exeunt Faustus and Mephistophilis.

---

105 *Statutes Decretal* papal decrees   106 *council . . . Trent* held between
concerning religious doctrine or eccle-   1545 and 1563.
siastical law.

Bruno.   Pope Adrian, let me have some right of law.
   I was elected by the Emperor.
Pope.   We will depose the Emperor for that deed
   And curse the people that submit to him.
   Both he and thou shalt stand excommunicate   130
   And interdict from church's privilege
   And all society of holy men.
   He grows too proud in his authority,
   Lifting his lofty head above the clouds,
   And like a steeple over-peers the church.   135
   But we'll pull down his haughty insolence,
   And as Pope Alexander, our progenitor,
   Trod on the neck of German Frederick,
   Adding this golden sentence to our praise,
   'That Peter's heirs should tread on emperors   140
   And walk upon the dreadful adder's back,
   Treading the lion and the dragon down
   And fearless spurn the killing basilisk,'
   So will we quell that haughty schismatic,
   And by authority apostolical   145
   Depose him from his regal government.
Bruno.   Pope Julius swore to princely Sigismond,
   For him and the succeeding popes of Rome,
   To hold the emperors their lawful lords.
Pope.   Pope Julius did abuse the church's rites,   150
   And therefore none of his decrees can stand.
   Is not all power on earth bestowed on us?
   And therefore, though we would, we cannot err.
   Behold this silver belt, whereto is fixed
   Seven golden keys fast sealed with seven seals   155
   In token of our sevenfold power from heaven,
   To bind or loose, lock fast, condemn or judge,
   Resign, or seal, or whatso pleaseth us.
   Then he and thou and all the world shall stoop,
   Or be assurèd of our dreadful curse   160
   To light as heavy as the pains of hell.

---

126 *Pope Adrian* Marlowe is thinking probably of Pope Hadrian IV (1154–
1159) who came into conflict with
Frederick Barbarossa, the Holy Roman
Emperor, whom he forced to submit to
him. What historicity there may be in
these scenes at the papal court is badly
confused.

137–138 *Pope Alexander . . . Frederick*
Pope Alexander III (1159–1181) successor to Hadrian IV, continued the struggle
against Frederick Barbarossa and forced

him to acknowledge the papal supremacy
at Canossa.

143 *basilisk* a mythical monster with
power to kill by its looks.

147 *Pope Julius . . . Sigismond* None
of the three popes named Julius was
contemporary with the Emperor Sigis-
mund, who lived from 1368 to 1437. Sigis-
mund did, however, in 1414 summon the
Council of Constance which sought to
end the Great Schism.

Enter Faustus and Mephistophilis, like the Cardinals.
Mephistophilis.   Now tell me, Faustus, are we not fitted well?
Faustus.   Yes, Mephistophilis, and two such cardinals
 Ne'er served a holy pope as we shall do.
 But whilst they sleep within the consistory,   165
 Let us salute his reverend fatherhood.
Raymond.   Behold, my lord, the cardinals are returned.
Pope.   Welcome, grave fathers. Answer presently:
 What have our holy council there decreed
 Concerning Bruno and the Emperor.   170
 In quittance of their late conspiracy
 Against our state and papal dignity?
Faustus.   Most sacred patron of the church of Rome,
 By full consent of all the synod
 Of priests and prelates it is thus decreed: 175
 That Bruno and the German Emperor
 Be held as Lollards and bold schismatics
 And proud disturbers of the church's peace.
 And if that Bruno by his own assent,
 Without enforcement of the German peers,   180
 Did seek to wear the triple diadem
 And by your death to climb Saint Peter's chair.
 The Statutes Decretal have thus decreed:
 He shall be straight condemned of heresy
 And on a pile of fagots burned to death.   185
Pope.   It is enough. Here, take him to your charge,
 And bear him straight to Ponte Angelo,
 And in the strongest tower enclose him fast.
 Tomorrow, sitting in our consistory
 With all our college of grave cardinals,   190
 We will determine of his life or death.
 Here, take his triple crown along with you,
 And leave it in the church's treasury.
 Make haste again, my good lord cardinals,
 And take our blessing apostolical.   195
Mephistophilis.   So, so. Was never devil thus blessed before.
Faustus.   Away, sweet Mephistophilis, be gone.
 The cardinals will be plagued for this anon.
   Exeunt Faustus and Mephistophilis [with Bruno].
Pope.   Go presently and bring a banquet forth,
 That we may solemnize Saint Peter's feast,   200
 And with Lord Raymond, King of Hungary,
 Drink to our late and happy victory.   *Exeunt.*

✳

177 *Lollards* followers of John Wyclif (1320?–1384), the English reformer.

III,ii.

A sennet [is sounded] while the banquet is brought in; and
    then enter Faustus and Mephistophilis in their own shapes.
Mephistophilis.   Now, Faustus, come, prepare thyself for mirth.
    The sleepy cardinals are hard at hand
    To censure Bruno, that is posted hence,
    And on a proud-paced steed, as swift as thought,
    Flies o'er the Alps to fruitful Germany,   5
    There to salute the woeful Emperor.
Faustus.   The Pope will curse them for their sloth today,
    That slept both Bruno and his crown away.
    But now, that Faustus may delight his mind
    And by their folly make some merriment,   10
    Sweet Mephistophilis, so charm me here
    That I may walk invisible to all
    And do whate'er I please unseen of any.
Mephistophilis.   Faustus, thou shalt. Then kneel down presently:
                Whilst on thy head I lay my hand   15
                And charm thee with this magic wand.
                First wear this girdle; then appear
                Invisible to all are here.
                The planets seven, the gloomy air,
                Hell and the Furies' forkèd hair,   20
                Pluto's blue fire, and Hecate's tree,
                With magic spells so compass thee
                That no eye may thy body see.
    So Faustus.   Now, for all their holiness,
    Do what thou wilt, thou shalt not be discerned.   25
Faustus.   Thanks, Mephistophilis. Now friars take heed
    Lest Faustus make your shaven crowns to bleed.
Mephistophilis.   Faustus, no more. See where the cardinals come.
    Enter Pope and all the Lords. Enter the Cardinals with a book.
Pope.   Welcome, lord cardinals. Come, sit down.
    Lord Raymond, take your seat. Friars attend,   30
    And see that all things be in readiness,
    As best beseems this solemn festival.
First Cardinal.   First, may it please your sacred holiness
    To view the sentence of the reverend synod
    Concerning Bruno and the Emperor?   35
Pope.   What needs this question? Did I not tell you
    Tomorrow we would sit i' th' consistory
    And there determine of his punishment?
    You brought us word even now; it was decreed
    That Bruno and the cursèd Emperor   40
    Were by the holy council both condemned
    For loathèd Lollards and base schismatics.
    Then wherefore would you have me view that book?

First Cardinal.   Your grace mistakes. You gave us no such charge.

Raymond.   Deny it not. We all are witnesses   45
  That Bruno here was late delivered you,
  With his rich triple crown to be reserved
  And put into the church's treasury.

Both Cardinals.   By holy Paul, we saw them not.

Pope.   By Peter, you shall die   50
  Unless you bring them forth immediately.
  Hale them to prison. Lade their limbs with gyves.
  False prelates, for this hateful treachery
  Cursed be your souls to hellish misery.

               [Exeunt the two Cardinals with Attendants.]

Faustus.   So, they are safe. Now, Faustus, to the feast.   55
  The Pope had never such a frolic guest.

Pope.   Lord Archbishop of Rheims, sit down with us.

Archbishop.   I thank your holiness.

Faustus.   Fall to. The devil choke you an you spare.

Pope.   Who's that spoke? Friars look about.   60

Friar.   Here's nobody, if it like your holiness.

Pope.   Lord Raymond, pray fall to. I am beholding
  To the Bishop of Milan for this so rare a present.

Faustus.   I thank you, sir.   *[He snatches the dish.]*

Pope.   How now? Who snatched the meat from me?   65
  Villains, why speak you not?
  My good Lord Archbishop, here's a most dainty dish
  Was sent me from a cardinal in France.

Faustus.   I'll have that too.   *[He snatches the dish.]*

Pope.   What Lollards do attend our holiness,   70
  That we receive such great indignity?
  Fetch me some wine.

Faustus.   Ay, pray do, for Faustus is a-dry.

Pope.   Lord Raymond, I drink unto your grace.

Faustus.   I pledge your grace.   *[He snatches the cup.]*   75

Pope.   My wine gone too? Ye lubbers, look about
  And find the man that doth this villainy,
  Or by our sanctitude, you all shall die.
  I pray, my lords, have patience at this
  Troublesome banquet.   80

Archbishop.   Please it your holiness, I think it be some ghost crept out
  of purgatory, and now is come unto your holiness for his pardon.

Pope.   It may be so.
  Go then, command our priests to sing a dirge
  To lay the fury of this same troublesome ghost.   85

               [Exit an attendant.]

  Once again, my lord, fall to.

               The Pope crosseth himself.

Faustus.   How now?

Must every bit be spicèd with a cross?
Nay then, take that.　　　　　　　　　　[*He strikes the Pope.*]

Pope.　O I am slain. Help me, my lords.　　　　　　　90
O come and help to bear my body hence.
Damned be this soul for ever for this deed.
　　　　　　　　　　　　Exeunt the Pope and his train.

Mephistophilis.　Now, Faustus, what will you do now? For I can tell
you you'll be cursed with bell, book, and candle.

Faustus.　Bell, book, and candle; candle, book, and bell,　　95
Forward and backward, to curse Faustus to hell.
　　　Enter the Friars with bell, book, and candle for the dirge.

First Friar.　Come, brethren, let's about our business with good devotion.　　　　　　　　　　　　　　　　　　[*They chant.*]

　　Cursed be he that stole his holiness' meat from the table.
　　　　Maledicat Dominus!　　　　　　　　　　　100
　　Cursed be he that struck his holiness a blow on the face.
　　　　Maledicat Dominus!
　　Cursed be he that struck Friar Sandelo a blow on the pate.
　　　　Maledicat Dominus!
　　Cursed be he that disturbeth our holy dirge.　　　105
　　　　Maledicat Dominus!
　　Cursed be he that took away his holiness' wine.
　　　　Maledicat Dominus! Et omnes sancti. Amen.

　　[*Faustus and Mephistophilis*] *beat the Friars, fling fireworks*
　　　　　　　　　　　among them, and exeunt.

　　　　Enter [*Robin,*] *the clown, and Dick, with a cup.*　　III,iii.

Dick.　Sirrah Robin, we were best look that your devil can answer the
stealing of this same cup, for the vintner's boy follows us at the hard
heels.

Robin.　'Tis no matter. Let him come. An he follow us, I'll so conjure
him as he was never conjured in his life, I warrant him. Let me　[5
see the cup.

　　　　　　　　　　Enter Vintner.

Dick.　Here 'tis. Yonder he comes. Now, Robin, now or never show thy
cunning.

Vintner.　O, are you here? I am glad I have found you. You are a couple
of fine companions. Pray, where's the cup you stole from the　[10
tavern?

III,ii.
　95 *Bell, book, and candle* used traditionally in the office of excommunication.

Robin. How, how? We steal a cup? Take heed what you say. We look
not like cup stealers, I can tell you.

Vintner. Never deny't, for I know you have it, and I'll search you.

Robin. Search me? Ay, and spare not. Hold the cup, Dick. [15
[*Aside to Dick.*] Come, come, search me, search me.

         [*The Vintner searches Robin.*]

Vintner. [*to Dick*]   Come on, sirrah, let me search you now.

Dick. Ay, ay, do, do. Hold the cup, Robin. [*Aside to Robin.*] I fear not
your searching. We scorn to steal your cups, I can tell you.

          [*The Vintner searches Dick.*]

Vintner. Never outface me for the matter, for sure the cup is be- [20
tween you two.

Robin. Nay, there you lie. 'Tis beyond us both.

Vintner. A plague take you! I thought 'twas your knavery to take it
away. Come, give it me again.

Robin. Ay, much. When? Can you tell? Dick, make me a circle, [25
and stand close at my back, and stir not for thy life. Vintner, you
shall have your cup anon. Say nothing, Dick, *O per se, O Demogorgon,
Belcher and Mephistophilis.*

    Enter Mephistophilis. [Exit the Vintner, in fright.]

Mephistophilis. Monarch of hell, under whose black survey
Great potentates do kneel with awful fear,   30
Upon whose altars thousand souls do lie,
How am I vexèd by these villains' charms!
From Constantinople have they brought me now,
Only for pleasure of these damnèd slaves.

Robin. By Lady, sir, you have had a shrewd journey of it. Will it [35
please you to take a shoulder of mutton to supper and a tester in
your purse, and go back again?

Dick. Ay, I pray you heartily, sir, for we called you but in jest, I promise you.

Mephistophilis. To purge the rashness of this cursèd deed,   40
First be thou turnèd to this ugly shape,
For apish deeds transformèd to an ape.

Robin. O brave, an ape! I pray sir, let me have the carrying of him
about to show some tricks.

Mephistophilis. And so thou shalt. Be thou transformed to a dog, [45
and carry him upon thy back. Away, be gone!

Robin. A dog? That's excellent. Let the maids look well to their por-
ridge pots, for I'll into the kitchen presently. Come, Dick, come.

     Exeunt [Robin and Dick,] the two clowns.

Mephistophilis. Now with the flames of ever-burning fire,
I'll wing myself and forthwith fly amain   50
Unto my Faustus, to the great Turk's court.   *Exit.*

          ***

III,iii.
36 *tester* sixpence.

Enter Chorus.   IV,Prologue.

Chorus.   When Faustus had with pleasure ta'en the view
　　Of rarest things and royal courts of kings,
　　He stayed his course and so returnèd home;
　　Where such as bare his absence but with grief—
　　I mean his friends and nearest companions—　　　　5
　　Did gratulate his safety with kind words,
　- And in their conference of what befell,
　　Touching his journey through the world and air,
　　They put forth questions of astrology,
　　Which Faustus answered with such learnèd skill　　10
　　As they admired and wondered at his wit.
　　Now is his fame spread forth in every land.
　　Amongst the rest, the Emperor is one—
　　Carolus the fifth—at whose palace now
　　Faustus is feasted 'mongst his noblemen.　　　　　15
　　What there he did in trial of his art
　　I leave untold, your eyes shall see performed.

　　　　　　　　　　　　　　　　　　　Exit.

Enter Martino and Frederick, at several doors.　　IV,i.

Martino.   What ho, officers, gentlemen,
　　Hie to the presence to attend the Emperor.
　　Good Frederick, see the rooms be voided straight;
　　His majesty is coming to the hall.
　　Go back, and see the state in readiness.　　　　　5
Frederick.   But where is Bruno, our elected Pope,
　　That on a fury's back came post from Rome?
　　Will not his grace consort the Emperor?
Martino.   O yes, and with him comes the German conjurer,
　　The learnèd Faustus, fame of Wittenberg,　　　　10
　　The wonder of the world for magic art;
　　And he intends to show great Carolus
　　The race of all his stout progenitors,
　　And bring in presence of his majesty
　　The royal shapes and warlike semblances　　　　　15
　　Of Alexander and his beauteous paramour.
Frederick.   Where is Benvolio?
Martino.   Fast asleep, I warrant you.

IV, Prologue.
　7 *conference* discussion.
　14 *Carolus* Charles V, King of Spain
(as Charles I from 1516 to 1556) and
Holy Roman Emperor from 1519 to 1556.

IV,i.
　2 *presence* presence chamber.
　5 *state* throne
　10 *fame* glory.
　16 *Alexander* Alexander the Great.

He took his rouse with stoups of Rhenish wine
So kindly yesternight to Bruno's health   20
That all this day the sluggard keeps his bed.
Frederick.   See, see, his window's ope. We'll call to him.
Martino.   What ho, Benvolio!
      Enter Benvolio above at a window, in his nightcap, buttoning.
Benvolio.   What a devil ail you two?
Martino.   Speak softly, sir, lest the devil hear you,   25
For Faustus at the court is late arrived,
And at his heels a thousand furies wait
To accomplish whatsoever the doctor please.
Benvolio.   What of this?
Martino.   Come, leave thy chamber first, and thou shalt see   30
This conjurer perform such rare exploits
Before the Pope and royal Emperor
As never yet was seen in Germany.
Benvolio.   Has not the Pope enough of conjuring yet?
He was upon the devil's back late enough,   35
And if he be so far in love with him,
I would he would post with him to Rome again.
Frederick.   Speak, wilt thou come and see this sport?
Benvolio.   Not I.
Martino.   Wilt thou stand in thy window and see it then?
Benvolio.   Ay, and I fall not asleep i' th' meantime.   40
Martino.   The Emperor is at hand, who comes to see
What wonders by black spells may compassed be.
Benvolio.   Well, go you attend the Emperor. I am content for this
once to thrust my head out at a window, for they say if a man be drunk
overnight the devil cannot hurt him in the morning. If that   [45
be true, I have a charm in my head shall control him as well as
the conjurer, I warrant you.
                         Exit [Frederick, with Martino. Benvolio remains
                                        at the window above].

                                                              IV,ii.
A sennet [is sounded. Enter] Charles, the German Emperor,
Bruno, [the Duke of] Saxony, Faustus, Mephistophilis, Frede-
rick, Martino, and Attendants.
Emperor.   Wonder of men, renowned magician,
Thrice-learnèd Faustus, welcome to our court.
This deed of thine, in setting Bruno free
From his and our professèd enemy,

---

19 *took . . . stoups* i.e., had a drinking   32 *the Pope* i.e., Bruno.
bout with brimming goblets.

Shall add more excellence unto thine art   5
Than if by powerful necromantic spells
Thou couldst command the world's obedience.
Forever be beloved of Carolus,
And if this Bruno thou hast late redeemed
In peace possess the triple diadem   10
And sit in Peter's chair despite of chance,
Thou shalt be famous through all Italy
And honored of the German Emperor.

Faustus.   These gracious words, most royal Carolus,
Shall make poor Faustus to his utmost power   15
Both love and serve the German Emperor
And lay his life at holy Bruno's feet.
For proof whereof, if so your grace be pleased,
The doctor stands prepared by power of art
To cast his magic charms that shall pierce through   20
The ebon gates of ever-burning hell,
And hale the stubborn Furies from their caves
To compass whatsoe'er your grace commands.

Benvolio. [*above*]   Blood, he speaks terribly, but for all that, I do not
greatly believe him. He looks as like a conjurer as the Pope to a   [25
costermonger.

Emperor.   Then, Faustus, as thou late did'st promise us,
We would behold that famous conqueror,
Great Alexander, and his paramour
In their true shapes and state majestical,   30
That we may wonder at their excellence.

Faustus.   Your majesty shall see them presently.
Mephistophilis, away,
And with a solemn noise of trumpets' sound
Present before this royal Emperor,   35
Great Alexander and his beauteous paramour.

Mephistophilis.   Faustus, I will.

                                        [*Exit.*]

Benvolio.   Well, master doctor, an your devils come not away quickly,
you shall have me asleep presently. Zounds, I could eat myself for
anger to think I have been such an ass all this while, to stand   [40
gaping after the devil's governor and can see nothing.

Faustus.   I'll make you feel something anon, if my art fail me not.
My lord, I must forewarn your majesty
That when my spirits present the royal shapes
Of Alexander and his paramour,
Your grace demand no questions of the king,   45
But in dumb silence let them come and go.

IV,ii.
     9 *redeemed* rescued.   25 *the Pope* i.e., Bruno.

Emperor. Be it as Faustus please; we are content.

Benvolio. Ay, ay, and I am content too. And thou bring Alexander and his paramour before the Emperor, I'll be Actæon and turn [50 myself to a stag.

Faustus. And I'll play Diana and send you the horns presently.

> [*A*] *sennet* [*is sounded*]. *Enter at one* [*door*] *the Emperor Alexander, at the other Darius. They meet* [*in combat*]. *Darius is thrown down; Alexander kills him, takes off his crown, and, offering to go out, his paramour meets him. He embraceth her and sets Darius' crown upon her head: and coming back, both salute the Emperor, who, leaving his state, offers to embrace them, which Faustus seeing, suddenly stays him. Then trumpets cease and music sounds.*

My gracious lord, you do forget yourself.
These are but shadows, not substantial.

Emperor. O pardon me. My thoughts are so ravishèd   55
With sight of this renownèd emperor,
That in mine arms I would have compassed him.
But, Faustus, since I may not speak to them,
To satisfy my longing thoughts at full,
Let me this tell thee: I have heard it said   60
That this fair lady, whilst she lived on earth,
Had on her neck a little wart or mole;
How may I prove that saying to be true?

Faustus. Your majesty may boldly go and see.

Emperor. Faustus, I see it plain,   65
And in this sight thou better pleasest me
Than if I gained another monarchy.

Faustus. Away! Be gone!

Exit show.

See, see, my gracious lord, what strange beast is yon, that thrusts his head out at window?   70

Emperor. O wondrous sight! See, Duke of Saxony,
Two spreading horns most strangely fastenèd
Upon the head of young Benvolio.

Saxony. What? Is he asleep or dead?

Faustus. He sleeps, my lord, but dreams not of his horns.   75

Emperor. This sport is excellent. We'll call and wake him.
What ho, Benvolio!

Benvolio. A plague upon you! Let me sleep a while.

Emperor. I blame thee not to sleep much, having such a head of thine own.   80

Saxony. Look up, Benvolio; 'tis the Emperor calls.

---

50 *Actæon* See note to *Edward II*, I,i, 67.

52, SD *Darius* King Darius III of Persia (336–330 B.C.) defeated at Granicus in 334 B.C. by the Greeks under Alexander the Great.

Benvolio.   The Emperor? Where? O zounds, my head!

Emperor.   Nay, and thy horns hold, 'tis no matter for thy head, for
that's armed sufficiently.

Faustus.   Why, how now, sir knight! What, hanged by the horns?   [85
This is most horrible. Fie, fie, pull in your head for shame. Let not all
the world wonder at you.

Benvolio.   Zounds, doctor, is this your villainy?

Faustus.   O say not so, sir. The doctor has no skill,
No art, no cunning, to present these lords   90
Or bring before this royal Emperor
The mighty monarch, warlike Alexander.
If Faustus do it, you are straight resolved
In bold Actæon's shape to turn a stag.
And therefore, my lord, so please your majesty,   95
I'll raise a kennel of hounds shall hunt him so
As all his footmanship shall scarce prevail
To keep his carcass from their bloody fangs.
Ho, Belimote, Argiron, Asterote!

Benvolio.   Hold, hold! Zounds, he'll raise up a kennel of devils,   [100
I think, anon. Good, my lord, entreat for me. 'Sblood, I am never able
to endure these torments.

Emperor.   Then, good master doctor,
Let me entreat you to remove his horns.
He has done penance now sufficiently.   105

Faustus.   My gracious lord, not so much for injury done to me, as to
delight your majesty with some mirth, hath Faustus justly requited
this injurious knight; which being all I desire, I am content to remove
his horns. Mephistophilis, transform him.

                     [Mephistophilis removes the horns.]
And hereafter, sir, look you speak well of scholars.   110

Benvolio. [aside]   Speak well of ye? 'Sblood, and scholars be such cuckold makers to clap horns of honest men's heads o' this order, I'll ne'er
trust smooth faces and small ruffs more. But an I be not revenged
for this, would I might be turned to a gaping oyster and drink nothing
but salt water.   115

                     [Exit Benvolio above.]

Emperor.   Come, Faustus. While the Emperor lives,
In recompense of this thy high desert,
Thou shalt command the state of Germany
And live beloved of mighty Carolus.

                                                    Exeunt.

Enter Benvolio, Martino, Frederick, and Soldiers.   IV,iii.

Martino.   Nay, sweet Benvolio, let us sway thy thoughts
From this attempt against the conjurer.
Benvolio.   Away! You love me not to urge me thus.
Shall I let slip so great an injury,
When every servile groom jests at my wrongs   5
And in their rustic gambols proudly say,
'Benvolio's head was graced with horns today'?
O, may these eyelids never close again
Till with my sword I have that conjurer slain.
If you will aid me in this enterprise,   10
Then draw your weapons and be resolute.
If not, depart. Here will Benvolio die,
But Faustus' death shall quit my infamy.
Frederick.   Nay, we will stay with thee, betide what may,
And kill that doctor if he come this way.   15
Benvolio.   Then, gentle Frederick, hie thee to the grove,
And place our servants and our followers
Close in an ambush there behind the trees.
By this, I know, the conjurer is near.
I saw him kneel and kiss the Emperor's hand   20
And take his leave, laden with rich rewards.
Then, soldiers, boldly fight. If Faustus die,
Take you the wealth; leave us the victory.
Frederick.   Come, soldiers. Follow me unto the grove.
Who kills him shall have gold and endless love.   25
                        Exit Frederick with the Soldiers.
Benvolio.   My head is lighter than it was by th'horns,
But yet my heart's more ponderous than my head
And pants until I see that conjurer dead.
Martino.   Where shall we place ourselves, Benvolio?
Benvolio.   Here will we stay to bide the first assault.   30
O, were that damnèd hell-hound but in place,
Thou soon shouldst see me quit my foul disgrace.
                        Enter Frederick.
Frederick.   Close, close, the conjurer is at hand
And all alone comes walking in his gown.
Be ready then, and strike the peasant down.   35
Benvolio.   Mine be that honor then. Now, sword, strike home.
For horns he gave I'll have his head anon.
                Enter Faustus with the false head.
Martino.   See, see, he comes.
Benvolio.   No words! This blow ends all.
Hell take his soul; his body thus must fall.   [*He stabs Faustus.*]
Faustus. [*falling*] Oh!   40

IV,iii.
   13 *quit* pay for.

Frederick.   Groan you, master doctor?
Benvolio.   Break may his heart with groans! Dear Frederick, see,
   Thus will I end his griefs immediately.
Martino.   Strike with a willing hand. His head is off.
                     [Benvolio strikes off Faustus' false head.]
Benvolio.   The devil's dead. The Furies now may laugh.   45
Frederick.   Was this that stern aspèct, that awful frown,
   Made the grim monarch of infernal spirits
   Tremble and quake at his commanding charms?
Martino.   Was this that damnèd head whose heart conspired
   Benvolio's shame before the Emperor?   50
Benvolio.   Ay, that's the head, and here the body lies,
   Justly rewarded for his villainies.
Frederick.   Come, let's devise how we may add more shame
   To the black scandal of his hated name.
Benvolio.   First, on his head, in quittance of my wrongs,   55
   I'll nail huge forkèd horns and let them hang
   Within the window where he yoked me first,
   That all the world may see my just revenge.
Martino.   What use shall we put his beard to?
Benvolio.   We'll sell it to a chimney-sweeper. It will wear out ten   [60
   birchen brooms, I warrant you.
Frederick.   What shall eyes do?
Benvolio.   We'll put out his eyes, and they shall serve for buttons to
   his lips to keep his tongue from catching cold.
Martino.   An excellent policy! And now, sirs, having divided him,   [65
   what shall the body do?
                              [Faustus rises.]
Benvolio.   Zounds, the devil's alive again.
Frederick.   Give him his head, for God's sake.
Faustus.   Nay, keep it. Faustus will have heads and hands,
   Ay, all your hearts, to recompense this deed.   70
   Knew you not, traitors, I was limited
   For four-and-twenty years to breathe on earth?
   And had you cut my body with your swords,
   Or hewed this flesh and bones as small as sand,
   Yet in a minute had my spirit returned,   75
   And I had breathed a man made free from harm.
   But wherefore do I dally my revenge?
   Asteroth, Belimoth, Mephistophilis!
             Enter Mephistophilis and other Devils.
   Go, horse these traitors on your fiery backs,
   And mount aloft with them as high as heaven;   80
   Thence pitch them headlong to the lowest hell.
   Yet stay. The world shall see their misery,
   And hell shall after plague their treachery.

71 *limited* given a specific term.

Go, Belimoth, and take this caitiff hence,
And hurl him in some lake of mud and dirt. 85
Take thou this other; drag him through the woods
Amongst the pricking thorns and sharpest briars,
Whilst with my gentle Mephistophilis
This traitor flies unto some steepy rock
That, rolling down, may break the villain's bones 90
As he intended to dismember me.
Fly hence. Dispatch my charge immediately.
Frederick.　Pity us, gentle Faustus. Save our lives.
Faustus.　Away!
Frederick.　　　He must needs go that the devil drives.
　　　　　　　　　　Exeunt Spirits with the Knights.
　　　　　Enter the ambushed Soldiers.
First Soldier.　Come, sirs, prepare yourselves in readiness. 95
Make haste to help these noble gentlemen:
I heard them parley with the conjurer.
Second Soldier.　See where he comes. Dispatch and kill the slave.
Faustus.　What's here? An ambush to betray my life?
Then, Faustus, try thy skill. Base peasants, stand, 100
For lo, these trees remove at my command
And stand as bulwarks 'twixt yourselves and me,
To shield me from your hated treachery.
Yet to encounter this your weak attempt,
Behold an army comes incontinent. 105
　　　　Faustus strikes the door, and enter a Devil playing on a
　　　　drum, after him another bearing an ensign, and divers
　　　　with weapons, Mephistophilis with fireworks. They set
　　　　upon the Soldiers and drive them out. [Exit Faustus.]

　　Enter at several doors Benvolio, Frederick, and Martino, their
　　heads and faces bloody and besmeared with mud and dirt, all
　　　　　　　having horns on their heads.
Martino.　What ho, Benvolio!
Benvolio.　Here! What, Frederick, ho!
Frederick.　O help me, gentle friend. Where is Martino?
Martino.　Dear Frederick, here,
Half smothered in a lake of mud and dirt,
Through which the Furies dragged me by the heels. 5
Frederick.　Martino, see! Benvolio's horns again.
Martino.　O misery! How now, Benvolio?

101 *remove* change their positions. 105 *incontinent* at once.

Benvolio.   Defend me, heaven. Shall I be haunted still?
Martino.   Nay, fear not man; we have not power to kill.   10
Benvolio.   My friends transformèd thus! O hellish spite!
    Your heads are all set with horns.
Frederick.   You hit it right.
    It is your own you mean. Feel on your head.
Benvolio.   Zounds, horns again!
Martino.   Nay, chafe not man. We all are sped.   15
Benvolio.   What devil attends this damned magician,
    That, spite of spite, our wrongs are doublèd?
Frederick.   What may we do, that we may hide our shames?
Benvolio.   If we should follow him to work revenge,
    He'd join long asses' ears to these huge horns,   20
    And make us laughing-stocks to all the world.
Martino.   What shall we then do, dear Benvolio?
Benvolio.   I have a castle joining near these woods,
    And thither we'll repair and live obscure
    Till time shall alter these our brutish shapes.   25
    Sith black disgrace hath thus eclipsed our fame,
    We'll rather die with grief than live with shame.

                                        Exeunt omnes.

                    Enter Faustus and Mephistophilis.   IV,v.
Faustus.   Now, Mephistophilis, the restless course
    That time doth run with calm and silent foot,
    Shortening my days and thread of vital life,
    Calls for the payment of my latest years.
    Therefore, sweet Mephistophilis, let us   5
    Make haste to Wittenberg.
Mephistophilis.   What, will you go on horseback, or on foot?
Faustus.   Nay, till I am past this fair and pleasant green,
    I'll walk on foot.

                                    [*Exit Mephistophilis.*]

                    Enter a Horse-Courser.
Horse-Courser.   I have been all this day seeking one Master   [10
    Fustian. Mass, see where he is. God save you, master doctor.

IV,iv.
  9 *haunted* (1) bewitched (2) hunted,
pursued (since he is a stag).
  15 *sped* provided (with horns).
IV,v.
  The first eleven lines of this scene,
omitted by Greg from his reconstruction
of the play, appear only in the 1604
quarto. While recognizing that they may
well be spurious, I have retained them
because they provide a transition to the
Horse-Courser episode and at the same
time remind the audience of the im-
pending tragedy of Faustus' death.
  11 *Fustian* The perversion of Faustus'
name is a deliberate attempt at humor.

Faustus. What, horse-courser! You are well met.

Horse-Courser. I beseech your worship, accept of these forty dollars.

Faustus. Friend, thou canst not buy so good a horse for so small a
     price. I have no great need to sell him, but if thou likest him   [15
     for ten dollars more, take him, because I see thou hast a good mind
     to him.

Horse-Courser. I beseech you, sir, accept of this. I am a very poor
     man and have lost very much of late by horse-flesh, and this bargain
     will set me up again.   20

Faustus. Well, I will not stand with thee. Give me the money.

          [*The Horse-Courser gives Faustus money.*]
     Now, sirrah, I must tell you that you may ride him o'er hedge and
     ditch, and spare him not. But, do you hear? In any case, ride him not
     into the water.

Horse-Courser. How sir? Not into the water? Why, will he not   [25
     drink of all waters?

Faustus. Yes, he will drink of all waters, but ride him not into the
     water—o'er hedge and ditch, or where thou wilt, but not into the
     water. Go, bid the hostler deliver him unto you, and remember what
     I say.   30

Horse-Courser. I warrant you, sir. O joyful day! Now am I a man
     made forever.

                                                              Exit.

Faustus. What art thou, Faustus, but a man condemned to die?
     Thy fatal time draws to a final end.
     Despair doth drive distrust into my thoughts.   35
     Confound these passions with a quiet sleep.
     Tush! Christ did call the thief upon the cross;
     Then rest thee, Faustus, quiet in conceit.

                                   He sits to sleep [*in his chair*].

                  Enter the Horse-Courser, wet.

Horse-Courser. O what a cozening doctor was this? I riding my
     horse into the water, thinking some hidden mystery had been in   [40
     the horse, I had nothing under me but a little straw and had much
     ado to escape drowning. Well, I'll go rouse him and make him
     give me my forty dollars again. Ho, sirrah doctor, you cozening
     scab! Master doctor, awake and rise, and give me my money again,
     for your horse is turned to a bottle of hay. Master doctor!   45

          He [*tries to wake Faustus, and in doing so*] *pulls off his leg.*
     Alas, I am undone! What shall I do? I have pulled off his leg.

                                           [*Faustus awakes.*]

Faustus. O, help, help! The villain hath murdered me.

21 *stand . . . thee* bargain.
26 *drink . . . waters* be ready for anything (a common proverb of the time).

38 *conceit* thoughts.
40 *mystery* quality.
44 *scab* scurvy fellow.
45 *bottle* bundle.

Horse-Courser. Murder or not murder, now he has but one leg, I'll
outrun him and cast this leg into some ditch or other.

Faustus. Stop him, stop him, stop him! Ha, ha, ha, Faustus hath [50
his leg again, and the horse-courser a bundle of hay for his forty
dollars.

Enter Wagner.

How now, Wagner, what news with thee?

Wagner. If it please you, the Duke of Anholt doth earnestly entreat
your company and hath sent some of his men to attend you with [55
provision fit for your journey.

Faustus. The Duke of Anholt's an honorable gentleman, and one to
whom I must be no niggard of my cunning. Come away.

Exeunt.

IV,vi.

*Enter [Robin, the] Clown, Dick, [the] Horse-Courser, and a
Carter.*

Carter. Come, my masters, I'll bring you to the best beer in Europe.
What ho, hostess! Where be these whores?

Enter Hostess.

Hostess. How now, what lack you? What, my old guests, welcome.

Robin. Sirrah, Dick, dost thou know why I stand so mute?

Dick. No, Robin; why is't?   5

Robin. I am eighteen pence on the score. But say nothing; see if she
have forgotten me.

Hostess. Who's this that stands so solemnly by himself? What, my old
guest?

Robin. O hostess, how do you? I hope my score stands still.   10

Hostess. Ay, there's no doubt of that, for methinks you make no haste
to wipe it out.

Dick. Why, hostess, I say, fetch us some beer.

Hostess. You shall presently. Look up into th'hall there, ho!

Exit.

Dick. Come, sirs, what shall we do now till mine hostess come?   15

Carter. Marry, sir, I'll tell you the bravest tale how a conjurer served
me. You know Doctor Fauster?

Horse-Courser. Ay, a plague take him. Here's some on's have cause to
know him. Did he conjure thee too?

Carter. I'll tell you how he served me. As I was going to Witten- [20
berg t'other day with a load of hay, he met me and asked me what
he should give me for as much hay as he could eat. Now, sir, I thinking that a little would serve his turn, bade him take as much as he

6 *on the score* in debt.   10 *stands still* does not go higher.

would for three farthings. So he presently gave me my money and
fell to eating; and as I am a cursen man, he never left eating till [25
he had eat up all my load of hay.

All. O monstrous! Eat a whole load of hay!

Robin. Yes, yes, that may be, for I have heard of one that has eat a
load of logs.

Horse-Courser. Now, sirs, you shall hear how villainously he [30
served me. I went to him yesterday to buy a horse of him, and he
would by no means sell him under forty dollars. So, sir, because I
knew him to be such a horse as would run over hedge and ditch and
never tire, I gave him his money. So when I had my horse, Doctor
Fauster bade me ride him night and day and spare him no time; [35
but, quoth he, in any case ride him not into the water. Now sir, I
thinking the horse had had some rare quality that he would not have
me know of, what did I but rid him into a great river, and when I
came just in the midst, my horse vanished away, and I sat straddling
upon a bottle of hay.   40

All. O brave doctor!

Horse-Courser. But you shall hear how bravely I served him for it. I
went me home to his house, and there I found him asleep. I kept a
hallooing and whooping in his ears, but all could not wake him.
I seeing that, took him by the leg and never rested pulling till [45
I had pulled me his leg quite off, and now 'tis at home in mine hostry.

Robin. And has the doctor but one leg then? That's excellent, for one
of his devils turned me into the likeness of an ape's face.

Carter. Some more drink, hostess.

Robin. Hark you, we'll into another room and drink a while, [50
and then we'll go seek out the doctor.

                                                    Exeunt.

                                                      IV,vii.

Enter the Duke of Anholt, his Duchess, Faustus, and Mephis-
tophilis, [Servants and Attendants].

Duke. Thanks, master doctor, for these pleasant sights. Nor know I
how sufficiently to recompense your great deserts in erecting that enchanted castle in the air, the sight whereof so delighted me, as nothing in the world could please me more.

Faustus. I do think myself, my good lord, highly recompensed in [5
that it pleaseth your grace to think but well of that which Faustus
hath performed. But, gracious lady, it may be that you have taken
no pleasure in those sights. Therefore, I pray you, tell me what is
the thing you most desire to have; be it in the world, it shall be

25 *cursen* christened.

yours. I have heard that great-bellied women do long for things   [10
are rare and dainty.

Duchess.   True, master doctor, and since I find you so kind, I will
make known unto you what my heart desires to have. And were it
now summer, as it is January, a dead time of the winter, I would
request no better meat than a dish of ripe grapes.   15

Faustus.   This is but a small matter. Go, Mephistophilis, away!

Exit Mephistophilis.

Madam I will do more than this for your content.

Enter Mephistophilis again with the grapes.

Here; now taste ye these. They should be good, for they come from a
far country, I can tell you.

Duke.   This makes me wonder more than all the rest, that at this   [20
time of year, when every tree is barren of his fruit, from whence you
had these ripe grapes.

Faustus.   Please it, your grace, the year is divided into two circles over
the whole world, so that when it is winter with us, in the contrary
circle it is likewise summer with them, as in India, Saba, and   [25
such countries that lie far east, where they have fruit twice a year.
From whence, by means of a swift spirit that I have, I had these
grapes brought, as you see.

Duchess.   And trust me, they are the sweetest grapes that e'er I tasted.

The Clown[s, Robin, Dick, the Carter, and the Horse-Courser,]
bounce at the gate within.

Duke.   What rude disturbers have we at the gate?   30
Go, pacify their fury. Set it ope,
And then demand of them what they would have.

[Exit a Servant.]

They knock again and call out to talk with Faustus.

[Enter Servant to them.]

Servant.   Why, how now, masters, what a coil is there?
What is the reason you disturb the duke.

Dick.   We have no reason for it; therefore a fig for him.   35

Servant.   What, saucy varlets, dare you be so bold?

Horse-Courser.   I hope, sir, we have wit enough to be more bold than
welcome.

Servant.   It appears so. Pray be bold elsewhere,
And trouble not the duke.

Duke.   What would they have?   40

IV,vii.

25 *Saba* Sheba.

29, SD The staging of this scene presents considerable difficulty. It may be
that while Faustus, the Duke, and the
Duchess are on the inner stage the
clowns appear on the outer platform and
knock at the side door. They may have
approached the platform from the theater
pit. A servant moves from the inner to
the outer stage to address them. This
explanation, however, makes it difficult
to account for the stage direction 'within'
since this refers usually to action on the
inner stage. *bounce* bang.

33 *coil* disturbance.

Servant.   They all cry out to speak with Doctor Faustus.

Carter.   Ay, and we will speak with him.

Duke.   Will you, sir? Commit the rascals.

Dick.   Commit with us! He were as good commit with his father as
   commit with us.   45

Faustus.   I do beseech your grace, let them come in;
   They are good subject for a merriment.

Duke.   Do as thou wilt, Faustus. I give thee leave.

Faustus.   I thank your grace.
                     Enter Robin, Dick, Carter, and Horse-Courser.
                                    Why, how now, my good friends?
   'Faith you are too outrageous, but come near;   50
   I have procured your pardons. Welcome all!

Robin.   Nay, sir, we will be welcome for our money, and we will pay
   for what we take. What ho! Give's half a dozen of beer here, and be
   hanged.

Faustus.   Nay, hark you; can you tell me where you are?   55

Carter.   Ay, marry can I: we are under heaven.

Servant.   Ay, but sir sauce-box, know you in what place?

Horse-Courser.   Ay, ay, the house is good enough to drink in. Zouns,
   fill us some beer, or we'll break all the barrels in the house and dash
   out all your brains with your bottles.   60

Faustus.   Be not so furious. Come, you shall have beer.
   My lord, beseech you give me leave a while:
   I'll gage my credit, 'twill content your grace.

Duke.   With all my heart, kind doctor. Please thyself;
   Our servants and our court's at thy command.   65

Faustus.   I humbly thank your grace. Then fetch some beer.

Horse-Courser.   Ay, marry, there spake a doctor indeed, and 'faith,
   I'll drink a health to thy wooden leg for that word.

Faustus.   My wooden leg? What dost thou mean by that?

Carter.   Ha, ha, ha! Dost hear him, Dick? He has forgot his leg.   70

Horse-Courser.   Ay, ay, he does not stand much upon that.

Faustus.   No, faith; not much upon a wooden leg.

Carter.   Good lord, that flesh and blood should be so frail with your
   worship! Do not you remember a horse-courser you sold a horse to?

Faustus.   Yes, I remember I sold one a horse.   75

Carter.   And do you remember you bid he should not ride into the
   water?

Faustus.   Yes, I do very well remember that.

Carter.   And do you remember nothing of your leg?

Faustus.   No, in good sooth.   80

Carter.   Then, I pray, remember your courtesy.

Faustus.   I thank you, sir.

---

50 *outrageous* violent.   81 *courtesy* curtsy, or leg.
71 *stand much* make much of (with a
quibble).

Carter.   'Tis not so much worth. I pray you, tell me one thing.

Faustus.   What's that?

Carter.   Be both your legs bedfellows every night together?   ' 85

Faustus.   Wouldst thou make a Colossus of me, that thou askest me such questions?

Carter.   No, truly, sir. I would make nothing of you, but I would fain know that.

Enter Hostess with drink.

Faustus.   Then, I assure thee, certainly they are.   90

Carter.   I thank you; I am fully satisfied.

Faustus.   But wherefore dost thou ask?

Carter.   For nothing, sir. But methinks you should have a wooden bedfellow of one of 'em.

Horse-Courser.   Why, do you hear, sir; did not I pull off one of [95 your legs when you were asleep?

Faustus.   But I have it again, now I am awake. Look you here, sir.

All.   O horrible! Had the doctor three legs?

Carter.   Do you remember, sir, how you cozened me and ate up my load of—   100
Faustus charms him dumb.

Dick.   Do you remember how you made me wear an ape's—
[*Faustus charms him dumb.*]

Horse-Courser.   You whoreson conjuring scab, do you remember how you cozened me with a ho—
[*Faustus charms him dumb.*]

Robin.   Ha' you forgotten me? You think to carry it away with your *hey-pass* and *re-pass;* do you remember the dog's fa—   105
[*Faustus charms him dumb.*] *Exeunt Clowns.*

Hostess.   Who pays for the ale? Hear you, master doctor, now you have sent away my guests, I pray who shall pay me for my a—
[*Faustus charms her dumb.*] *Exit Hostess.*

Duchess.   My lord,
We are much beholding to this learnèd man.

Duke.   So are we, madam, which we will recompense   110
With all the love and kindness that we may.
His artful sport drives all sad thoughts away.

Exeunt.

V,i.

*Thunder and Lightning. Enter Devils with covered dishes.
Mephistophilis leads them into Faustus' study. Then enter
Wagner.*

---

86 *Colossus* a giant statue said to have   to the ancient harbor of Rhodes.
stood with its legs astride at the entrance   104 *carry it away* come off best.

Wagner. I think my master means to die shortly.
  He has made his will and given me his wealth,
  His house, his goods, and store of golden plate,
  Besides two thousand ducats ready coined.
  I wonder what he means. If death were nigh,   5
  He would not frolic thus. He's now at supper
  With the scholars, where there's such belly-cheer
  As Wagner in his life ne'er saw the like.
  And see where they come; belike the feast is done.

                                                        Exit.

        Enter Faustus, Mephistophilis, and two or three Scholars.

First Scholar. Master Doctor Faustus, since our conference about [10
fair ladies, which was the beautifulest in all the world, we have determined with ourselves that Helen of Greece was the admirablest
lady that ever lived. Therefore, master doctor, if you will do us so
much favor as to let us see that peerless dame of Greece, whom all
the world admires for majesty, we should think ourselves much [15
beholding unto you.

Faustus. Gentlemen,
  For that I know your friendship is unfeigned,
  And Faustus' custom is not to deny
  The just requests of those that wish him well,   20
  You shall behold that peerless dame of Greece,
  No otherwise for pomp and majesty
  Than when Sir Paris crossed the seas with her
  And brought the spoils to rich Dardania.
  Be silent then, for danger is in words.   25
        *Music sounds. Mephistophilis brings in Helen; she passeth
                          over the stage.*

Second Scholar. Was this fair Helen, whose admirèd worth
  Made Greece with ten years war afflict poor Troy?
  Too simple is my wit to tell her praise,
  Whom all the world admires for majesty.

Third Scholar. No marvel though the angry Greeks pursued   30
  With ten years' war the rape of such a queen,
  Whose heavenly beauty passeth all compare.

First Scholar. Since we have seen the pride of nature's works
  And only paragon of excellence,
  We'll take our leaves, and for this blessèd sight   35
  Happy and blest be Faustus evermore.

Faustus. Gentlemen, farewell; the same wish I to you.

                                                Exeunt Scholars.

                    Enter an Old Man.

Old Man. O gentle Faustus, leave this damned art,

V,i.
  9 *belike* no doubt.   24 *Dardania* Troy.

This magic that will charm thy soul to hell
And quite bereave thee of salvation.   40
Though thou hast now offended like a man,
Do not persevere in it like a devil.
Yet, yet, thou hast an amiable soul,
If sin by custom grow not into nature.
Then, Faustus, will repentance come too late;   45
Then thou art banished from the sight of heaven.
No mortal can express the pains of hell.
It may be this my exhortation
Seems harsh and all unpleasant; let it not,
For, gentle son, I speak it not in wrath   50
Or envy of thee, but in tender love
And pity of thy future misery.
And so have hope that this my kind rebuke,
Checking thy body, may amend thy soul.

Faustus.   Where art thou, Faustus? Wretch, what hast thou done?   55
Damned art thou, Faustus, damned; despair and die!
Hell claims his right, and with a roaring voice
Says, 'Faustus, come; thine hour is almost come';
And Faustus now will come to do thee right.
                    Mephistophilis gives him a dagger.

Old Man.   O stay, good Faustus, stay thy desperate steps.   60
I see an angel hovers o'er thy head,
And with a vial full of precious grace
Offers to pour the same into thy soul.
Then call for mercy and avoid despair.

Faustus.   Ah, my sweet friend, I feel thy words   65
To comfort my distressèd soul.
Leave me a while to ponder on my sins.

Old Man.   Faustus, I leave thee, but with grief of heart,
Fearing the enemy of thy hapless soul.
                                        Exit.

Faustus.   Accursèd Faustus, where is mercy now?   70
I do repent, and yet I do despair.
Hell strives with grace for conquest in my breast.
What shall I do to shun the snares of death?

Mephistophilis.   Thou traitor, Faustus, I arrest thy soul
For disobedience to my sovereign lord.   75
Revolt, or I'll in piecemeal tear thy flesh.

Faustus.   I do repent I e'er offended him.
Sweet Mephistophilis, entreat thy lord
To pardon my unjust presumption,
And with my blood again I will confirm   80
The former vow I made to Lucifer.

43 *amiable* worthy of divine love or   51 *envy of* ill-will towards.
grace.   54 *Checking* admonishing.

Mephistophilis. Do it then, Faustus, with unfeignèd heart,
  Lest greater dangers do attend thy drift.
                        [*Faustus stabs his arm and writes on a
                              paper with his blood.*]
Faustus. Torment, sweet friend, that base and agèd man
  That durst dissuade me from thy Lucifer,   85
  With greatest torment that our hell affords.
Mephistophilis. His faith is great; I cannot touch his soul,
  But what I may afflict his body with
  I will attempt, which is but little worth.
Faustus. One thing, good servant, let me crave of thee   90
  To glut the longing of my heart's desire—
  That I may have unto my paramour
  That heavenly Helen which I saw of late,
  Whose sweet embracings may extinguish clear
  Those thoughts that do dissuade me from my vow,   95
  And keep mine oath I made to Lucifer.
Mephistophilis. This, or what else my Faustus shall desire,
  Shall be performed in twinkling of an eye.
        Enter Helen again, passing over [*the stage*] *between two Cupids.*
Faustus. Was this the face that launched a thousand ships
  And burnt the topless towers of Ilium?   100
  Sweet Helen, make me immortal with a kiss.

                                    [*She kisses him.*]

  Her lips suck forth my soul. See where it flies!
  Come, Helen, come, give me my soul again.
  Here will I dwell, for heaven is in these lips,
  And all is dross that is not Helena.   105
                  [*Enter the Old Man.*]
  I will be Paris, and for love of thee
  Instead of Troy shall Wittenberg be sacked;
  And I will combat with weak Menelaus
  And wear thy colors on my plumèd crest.
  Yea, I will wound Achilles in the heel   110
  And then return to Helen for a kiss.
  O, thou art fairer than the evening's air,
  Clad in the beauty of a thousand stars.
  Brighter art thou than flaming Jupiter
  When he appeared to hapless Semele,   115
  More lovely than the monarch of the sky

---

82 *unfeignèd* honest
83 *drift* purpose.
108 *Menelaus* the husband of Helen
of Troy.
110 *Achilles* the Greek hero of the
Trojan war, wounded in the heel by
Paris.

115 *Semele* the daughter of Cadmus
and Harmonia who was beloved by Zeus
to whom she bore the child, Dionysus.
116–117 *monarch . . . arms* No such
episode is recorded in Greek mythology.
Arethusa was a nymph, one of the
Nereids, who governed a fountain on the
isle of Ortygia near Syracuse.

In wanton Arethusa's azured arms,
And none but thou shalt be my paramour.

                              Exeunt [all but the Old Man].

Old Man.   Accursèd Faustus, miserable man,
  That from thy soul exclud'st the grace of heaven   120
  And fliest the throne of his tribunal seat!

                          Enter the Devils.

Satan begins to sift me with his pride.
As in this furnace God shall try my faith,
My faith, vile hell, shall triumph over thee.
Ambitious fiends, see how the heavens smiles   125
At your repulse and laughs your state to scorn.
Hence hell, for hence I fly unto my God.

                                            Exeunt.

                              *

                                                        V,ii.

  Thunder. Enter [above] Lucifer, Beëlzebub, and Mephistophilis.

Lucifer.   Thus from infernal Dis do we ascend
  To view the subjects of our monarchy,
  Those souls which sin seals the black sons of hell,
  'Mong which as chief, Faustus, we come to thee,
  Bringing with us lasting damnation   5
  To wait upon thy soul. The time is come
  Which makes it forfeit.
Mephistophilis.   And this gloomy night,
  Here in this room will wretched Faustus be.
Beëlzebub.   And here we'll stay
  To mark him how he doth demean himself.   10
Mephistophilis.   How should he, but in desperate lunacy?
  Fond worldling, now his heart-blood dries with grief;
  His conscience kills it, and his laboring brain
  Begets a world of idle fantasies
  To over-reach the devil. But all in vain;   15
  His store of pleasures must be sauced with pain.
  He and his servant, Wagner, are at hand.
  Both come from drawing Faustus' latest will.
  See where they come.

                     Enter Faustus and Wagner.

Faustus.   Say, Wagner, thou hast perused my will;   20
  How dost thou like it?
Wagner.   Sir, so wondrous well

  126 *state* royal power.   16 *sauced* paid for.

V,ii.
  1 *Dis* Hades, or hell.

As in all humble duty I do yield
My life and lasting service for your love.
Enter the Scholars.
Faustus. Gramercies, Wagner. Welcome, gentlemen.
　　　　　　　　　　　　　　　　　　　　[Exit Wagner.]
First Scholar. Now, worthy Faustus, methinks your looks are changed. 25
Faustus. Ah, gentlemen!
Second Scholar. What ails Faustus?
Faustus. Ah, my sweet chamber-fellow, had I lived with thee, then had
I lived still, but now must die eternally. Look, sirs; comes he not?
Comes he not?　　　　　　　　　　　　　　　　　　　　30
First Scholar. O my dear Faustus, what imports this fear?
Second Scholar. Is all our pleasure turned to melancholy?
Third Scholar. He is not well with being over-solitary.
Second Scholar. If it be so, we'll have physicians, and Faustus shall be
cured.　　　　　　　　　　　　　　　　　　　　　　35
Third Scholar. 'Tis but a surfeit sir; fear nothing.
Faustus. A surfeit of deadly sin that hath damned both body and
soul.
Second Scholar. Yet Faustus, look up to heaven, and remember mercy
is infinite.　　　　　　　　　　　　　　　　　　　　40
Faustus. But Faustus' offence can ne'er be pardoned. The serpent that
tempted Eve may be saved, but not Faustus. Ah gentlemen, hear me
with patience and tremble not at my speeches. Though my heart
pants and quivers to remember that I have been a student here these
thirty years, O, would I had never seen Wittenberg, never read [45
book. And what wonders I have done, all Germany can witness—yea,
all the world—for which Faustus hath lost both Germany and the
world, yea heaven itself, heaven the seat of God, the throne of the
blessed, the kingdom of joy, and must remain in hell for ever. Hell,
ah hell for ever! Sweet friends, what shall become of Faustus, [50
being in hell for ever?
Second Scholar. Yet Faustus, call on God.
Faustus. On God, whom Faustus hath abjured? On God, whom
Faustus hath blasphemed? Ah, my God, I would weep, but the devil
draws in my tears. Gush forth blood instead of tears, yea life and [55
soul. O, he stays my tongue! I would lift up my hands, but see, they
hold 'em; they hold 'em.
All. Who, Faustus?
Faustus. Why, Lucifer and Mephistophilis. Ah, gentlemen, I gave them
my soul for my cunning.　　　　　　　　　　　　　　60
All. God forbid!
Faustus. God forbade it indeed, but Faustus hath done it. For the
vain pleasure of four and twenty years hath Faustus lost eternal joy
and felicity. I writ them a bill with mine own blood. The date is

24 *Gramercies* thanks.

expired. This is the time, and he will fetch me.   65

First Scholar.   Why did not Faustus tell us of this before, that divines
   might have prayed for thee?

Faustus.   Oft have I thought to have done so, but the devil threatened
   to tear me in pieces if I named God, to fetch me, body and soul, if
   I once gave ear to divinity. And now 'tis too late. Gentlemen   [70
   away, lest you perish with me.

Second Scholar.   O, what may we do to save Faustus?

Faustus.   Talk not of me, but save yourselves and depart.

Third Scholar.   God will strengthen me; I will stay with Faustus.

First Scholar.   Tempt not God, sweet friend, but let us into the   [75
   next room and there pray for him.

Faustus.   Ay, pray for me, pray for me; and what noise soever you
   hear, come not unto me, for nothing can rescue me.

Second Scholar.   Pray thou, and we will pray that God may have mercy
   upon thee.   80

Faustus.   Gentlemen, farewell. If I live till morning, I'll visit you; if
   not, Faustus is gone to hell.

All.   Faustus, farewell.

                                          Exeunt Scholars.

Mephistophilis.   [*above*]   Ay, Faustus, now thou hast no hope of heaven;
   Therefore despair. Think only upon hell,   85
   For that must be thy mansion, there to dwell.

Faustus.   O thou bewitching fiend, 'twas thy temptation
   Hath robbed me of eternal happiness.

Mephistophilis.   I do confess it, Faustus, and rejoice.
   'Twas I, that when thou wert i' the way to heaven,   90
   Damned up thy passage. When thou took'st the book
   To view the Scriptures, then I turned the leaves
   And led thine eye.
   What, weep'st thou? 'Tis too late. Despair! Farewell!
   Fools that will laugh on earth must weep in hell.   95

                                               Exit.

      Enter the Good Angel and the Bad Angel at several doors.

Good Angel.   Ah, Faustus, if thou hadst given ear to me,
   Innumerable joys had followed thee;
   But thou didst love the world.

Bad Angel.   Gave ear to me,
   And now must taste hell's pains perpetually.

Good Angel.   O what will all thy riches, pleasures, pomps   100
   Avail thee now?

Bad Angel.   Nothing but vex thee more,
   To want in hell, that had on earth such store.

                          Music while the throne descends.

Good Angel.   O, thou hast lost celestial happiness,
   Pleasures unspeakable, bliss without end.
   Hadst thou affected sweet divinity,   105

Hell or the devil had had no power on thee.
Hadst thou kept on that way, Faustus, behold
In what resplendent glory thou hadst sat
In yonder throne, like those bright shining saints,
And triumphed over hell. That hast thou lost,   110
And now, poor soul, must thy good angel leave thee.
                                        [*The throne ascends.*]
The jaws of hell are open to receive thee.

                                                Exit.

                                        Hell is discovered.

Bad Angel.   Now, Faustus, let thine eyes with horror stare
Into that vast perpetual torture-house.
There are the Furies tossing damnèd souls   115
On burning forks; their bodies boil in lead.
There are live quarters broiling on the coals,
That ne'er can die. This ever-burning chair
Is for o'er-tortured souls to rest them in.
These that are fed with sops of flaming fire   120
Were gluttons and loved only delicates
And laughed to see the poor starve at their gates.
But yet all these are nothing; thou shalt see
Ten thousand tortures that more horrid be.
Faustus.   O, I have seen enough to torture me.   125
Bad Angel.   Nay, thou must feel them, taste the smart of all.
He that loves pleasure must for pleasure fall.
And so I leave thee, Faustus, till anon;
Then wilt thou tumble in confusion.

                                                Exit.

              [*Hell disappears.*] *The clock strikes eleven.*
Faustus.   Ah Faustus,   130
Now hast thou but one bare hour to live,
And then thou must be damned perpetually.
Stand still, you ever-moving spheres of heaven,
That time may cease and midnight never come.
Fair nature's eye, rise, rise again, and make   135
Perpetual day; or let this hour be but
A year, a month, a week, a natural day,
That Faustus may repent and save his soul.
O lente, lente currite noctis equi!
The stars move still; time runs; the clock will strike;   140
The devil will come, and Faustus must be damned.
O, I'll leap up to my God! Who pulls me down?
See, see, where Christ's blood streams in the firmament!
One drop would save my soul, half a drop! Ah, my Christ!

139 *O . . . equi* O slowly, slowly, run   you horses of night (adapted from Ovid's
Amores).

Rend not my heart for naming of my Christ!   145
Yet will I call on him. O, spare me, Lucifer!
Where is it now? 'Tis gone. And see where God
Stretcheth out his arm and bends his ireful brows.
Mountains and hills, come, come, and fall on me,
And hide me from the heavy wrath of God.   150
No, no!
Then will I headlong run into the earth.
Earth, gape! O no, it will not harbor me!
You stars that reigned at my nativity,
Whose influence hath allotted death and hell,   155
Now draw up Faustus like a foggy mist
Into the entrails of yon laboring cloud,
That when you vomit forth into the air,
My limbs may issue from your smoky mouths,
So that my soul may but ascend to heaven.   160

The watch strikes.

Ah, half the hour is past; 'twill all be past anon.
O God,
If thou wilt not have mercy on my soul,
Yet for Christ's sake, whose blood hath ransomed me,
Impose some end to my incessant pain.   165
Let Faustus live in hell a thousand years,
A hundred thousand, and at last be saved.
O, no end is limited to damnèd souls.
Why wert thou not a creature wanting soul?
Or why is this immortal that thou hast?   170
Ah, Pythagoras' *metempsychosis,* were that true,
This soul should fly from me and I be changed
Into some brutish beast. All beasts are happy,
For, when they die
Their souls are soon dissolved in elements,   175
But mine must live still to be plagued in hell.
Cursed be the parents that engendered me!
No, Faustus, curse thyself, curse Lucifer
That hath deprived thee of the joys of heaven.

The clock strikes twelve.

O, it strikes, it strikes! Now, body, turn to air,   180
Or Lucifer will bear thee quick to hell.
O soul, be changed to little water-drops,
And fall into the ocean, ne'er be found!

Thunder, and enter the Devils.

My God, my God, look not so fierce on me!
Adders and serpents, let me breathe a while!   185

---

171 *metempsychosis* belief in the trans-   Greek philosopher, Pythagoras of Samos.
migration of souls, associated with the   181 *quick* alive.

Ugly hell, gape not! Come not, Lucifer!
I'll burn my books! Ah, Mephistophilis!

Exeunt [Faustus and Devils].

Enter the Scholars.	V,iii.

First Scholar.   Come, gentlemen, let us go visit Faustus,
For such a dreadful night was never seen
Since first the world's creation did begin.
Such fearful shrieks and cries were never heard.
Pray heaven the doctor have escaped the danger.   5
Second Scholar.   O help us, heaven! See, here are Faustus' limbs,
All torn asunder by the hand of death.
Third Scholar.   The devils whom Faustus served have torn him thus;
For 'twixt the hours of twelve and one, methought
I heard him shriek and call aloud for help,   10
At which self time the house seemed all on fire
With dreadful horror of these damnèd fiends.
Second Scholar.   Well, gentlemen, though Faustus' end be such
As every Christian heart laments to think on,
Yet for he was a scholar, once admired   15
For wondrous knowledge in our German schools,
We'll give his mangled limbs due burial;
And all the students, clothed in mourning black,
Shall wait upon his heavy funeral.

Exeunt.

	Epilogue.
Enter Chorus.	

Chorus.   Cut is the branch that might have grown full straight,
And burnèd is Apollo's laurel bough
That sometime grew within this learnèd man.
Faustus is gone. Regard his hellish fall,
Whose fiendful fortune may exhort the wise   5
Only to wonder at unlawful things,
Whose deepness doth entice such forward wits
To practise more than heavenly power permits.

[*Exit.*]

Terminat hora diem; terminat author opus.

V,iii.   **Epilogue.**
  19 *wait upon* be present at. *heavy*   9 *Terminat . . . opus* The hour ends
sorrowful.   the day; the author ends his work.

Textual Notes

Doctor Faustus was first printed for Thomas Bushell in 1604, in a black letter quarto of which one copy is today extant, in the Malone collection in the Bodleian. Sir Walter Greg has argued that this represents a memorial reconstruction of the original version of the play, shortened for performance in the provinces and subjected to a good deal of debasement and interpolation. This version was reprinted in 1609 and 1611. In 1616 appeared a new and enlarged edition of the play, printed for John Wright. This, Greg has held, was prepared from Marlowe's own drafts from which the theater prompt book had been transcribed. In the course of prompt book preparation the manuscript itself must have undergone a good deal of revision. It was, moreover, incomplete, perhaps damaged and illegible in parts. In preparing it for the press, an editor was obliged to reproduce many passages from the earlier text as reprinted in the 1611 quarto. He also made a number of cuts and alterations, some of them to remove what he regarded as profanity. This edition was reprinted with corrections, many of them having considerable authority, in 1619, and again in 1620, 1624, 1628, and 1631.

We thus have two widely divergent versions of the play, neither of which reproduces the text as Marlowe—and the collaborator with whom he must have worked—had left it. The present edition is based on the quarto of 1616, which, with Greg and F. S. Boas, I would regard as the more authoritative. Readings from the 1604 quarto have been adopted where this text was used as copy for the 1616 quarto and where there are obvious omissions and alterations in the 1616 quarto. Readings from the 1619 and later quartos have been adopted when they correct obvious misprints in the 1616 text. I have been guided in many of these matters by Sir Walter Greg's conjectural reconstruction of the play, published in 1950, and by his superb edition of the parallel texts, *Marlowe's Doctor Faustus 1604–1616,* of the same year. The 1616 quarto has been departed from in the following instances:

Prologue.

12 *Rhode* (Boas) Rhodes (1619)
16 *The . . . graced* (1604) omitted 1616
18 *whose . . . disputes* (1604) and sweetly can dispute (1616)

I,i.

12 *On cay mae on* (1604) Oeconomy (1616). *Galen* (1604) and Galen (1616)
13 *Seeing . . . medicus* (1604) omitted 1616
19 *Is . . . aphorisms* (1604) omitted 1616
22 *divers* (1619) thousand (1616)
44 *there's* (1604) there is (1616)
52 *signs* (Greg) scenes (1604) omitted 1616. *and* (1604) omitted 1616
55 *of* (1604) and (1616)
60 *Nor . . . clouds* (1604) omitted 1616
64 *try thy* (1604) tire my (1616)
70, SD *Enter . . . Angel* (1604) Enter the Angell and Spirit (1616)
76 *treasury* (1604) treasure (1616)
83 *India* (1619) Indian (1616)
91 *silk* (Dyce) skill (1616, 1604)
97 *Antwerp's* (1604) Anwerpe (1616)
104–106 *Yet . . . skill* (1604) omitted 1616
109–110 *Divinity . . . vile* (1604) omitted 1616
110 *vile* vilde (1604)
116 *Swarm* (1604) Sworn (1616)
119 *shadows* (1604) shadow (1616)
127 *Lapland* (1604) Lopland (1616)
130 *in* (1604) has (1616)
133 *stuffs* (1604) stuff'd (1616)
142 *renowned* renowm'd (1616)
152 *lusty* (1604) bushy (1616)
155 *Abanus'* (Greg) Albanus (1616)
167, SD Exeunt om. (1616)

I,iii.

SD *Enter . . . conjure* (1604) Faustus to them with this speech (1616)
12 *erring* (1604) euening (1616)
16 *Dei* (1604) dii (1616)
19 *Mephistophilis . . . moraris* (Boas) Mephistophilis, Dragon, quod tumeraris (1616)
22 *dicatus* (1619) dicatis (1604, 1616)
32–34 *Now . . . imagine* (1604) omitted 1616. *Now* (Bullen) No (1604)
34 *redis* (Boas) regis (1604)
44 *hither* (1619) now hither (1616)
45 *speeches* (1604) omitted 1616
46 *accidens* (1624) accident (1616)
53 *the Trinity* (1604) all godlincsse (1616)

55–56 *So . . . principle* one line in 1616
71 *fell* (1604) liue (1616)
77 *who* (1604) that (1616)
82 *strike* (1604) strikes (1616)
96 *aid* (1604) to aid (1616)
112 *desire* (1604) desir'd (1616)

I,iv.

2 *Robin* Clo. (1616) and throughout scene
3 *such pickedevants* (1604) beards (1616)
28 *again* (1619) omitted 1616

II,i.

2 *And canst* (1604) Canst (1616)
9 *Ay . . . again* (1604) omitted 1616
10 *To God* (1604) Why (1616)
10–11 *To . . . appetite* one line in 1616
15 *Bad Angel* Euill An (1616)
20 *men* (1604) them (1616)
31 *Mephistophilis* (1604) omitted 1616
38–39 *Stay . . . lord* (Boas) Stay . . . me,/ What . . . Lord (1616)
42 *others* (1604) other (1616)
52–54 *Lo . . . Lucifer's* (1604) prose in 1616. *I* (1604) Faustus hath (1616). *mine arm* (1604) his arme (1616). *my proper* (1604) his proper (1616). *my soul* (1604) his soule (1616)
66 *Ah* (1604) O (1616)
77 *God* (1604) heaven (1616)
92 *made* (1604) both (1616)
96–97 *at his command* (1604) by him commanded (1616)
102 *form or shape* (1604) shape and forme (1616)
106 *the . . . inviolate* (1604) these Articles aboue written being inviolate (1616)
108 *or goods* (1604) omitted 1616
113 *will I* (1604) I will (1616). *with* (1604) omitted 1616
138–141 *But . . . wife* prose in 1616 and 1604
138 *off* (1604) omitted 1616
142–143 *Mephistophilis . . . one* (1604) omitted 1616
145 *Sit . . . come* (1604) omitted 1616
145, SD *Enter . . . fireworks* (1604) He fetches in a woman deuill (1616)
147 *how dost thou like thy* (1604) wilt thou have a (1616)
157 *Hold* (1604) Here (1616). *thoroughly* (1604) well (1616)

II,ii.

6 *'tis* (1604) it is (1616)

7 *breathes* (1619) breathe (1616)
17 *Bad Angel* Evil Angil (1616). SD
Exeunt Exit (1616)
20–21 *But . . . knives* (1604) omitted
1616. *thunder* (Greg) thunders (1604)
22 *Poison, guns* (1604) Swords, poyson
(1616)
44 *erring* (1604) euening (1616)
44–45 *But . . . tempore* one line in
1616
55–56 *suppositions* (1604) questions
(1616)
77–78 *'Tis . . . late* one line in 1616
88–89 *I . . . hell* one line in 1616
96 *I* (1604) Faustus (1616). *in* (1604)
for (1616)
98–100 *Never . . . down* (1604) omitted 1616
116 *lips* (1604) omitted 1616
136 *this* (1604) these (1616)
146 *jolly* (1604) ancient (1616)
146–147 *and . . . city* (1604) omitted
1616
147 *Mistress* (1604) omitted 1616
153–156 *where . . . Lechery* (1604)
omitted 1616
173, SD Exeunt omnes (1616)

II,iii.

1 *Robin* omitted 1616

III, Prologue.

1–2 *Learnèd . . . astronomy* one line
in 1616
8 *tropics* (Greg) Tropick (1616)

III,i.

7 *Rhine* (1604) Rhines (1616)
12 *Quarters . . . equivalents* (1604)
omitted 1616 *equivalents* equiuolence
(1604)
16 *rest* (1604) East (1616)
17 *midst* (1604) one (1616)
37 *four* (1604) two (1616)
43 *match* (1604) watch (1616)
55 *in state and* (1619) this day with
(1616)
77 *cunning* (1624) comming (1616) and
in line 81
125, SD *Exeunt* Exit (1616)
155 *keys* (Boas) seales (1616)

III,ii.

58 *Archbishop* Bish. (1616) and in line
81
61 *Friar . . . holiness* (1604) omitted
1616
62 *Pope* (1604) omitted 1616

71–72 *That . . . wine* one line in
1616
74 *Raymond* (1619) Kaymond (1616)
86 *Once . . . to* (1604) omitted 1616
86, SD *The . . . himself* (1604) omitted 1616
87–88 *How . . . cross* one line in 1616
101 *blow on the* (1604) blow the (1616)
108 *Et . . . Amen* (1604) omitted 1616

III,iii.

29–31 *Monarch . . . lie* (1604) you
Princely Legions of infernall rule (1616)

IV, Prologue.

1–17 *When . . . performed* (1604)
omitted 1616

IV,ii.

25 *like a* (1619) a (1616)

IV,iii.

27 *heart's* (1619) heart (1616)
70 *Ay, all* (Dyce) I call (1616)
105, SD Exeunt omnes (1616)

IV,iv.

14 *Zounds* (1619) Zons (1616)
25 *these* (1619) this (1616)

IV,v.

SD Enter Faustus, and the Horse-
Courser, and Mephistophilis (1616)
1–11 *Now . . . doctor* (1604) omitted
1616
1–2 *Now . . . foot* Now . . . time/
doth . . . foot (1604)
5–6 *Therefore . . . Wittenberg* one
line in 1604
54 *Anholt* (Boas) Vanholt (1616) and
in line 57

IV,vi.

3 *guests* (1619) Guesse (1616)
4 *Robin* Clow. (1616) and throughout
scene
37 *rare quality* (1619) quality (1616)
51, SD Exeunt omnes (1616)

IV,vii.

SD *Anholt* (Boas) Vanholt (1616) and
throughout scene
12 *Duchess* Lady (1616) and throughout
scene
49, SD *Robin* Clowne (1616) and
throughout scene
107 *guests* (1619) guesse (1616)

V,i.

1–9 *I . . . done* prose in 1616
17–18 *Gentlemen . . . unfeigned* one line in 1616
19 *And Faustus'* (1604) It is not Faustus (1616)
20 *requests* (1604) request (1616)
25, SD *sounds* (1604) sound (1616)
28 *Too . . . praise* speech given to Third Scholar in 1616
28 *praise* (1604) worth (1616)
30–32 *Third Scholar . . . compare* (1604) omitted in 1616
33 *Since* (1604) Now (1616). *works* (1604) worke (1616)
34 *And . . . excellence* (1604) omitted 1616
56 *Damned . . . die* (1604) omitted 1616
61 *hovers* (1604) hover (1616)
65 *Ah, my sweet* (1604) O (1616)
65–66 *Ah . . . soul* one line in 1616
70 *where . . . now* (1604) wretch, what hast thou done? (1616)
82 *Mephistophilis* (1604) omitted in 1616
84 *Faustus* (1604) omitted in 1616
94 *embracings* (1604) embraces (1616)
96 *mine oath* (1604) my vow (1616)
117 *azured* (1604) azure (1616)
119–127 *Old Man . . . God* (1604) omitted 1616

V,ii.

26 *Ah* (1604) O (1616)
28–30 *Ah . . . not* (1604) verse in 1616
42 *Ah* (1604) O (1616). *hear me* (1604) hear (1616)
44 *pants and quivers* (1604) pant & quiuer (1616)
50 *ah* (1604) O (1616)

54 *Ah* (1604) O (1616)
59 *Ah* (1604) O (1616)
61 *God* O God (1616)
76 *there pray* (1604) pray (1616)
96 *Ah* (Greg) O (1616)
108 *sat* set (1616)
116 *boil* (1620) broyle (1616)
130 *Ah* (1604) O (1616)
136–137 *be but/ A year* (Boas) be but a yeare/ A month (1604, 1616)
142 *my God* (1604) heaven (1616)
143 *See . . . firmament* (1604) omitted 1616
144 *would . . . Ah* (1604) of blood will save me; o (1616)
147–148 *'Tis . . . brows* (Dyce) tis gone:/ And see . . . arm,/ And . . . brows (1604). gone./ And see a threatning Arme, an angry Brow. (1616)
150 *God* (1604) heauen (1616)
151 *No, no!* (1604) No? (1616)
151–152 *No . . . earth* one line in 1604 and 1616
153 *Earth, gape* (1604) Gape earth (1616)
160 *So that* (1604) But let (1616). *may but* (1604) mount, and (1616)
161 *Ah* (1604) O (1616)
162–163 *O . . . soul* one line in 1604 O, if my soule must suffer for my sinne (1616)
164 *Yet . . . me* (1604) omitted 1616
168 *O, no* (1604) No (1616)
171 *Ah* (1604) Oh (1616)
173–174 *Into . . . die* (Eds.) Into . . . beast./ All die (1616)
180 *O, it* (1604) It (1616)
182 *to* (Greg) into (1604, 1616). *little* (1604) small (1616)
184 *My God, my God* (1604) O mercy heauen (1616)
187 *Ah* (1604) oh (1616)

The Major Critics

Faustus

UNA M. ELLIS-FERMOR

"Thinkest thou that I who saw the face of God,
And tasted the eternal joyes of heaven,
Am not tormented with ten thousand hels
In being depriv'd of everlasting blisse?"

(*Ll.* 313–16)   [I, iii, 77–80]

These lines, spoken by Mephistopheles near the beginning of the
play, have the ring of intense feeling that characterises Marlowe's
utterance when his deepest and most passionate experience is revealed. And the experience which these lines summarise is perhaps the greatest event in Marlowe's biography; from it the play
of *Faustus* inevitably sprang. It matters little in what formula it
is expressed; the tragedy indicated here is /61/ as old as humanity and universal. Wherever civilisation has freed men from
absorption in the means of material life and has left leisure for
reflexion, there has followed, sooner or later, the need to inter-

Reprinted from *Christopher Marlowe* (London: Methuen & Co., 1927), pp. 61–87.
Miss Ellis-Fermor, as was common at the time she wrote, used a text of *Faustus*
based on the quarto of 1604, as contained in *The Works of Christopher Marlowe*, ed.
C. F. Tucker Brooke (Oxford, 1910).

pret or explain the universe and the meaning of man's being. For the possession of this understanding is the next vital thing after man's daily bread. It may be arrived at by thought and reasoning for one man, and for another exist rather as a sense of harmony drawn in with the air he breathes, unformulated, yet in fact the vital principle of his life. It is the loss, then, of this sense of unity, of this harmony between his mind and the universal forces surrounding him, which is the essence of spiritual tragedy, and it is of a loss of this kind that *Faustus* is the record. We feel in this play that the protagonist (and the poet himself whom he so closely shadows) has lost his sense of secure contact; his lines of communication are broken. The central idea of the play is an idea of loss. Marlowe does not tell us precisely what this is, for the plain reason that he did not know. The catastrophe is too recent; *Faustus* is written hard upon the heels of the event. But the passionate agony of the play is an agony of loss and it finds a fitting form for its expression in the medieval idea of a lost soul. Beyond this clear, transcendent passion of regret and despair, this realisation that "All places shall be hell that is not heaven," all is confusion. And this again is natural, for the poet, in a bewildering chaos of conflicting emotions, is searching for the meaning of the calamity that has befallen him. He offers in *Faustus* a series of explanations, some of which seem, in the light of his earlier and of his later work, to be the true ones, some of which contradict these and are a kind of apostasy in which Marlowe denies his fundamental creed. Most deeply of all he resents and blames that servitude to the dry and barren learning which he rightly perceives has led him somehow astray, though the error is too complete for him to see what it is that he should have followed in its stead or, even, at this stage, to hope for a /62/ recovery of the way. This he expresses very truly as the loss of the soul—the cutting off of the personality from its natural sources of inspiration and of faith. What these sources were, he does not know and cannot tell us; only, of the loss there is no question; the pain reveals the presence of disease, but does not diagnose it. In his further attempts at diagnosis he, as often as not, gives what must have appeared to him later as an altogether wrong explanation: he accepts, with a half-cowed and sometimes almost frantic submission, the conventional idea that it is his rejection of the superstitions of his contemporaries that has ruined him. It is here, I think, that there is apostasy.

When he presents Faustus growing despearate as he realises the barrenness of the learning upon which the best years of his life have been spent, or exclaiming: "Would I had never seen *Wertenberge,* never read booke": it is consistent with the Marlowe of *Tamburlaine* and of *Hero and Leander,* and we understand the tragedy implied. When, however, he numbers among the wiles of Mephistopheles, the destroyer, the beautiful vision of Helen and that "sweet pleasure" that "conquered deep despair," he is denying the two truest elements in his own nature, an instinct for beauty so fine that it trembles upon the very borders between the sensuous and the spiritual, and a ruthless, scientific honesty of thought and devotion to truth that mark his nature as profoundly religious.

Faustus, the great scholar of Würtemberg, reveals in his first speech the mind of a man who has gained enough knowledge and spent years enough in thought to realize that knowledge and philosophy leave him still unsatisfied. The predominant mood of the first scene is that of a man who awakes from a dream of mountain-tops to find himself still in the plains, or of a man who, having reached the mountain-top, is more than ever oppressed by his earth-bound nature and by the mocking distance of the skies towards which he had seemed to be climbing: "Yet art /63/ thou still but *Faustus,* and a man!" For Faustus has never accepted the conditions of his human nature; the object of all his studies has been to transcend them, and each branch of medieval learning—logic, physic, law, divinity—as it comes up in its turn for review, is rejected because he sees that its highest reach falls short of that infinity for which he craves with an unformulated desire. Surveying his experience—a lifetime spent in the endeavour to make reason adequate to infinity—he dismisses his past labour as a delusion. He does not impute his failure to the limitations of his spirit, but to the limitation of the methods by which he has pursued his end:

> "Philosophy is odious and obscure,
> Both Law and Phisicke are for pettie wits,
> Divinitie is basest of the three . . ."[1]

---

[1] *Faustus, ll.* 134–6. [I, ii, 107–9]

Partly in the recklessness which is the natural reaction from his former patience, partly in the desire for consolation, he abandons the systematic search for that final understanding the desire for which has led him forward, yet eluded him, all his life, and plunges defiantly into the practice of magic. With the aid of Cornelius and Valdes he summons Mephistopheles, who opens for him the world of Black Magic, and offers yet another means of delusion, perhaps the only one which still has power to distract him. Faustus readily promises to give his soul for the power to command Mephistopheles and control elemental spirits for twenty-four years. Yet the futility of this final aberration is revealed in the very scene in which the promise is made. The first thing which Faustus asks of Mephistopheles is knowledge—that very knowledge upon which he had apparently turned his back. "Tell me," he begins. "What is that *Lucifer* thy Lord? . . . Where are you damn'd? . . . How comes it then that thou art out of hel?" In the next scene he would have a book /64/ to tell him of the movements of all planets and another of all plants that grow on the earth. Faustus is dazzled by the material power that Magic puts into his hands, and dreams of being "great Emperor of the world" and walling all Germany with brass; but from time to time, like a deep undertone, is heard that desire which has moved him all his life, which Mephistopheles can not satisfy:

> *Faustus:* . . . tell me who made the world?
> *Meph:* . . . I will not
> *Faustus:* Sweete Mephastophilus, tell me.
> *Meph:* Move me not, for I will not tell thee.[2]

By this time it is clear that Magic will bring him no nearer to the understanding he desires than did the laborious pursuit of Knowledge, and that Faustus is in the grip of yet another and more ironic delusion. For the rest of his life his mind is in ever-increasing conflict; his evil angel and the potentates of Hell urge him on, by alternate threats and seductions, in courses that lead him more and more deeply into their power, while in moments of agonised reaction his good angel stirs in him contrition almost immediately overwhelmed by despair. These alternating moods continue, with increasing violence, up to the last scene; a ma-

[2] *Ll.* 678-81. [II, ii, 67-70]

cabre and sombre series of contradictory passions: triumph, mirth, terror, repentance, despair and recklessness, until Faustus is beyond repentance, beyond salvation, and looks back over his last delusion with clear eyes for a moment before terror blots out all other emotions and all thought. It is a profoundly significant story, whatever interpretation we assume to lie behind the symbols.

Out of such conflict of emotion and thought the great fragment of *Faustus* is produced. It is the battleground of the forces more or less spontaneously at work in *Tamburlaine,* and of those hitherto obscure, but easily imagined habits of mind and thought inculcated by the bitter years /65/ of tutelage to an empty and unreal mental discipline. What was the natural bent of Marlowe's mind in his early years we may see in the rhapsodic, lyrical passages of his first play; of the perversion of that mind under the influence of contemporary scholarism and theological dogma we have no record beyond the bitter attacks on Christians in *Tamburlaine,* until we come to the picture of catastrophe and confusion in *Faustus. Faustus* remains, then, an almost unmatched record of spiritual tragedy in a medium capable of isolating the spiritual elements and preserving them unmixed with any of the other elements of life. The play reflects constantly back to *Tamburlaine,* and we, viewing it, may look constantly on to *Hero and Leander;* to the poetic aspiration of the one and the sensuous security of the other it is related by isolated outcrops, the invocation to Helen and such lines as:

> "Have not I made blinde *Homer* sing to me
> Of *Alexanders* love and *Enons* death,
> And hath not he that built the walles of *Thebes,*
> With ravishing sound of his melodious harp
> Made musicke with my *Mephastophilis?*"[3]

Tamburlaine was a young man's vision: "We may become immortal like the gods"; *Faustus* is an intense and passionate expression of the despair that follows upon the clouding-over of the vision of "the face of God," whose loss made all places hell. And so perhaps our second impression of *Faustus,* after that of the clear, uncomplicated passion of loss, is of a purely negative

[3] *Ll.* 637–41. [II, ii, 26–30]

play, which is often only a denial or condemnation of the aspirations of *Tamburlaine:*

> *Faustus:* Tell me what is that *Lucifer* thy Lord?
> *Meph:*   Arch-regent and commander of all spirits.
> *Faustus:* Was not that *Lucifer* an Angell once?
> *Meph:*   Yes *Faustus,* and most dearely lov'd of God.
> *Faustus:* How comes it then that he is prince of divels? /66/
> *Meph:*   O by aspiring pride and insolence,
>   For which God threw him from the face of heaven.
> *Faustus:* And what are you that live with *Lucifer?*
> *Meph:*   Unhappy spirits that fell with *Lucifer,*
>   Conspir'd against our God with *Lucifer;*
>   And are for ever damnd with *Lucifer.*
> *Faustus:* Where are you damn'd?
> *Meph:*   In hell.
> *Faustus:* How come it then that thou art out of hel?
> *Meph:*   Why this is hel, nor am I out of it: . . .[4]

This is reaction, a withdrawal from his boldest thoughts, a re-
treat upon conventional interpretations, which, being once left
behind and abandoned, will no longer shelter him. And so the
action of the play takes place in a kind of No-man's-land, between two armies of ideas to neither of which Marlowe wholly
belongs. It is a faithful revelation of a mind in transition between two conceptions of the universe. As Faustus wavers between his good and evil angels, between God and the devil, so we
may see Marlowe hesitating between the submissive acceptance
of a dogmatic system and a pagan simplicity of outlook to which
instinct and temperament prompted him.

> *Faustus:* "My hearts so hardned I cannot repent,
>   Scarse can I name salvation, faith, or heaven,
>   But feareful ecchoes thunders in mine eares,
>   Faustus, thou art damn'd . . .
>   And long ere this I should have slaine my selfe,
>   Had not sweete pleasure conquerd deepe dispaire,
>   Have not I made blinde *Homer* sing to me
>   Of *Alexanders* love, and Enons death . . .
>   Why should I dye then, or basely dispaire?
>   I am resolv'd *Faustus* shal nere repent."[5]

[4] *Ll.* 298–312. [I, iii, 63–76]
[5] *Ll.* 629–43 *passim.* [II, ii, 18–32 *passim*]

Yet in spite of this turmoil of ideas, the emotional quality of the play has a clarity almost unsurpassed in the range of the literature of passion. Since it was primarily the conflict of ideas that caused the suffering in Marlowe's mind, no amount of confusion here can do anything but heighten the tragic intensity of an action that takes place, /67/ as it were, on a plane above that of the intellect. It is the peculiar nature of this play—arising, indeed from the peculiar balance of faculties in Marlowe's mind—that it gives us a record of absolute emotion hardly reached by any other work of art. It is one of the everlasting paradoxes of art that an experience must be viewed from the outside before it can be formed into a work of art, but that, in so far as the poet does detach himself, in so far the intensity of the emotion diminishes. A battle, a shipwreck, a sandstorm in the desert is not a work of art. The experience has an intensity, an absoluteness beside which a work of art shrivels up and is meaningless. The aim of the tragic artist is to combine as nearly as possible this maximum of emotion which excludes the idea of art, with the degree of detachment necessary to give that form which distinguishes art from raw life. This approximation Marlowe has achieved in *Faustus* to an almost unparalleled degree. It seems, when we look back upon it, to have been created as nearly out of the heart of the experience and as nearly at the moment of sensation as it is possible for art to be. It is this that makes even the transmitted experience of the last scene almost unbearable.

> "The starres moove stil, time runs, the clocks wil strike,
> The divel wil come, and Faustus must be damnd.
> O Ile leape up to my God: who pulles me downe?
> See see where Christs blood streames in the firmament.
> One drop would save my soule, halfe a drop, ah my Christ.
> Ah rend not my heart for naming of my Christ,
> Yet wil I call on him: oh spare me *Lucifer!*
> Where is it now? tis gone: And see where God
> Stretcheth out his arme, and bends his irefull browes:
> Mountaines and hilles, come, come, and fall on me,
> And hide me from the heavy wrath of God.
> No, no.
> Then wil I headlong runne into the earth:
> Earth gape. O no, it wil not harbour me:

You starres that raignd at my nativitie,
Whose influence hath alotted death and hel,
Now draw up Faustus like a foggy mist,
Into the intrailes of yon labring cloude,
That when you vomite foorth into the ayre, /68/
My limbes may issue from your smoaky mouthes,
So that my soule may but ascend to heaven:
Ah, halfe the houre is past:
Twil all be past anone:
Oh God,
If thou wilt not have mercy on my soule,
Yet for Christs sake, whose bloud hath ransomd me,
Impose some end to my incessant paine.
Let Faustus live in hel a thousand yeeres,
A hundred thousand, and at last be sav'd."[G]

When the old German story of the *Faustbuch* fell into Marlowe's hands it must have come with startling significance as the symbol of the conflict in progress in his own mind. The story of the man who sells his soul to the devil is of undying vitality and can be made to comprehend the whole of human experience—as indeed Goethe came very near to making it. The question with Marlowe is, then, what did he read into the formula thus offered him?

Several suggestions may be made, perhaps none of them better than conjectures more or less wide of the mark. Yet, to the modern mind, much is suggested by the relationship between *Tamburlaine* and *Faustus*. Behind the poetry of this first play there is apparent an instinct for abstract thought, strong enough to draw his attention away from any other theme, never quite strong enough to carry him clear of all other interests into the region of pure metaphysics. In process of time this results in a peculiar and highly individual attitude to life and Marlowe becomes preoccupied with man in his spiritual and intellectual aspects, taking no interest in the relations of man to man, or in the characteristics of individual men. Thus he came to concentrate more and more upon that intense inner life, so that the only things that had the power to touch him belonged to the world of thought. It was from this world therefore that the catasrophe of his early life came upon him. It was a tragedy of the mind, such as befalls a

[G] *Ll.* 1429–57. [V, ii, 140–167]

Carlyle or a Goethe, all independent of external circumstances. Marlowe had been bred a scholar and a theologian /69/ and was of a profoundly religious temperament. Though he had refused to take the Church for his profession and had scoffed at it bitterly enough in *Tamburlaine*, this rejection had gone no further than to the dogmatic system of the Christian religion which Marlowe saw around him in a debased form. It is one thing for a man to reject his generation's interpretation of a particular religion but another to find himself suddenly robbed of faith in those fundamental notions upon which religion in general—and so life, purpose, hope—is built. This is the moment of terror, confusion and desolation, when the horror and meaninglessness of the jumbled elements of the world bring the mind to the verge of madness. "Nothing is but what is not," and the scene upon which the exhausted imagination looks out is like that of a country devastated by flood or earthquake. All the known landmarks are down; nothing appears from horizon to horizon but wreckage and a still shifting, unstable surface in which no fixed point can be found and no distance measured.

It was, for Carlyle, the perception of an everlasting 'No.' For Marlowe it was the sense of something lost that can never be regained, of the significance gone from the heart of life, taking purpose and hope with it. And because he was trained in the theological dogma of his day he used its terminology, and turning back to find wherein the cause lay, fastened upon the "aspiring pride and insolence" and related the whole story under the symbolism of the old German legend of the scholar who lost his soul through seeking to know "more than heavenly power permits." The play, then, is an attempt to give a faithful portrait of this condition of mind and, at the same time, a comment upon it. The feelings and thoughts of Faustus furnish the one; the conduct of the action and his catastrophic fate, the other. The intrinsic worth of the play lies almost wholly in the first, for the significance of which it is hard to find fit words. But Marlowe's comment upon Faustus's career is rich in autobiographical /70/ suggestion and affords a rare revelation of a mind in reaction against its own former boldness, of a high spirit temporarily shaken into abjectness by spiritual fear.

In the opening scene of the play, where Faustus, sitting in his study, surveys the sum of his ideas and of his achievements, we meet a man who has reached a pausing place in life. He has been sustained by an aspiration, undefined but powerful which has been forced into a certain way of thought until the moment comes when he looks for the idea that first animated him and can no longer perceive it; nor can he at first understand why he has lost it. It is time for a revision of the situation; Faustus must 'settle' his studies and look over the stock of his mind. For the first time he is dimly conscious that the ground is not secure beneath him and that it behoves him to consider how sure are the foundations of those "professions" upon which he has built up his faith, career and reputation.

He despatches the practical aspect of the situation in one reach of thought. It is easy enough to be a divine in show. But the question what he professes within his own mind still confronts him as it confronts every honest man at least once, and some not once, nor twice, but continually throughout their lives. The first answer that occurs is that Faustus has 'taken all knowledge to be his province,' that he will 'level at the end of every art,' in other words that he, like Bacon after him, will contemplate the ends, the purposes and the relationships of all forms of knowledge, that he is a native of that country where sciences become Science, where departments of knowledge become Knowledge:

> Faustus. "Settle thy studies Faustus, and beginne
> To sound the deapth of that thou wilt professe:
> Having commencde, be a Divine in shew,
> Yet levell at the end of every Art,
> And live and die in Aristotles workes:"[7] /71/

In pursuit of this idea he turns to consider Philosophy or Logic. There is enough in Aristotle's thought for a man to spend his life in its contemplation. In the Analytics he had imagined for a time that he found an expression of his inspiration. What is the "end" of this art? Where and how does it become universal knowledge?

> "Is to dispute well, Logickes chiefest end,
> Affoords this Art no greater myracle?
> Then reade no more, thou hast attaind the end;
> A greater subject fitteth Faustus wit; . . ."[8]

[7] Ll. 29–33. [I, i, 1–5]   [8] Ll. 36–9. [I, i, 8–11]

There is something limited and futile in that. It will not lift man far. The earlier vision of infinite possibility here must have been a delusion or a mistake. There is nothing in deductive logic to warrant the idea that through it man may touch infinity.

Faustus must have a wider range for his thought; this is circumscribed and slavish. What of medicine?

> "Seeing, *ubi desinit philosophus, ibi incipit medicus*.
> Be a physition *Faustus,* heape up golde,
> And be eternizde for some wondrous cure."⁹

There is opportunity of discovery there that stretches out to unlimited possibility. The experimental scientist, the inductive thinker, begins where the formalist, the pure logician, leaves off. Besides, in this art there is wordly glory and wealth to be won.

So much for its nature and practical application. But at what point does this form of knowledge touch absolute knowledge? What is its highest reach?

> "*Summum bonum medicinæ sanitas,*
> The end of physicke is our bodies health:
> Why *Faustus,* hast thou not attaind that end?
> Is not thy common talke sound Aphorismes?
> Are not thy billes hung up as monuments, /72/
> Whereby whole Citties have escapt the plague,
> And thousand desprate maladies beene easde,
> Yet art thou still but *Faustus,* and a man.
> Couldst thou make men to live eternally?
> Or being dead, raise them to life againe?
> Then this profession were to be esteemd.
> Physicke, farewell, . . ."¹⁰

Faustus has fame as a doctor, but what of that? Man's estate is in no way altered by his high achievements in this art. It leaves him but a man and others but men. There is no key to any profound secret there. If this art is of any dignity it should, in the hands of Faustus, yield up the secret of eternal life at least. So only could it show itself worthy of the passion and profundity of his question.

Faustus turns back again to the realm of the mind. Man's greatest dignity and triumph is in thought. And one of the high-

---

⁹ *Ll.* 41–3. [I, i, 13–15]
¹⁰ *Ll.* 44–55. [I, i, 16–27]

est concepts of this thought is the idea of Law. Here is Justinian's *Institute:*

> "*Si una eademque res legatur duobus,*
> *Alter rem, alter valorem rei.*
> A pretty case of paltry legacies:
> *Exhaereditare filium non potest pater nisi:*
> Such is the subject of the institute
> And universall body of the law:
> This study fittes a mercenary drudge,
> Who aimes at nothing but externall trash;
> Too servile and illiberall for me:"[11]

Again, there is the particular for the general, the petty, concrete detail instead of the magic universal formula. There is no
knowledge in these pedantic groupings of facts. There is no inward significance, only "outward trash."

To find the great and universal concepts a man must turn to
divinity after all:

> "When all is done, Divinitie is best.
> *Jeromes* Bible, *Faustus,* view it well.
> *Stipendium peccati mors est:* ha, *Stipendium, &c.*
> The reward of sinne is death: thats hard.
> *Si peccasse negamus, fallimur, et nulla est in nobis veritas.* /73/
> If we say that we have no sinne,
> We deceive our selves, and theres no truth in us.
> Why then belike
> We must sinne, and so consequently die.
> I, we must die an everlasting death:
> What doctrine call you this, *Che sera, sera,*
> What wil be, shall be? Divinitie, adieu, . . ."[12]

Yet there are the two horns of a dilemma. Each statement is irre-
futable and the sum of them is death. This is no better than the
syllogism that contained its conclusion in its major premise. Divinity, then, is no better than logic.

Finally, Faustus turns away from these barren sciences. There
is no way there to absolute knowledge, no key to the secrets of
the universe, no answer to patient investigation, thought and
reasoning. Perhaps—

> "The oracles are dumb, or cheat
> Because they have no secret to express."

[11] *Ll.* 56–64. [I, i, 28–36]   [12] *Ll.* 65–76. [I, i, 37–49]

Heaven may be more readily reached by letting the fancy range. There is a world of experience, of entertainment, of food for contemplation in the dreams of the old magicians. Seeing that there is no result from the arduous and honest search for truth, why not instead these pleasant, fantastic dreams?

> "These Metaphisickes of Magicians,
> And Negromantike bookes are heavenly:
> Lines, circles, sceanes, letters, and characters:
> I, these are those that *Faustus* most desires.
> O what a world of profit and delight,
> Of power, of honor, of omnipotence
> Is promised to the studious Artizan?
> All things that moove betweene the quiet poles
> Shalbe at my commaund, Emperours and Kings
> Are but obeyd in their severall provinces:
> Nor can they raise the winde, or rend the cloudes:
> But his dominion that exceedes in this,
> Stretcheth as farre as doth the minde of man.
> A sound Magician is a mighty god:"[13] /74/

These are fruitful metaphysics; here is a heaven of suggestion. All that man could not reach by arduous thought lies here. Faustus will withdraw into this imagined world where the philosopher may at last reap his reward where "all things that move between the quiet poles" are in his power, and he may control everything that the mind of man can conceive. Here a man is, in imaginative creation, the equal of God.

The magic that Faustus practises is magic that has been practised since the beginning of the history of thought by those who have followed the wrong road, and, discovering it, have not known where to find the right. Knowledge and the pursuit of truth are hard, barren and often fruitless, if sought in the way that is not natural or spontaneous to the mind at work. So Marlowe found, so Faustus. But let a man once turn his back upon this effort, and the world of dreams is rich, enthralling; there a poor scholar may be Tamburlaine and conqueror of the world, surrounded by images of such splendour that the external world is dim as though seen through a veil, by echoes so triumphant that the voices of that world come muffled and as from a great distance. In his first discovery of this kingdom of the mind, man's

[13] *Ll.* 77–90. [I, i, 50–63]

pride 'dares God out of Heaven,' for is not he himself a god, as securely throned?

The way into this country is, moreover, made peculiarly clear by the perception of the mockery of the conditions under which the game of life is played. For man's career, free though it appear, is only that of an animal in a trap, the conclusion prearranged. Marlowe's criticism of the life of man, in this play, rests upon the cruel and ironic paradox which is the climax of this speech. "The reward of sin is death. . . . If we say that we have no sin, we deceive ourselves," with the pitilessly logical deduction, "Why, then, belike man must sin and so die."

This, then, though it is by no means consistently adhered to, is an interpretation to which Marlowe refers. It is in this mood that the action is conceived. It is Marlowe's /75/ verdict upon man's position as the plaything of the gods.

That side of Marlowe's mind which was logical, ruthless and scientific, which had been trained in gloomy theology and the Hebrew doctrine of retribution, was conscious of two laws. First, that sin is the cause of death; or, rather, that sin is death of the spirit. Second, that sin is inherent in everything men do; that day by day they are conscious of thought, act or attitude of mind that has dealt a blow at the life of the spirit. But here Marlowe seems to stop, with the conclusion, "Why, then, belike we must sin and so die." This is the point at which we might imagine the clear, penetrating intellect of a thoughtful Jew before the Christian era coming to a stand in the teaching of the Pharisaic Law to which Marlowe's theology was closely akin. It is a curious thing that the sound sense, the clarity, the reasonableness of the ideas of Christ never seem to have called a response from similar qualities in Marlowe's own mind. The explanation, perhaps, lies in that indifference to the emotion of love which distinguishes Marlowe's mind in all its processes and all its conclusions. It was impossible for him to see in the factor of love a force which could oppose sin and death with a reality greater than their own. To him it was presumably no more than a shadowy doctrine of the schools, dim and meaningless from wearisome repetition. Small wonder, then, that such a man, when he speaks of the soul and its struggle speaks with the finality and harshness of a Pharisee. And here his virtues are his enemies. The logical clearness, the passionate desire for truth, the unswerving courage of his mind, all play their part in hastening the conclusion. And the fitting result is that drama which takes for its theme the reflection: "The reward of sin is death. That's hard." There is no comment; no effort to reject it or deny it. Hard it indeed is, and hard it remains. It is an unbending mind that can carry its thought through to such a conclusion and accept it. The infinite is above man, a standard which he can /76/ never reach, failure to reach which nevertheless is its own pitiless punishment. Life is a game at which man must be caught out sooner or later because it is implicit in the rules of the game that he should fail sooner or later. The gulf between man's nature and his ideals is unbridgeable. The whole process is a gigantic intellectual cheat. The reason may hold out delusive hopes for a time, but the conclusion was implied in the major premise. Man is doomed before he begins. Here then, is Faustus's answer to Tamburlaine. It is to be found in the mood which initiates the action of the play:

> "The sense that every struggle brings defeat
> Because Fate holds no prize to crown success;
> That all the oracles are dumb, or cheat,
> Because they have no secret to express;
> That none can pierce the vast black veil uncertain
> Because there is no light beyond the curtain;
> That all is vanity and nothingness."

And while we listen to Marlowe, it is impossible to see an error in this picture. It is all true. It is complete and perfect within itself.

But the great creative thinkers have met the problem differently and we have Goethe's word delivered upon the same theme to lay beside Marlowe's. And what Goethe says is only part of what has been said by Æschylus, or Socrates, or Christ. The writer of *Faust* does not limit his world to a picture of man at death-grips with a scientific law of sin and retribution, inevitable in its workings and worshipped by him as God. True, the law is inevitable, but it is liable, like all laws, to modification by causes working outside it and enveloping it. It is the perception of these enveloping forces and the reinterpretation of the same fragment of life in the light of that perception, that is Goethe's comment upon Marlowe's statement. Just so does the idea of

Christ envelop, not deny the law of sin and death, for if sin is
death, love is life. But whereas Goethe announces this clearly, for
Marlowe only the /77/ first half of this truth was visible when he
wrote *Faustus.*

Immediately from this arises the conception of God that we
find in *Faustus.* There is no longer, as in *Tamburlaine,* a variety
of suggestions behind the name. God is always for Faustus the
Hebrew law-giver, pitiless, just, mechanical and unimaginative.
Only once, in the mouth of Mephistopheles, is he referred to, as
so often in *Tamburlaine,* as the spirit that pervades the universe
and inspires the highest of man's faculties. "I," says Mephistopheles, looking back upon the Marlowe of *Tamburlaine,* "who
saw the Face of God. . . ." "I," that is "Whose mind was filled
with vision and with aspiration. . . ." Apart from this single reference, Marlowe chooses the first formula and uses the word
'God' to stand for the law, as yet undefined, by which sin is pun-
ished with spiritual death. The sin for which punishment is
meted out to Faustus is more often alluded to than explained.
The Old Man in the scene before the last gives a moving description—in purely general terms, however—of:

> ". . . such flagitious crimes of hainous sinnes,
>   As no commiseration may expel."[14]

But he leaves us, nevertheless, wondering to what he is referring.
Faustus, as far as we have been able to follow him, has been foolish and frivolous, but never criminal. Perhaps Marlowe knows
too little of what is in the heart of man to give a convincing picture of sin. Perhaps, also, the words of the Old Man are merely
symbols that have to be interpreted before we reach Marlowe's
meaning. Elsewhere in the play, he says, plainly enough, that
Lucifer's fall came about through 'aspiring pride and insolence,'
and it is probable that Marlowe, looking back upon the high
thoughts of Tamburlaine, sees in them that pride of mind that
he describes as sin. He endows Faustus, then, /78/ with similar
qualities, letting them bring about his doom, a doom which fur-
nishes a comment upon Tamburlaine no less than upon Faustus.

Underlying this, there is perhaps the further idea that is half
revealed in the opening speech, the idea of the conflict between

---

[14] *Ll.* 1281–2. [V, i, 39–40]

truth and delusion. Faustus abandons the search for truth because the road by which he is endeavouring to approach it is arduous and barren, letting himself sink into delusions which
soothe and entertain him, but lead nowhere. This tragedy is eternal and some aspect of eternal truth must be the genesis of work
written, as is *Faustus,* with the heart's blood of the poet. The
form in which Marlowe tried to clothe this idea—the symbols of
a dogmatic system in which angels and devils dispute for a man's
soul, did not, perhaps fit it closely enough to let him express it
clearly. As in *Tamburlaine,* the form tends to betray the idea
rather than to elucidate it.

After all, all attempts to explain the cause of the state of mind
so unerringly revealed in *Faustus* are of less importance than a
realisation of the central truth which preoccupied Marlowe himself—the truth that, from one cause or another, catastrophe had
overtaken his mind and that he felt himself cut off from the inspiration that had sustained him. Nothing is more unlikely than
that a man, while still in the grip of such a catastrophe, could
define the cause of it rightly; beside the overwhelming power of
the single idea, Marlowe's explanations and his references to sin
and evil are insignificant, and would, undoubtedly, have been
denied by him at the later and saner period of his life which saw
the writing of *Hero and Leander.* At present, in *Faustus,* he is
suffering a spiritual catastrophe and imputing his fall to sin.
Later, I imagine, when he ceased to impute it to sin, he probably
saw clearly what he had dimly felt in *Faustus:* that his mind had
been denied the things needful to its development and had been
forced to submit itself to years of fruitless and unproductive /79/
effort. Later still he recovered part, at least, of what had been
lost and wrote *Hero and Leander.*

But at the time of the writing of *Faustus,* this element is curiously misunderstood by the poet himself. The spontaneous love
of beauty, which had been clear in *Tamburlaine,* owes allegiance
to no moral code; it springs into being unsolicited and irresponsible; it is powerful and yet unexplained. Faustus sees Helen of
Troy and the thoughts of death and hell vanish. Sin is meaningless and the ministers of vengeance powerless. More than once,
for Faustus, "sweet pleasure conquered deep despair," and the
singing of blind Homer, the tale of "Alexander's love or Œnon's

death" has made him laugh away the idea of repentance and "confound hell in Elysium." Some of the best of Marlowe is in this mood of Faustus. There is a serene confidence about these utterances, steadier than the raptures of Tamburlaine, and a certain sweetness which has more repose than the exaltations of the earlier play. But this quality only appears for an instant through the wreckage of hope and passion and then disappears, not to be seen again until it is revealed as the master quality of his mind in *Hero and Leander*. Faustus is at peace, not when he is bending his mind to the stern task of abstract thought and the contemplation of pure reason, not when he is allowing himself to be immersed in the delusions of Mephistopheles' magic, but when, looking at the face of Helen, he enters that pagan world to which his mind truly belonged.

But unable in *Faustus* to follow or trust to these instincts, Marlowe draws back in fear from the irresponsible, unmoral quality of these emotions. He dare not be a law to himself, for that self he is only beginning to re-discover. He has not yet experienced mental freedom, though the desire for it has driven him into desperate terms. Now that the chains have fallen off, his nerve is broken, he would have them back again and is more afraid of the unknown freedom than of the familiar slavery. "The God thou /80/ servest is thine own appetite," he exclaims and turns back.

Mephistopheles expresses a bolder mood when he says that Heaven is:

" . .. not halfe so faire as thou,
Or any man that breathes on earth."[15]

But upon the heels of this follows the thought: "I will renounce this magic and repent." Marlowe, in love with the beauty and the splendour of man, stops short out of momentary timidity when he might have found in the worship of the spirit of man, for which he was peculiarly framed, that divine element whose loss he mourned.

One idea, however, rises clear: Marlowe's picture of hell, that hell which "is not circumscribed in one self place," but is a state of mind, a man's outlook upon the world. Mephistopheles, who

[15] *Ll.* 617–18. [II, ii, 6–7]

is also Marlowe, gives us the clue to it in his first description of hell. The poet who "saw the face of God" now sees it no more. It is the world-old lament over clouded vision. Wordsworth stoically notes something "gone that nothing can restore." Virgil mourns, "*neque auras dispiciunt clausæ tenebris et carcere cæco.*" It is a sharp pain, this, that life keeps especially for poets and, in measure as a man is a poet, in such degree will the catastrophe seem final when it befalls him. More than ever was it bitter to Marlowe, for his poetry was, as we have seen in *Tamburlaine,* a poetry of ideas. His vision was literally a looking upon "the face of God." It is not, with him, the pansy at his feet that has lost its magic, nor the passions and joys of man that have decayed or flagged, it is that purer spiritual passion of idea which has in some way been contaminated.

The loss and isolation were probably intensified in Marlowe's case by the singleness of this youthful vision. The sphere of his passion had been limited in its scope if /81/ exalted in its reach. He apparently loved neither earth nor man for themselves; his dauntless soul had "tasted the eternal joys of heaven," which had left all other joys tasteless and all places "hell, which are not heaven." He possessed a rare combination of faculties to which alone such a catastrophe is possible, and he had developed apparently that habit of mind (not unknown to the severer mystics of the Catholic Church, such as St. Juan of the Cross) which assumes that man can only fulfil the will of his Creator by eliminating or by transcending his humanity.

Through this tangle of ideas Marlowe cuts his way, sometimes successfully, sometimes unsuccessfully, his strength lying in his clarity, honesty and fearlessness of thought, his weakness in the limited field of his sympathies. Had he understood more, or less, of what is in man, he would have escaped the bitterest part of his experience; but that very combination of clear single-mindedness and narrowness of outlook gave him the key to the catastrophe of Faustus.

The form of *Faustus* is a little like that of all ruins—the design is not obvious, but it can be perceived. If the roof of a cathedral were broken in several places and patched with rococo work and frivolous, degenerate ornaments, no architect would be deceived. Rather, his first thought would take the form of Goethe's exclamation: "Wie gross ist alles angelegt!" The ribs of the original arches can be discerned, though their continuity is broken and their surface deformed. At a distance, the proposed design still gives an impression of balance, of proportion, of magnitude. So with Faustus, though Marlowe's action never appears continuously and the flow of his blank verse is broken even in the last scene.

We can trace six main episodes in the play, roughly equivalent to six acts, followed by a catastrophe. In the first scene, Faustus surveys his position and makes the choice that begins the action and sets the play moving /82/ towards the crisis. In the next, he takes the first significant step and summons Mephistopheles as he had determined in the scene before. Still his mind is rising in its purpose and its desires. In the third great scene comes the crisis, the selling of his soul, with the vacillation attendant upon a crisis, leaving us uncertain which way the action will move. In the next scene of importance, Faustus's regrets begin and the evil powers double their efforts and triumph, so that the action, instead of swaying to and fro in balanced conflict, now sets downward. The two choruses and the next few scenes represent, as far as we can judge them, a period of quiescence during which Faustus exploits the resources of the universe. It is a period also of disintegration and of loss of ideals after the upward movement of the first three scenes; even the approach of the end fails to rouse him. The last struggle of the good forces fills the next scene where the Old Man pleads with Faustus as the two Angels had done in the first half, and where the forces of evil make their most strenuous effort and gain their final triumph. This period of contest ends, as did the first, with the signing of the bond, and the whole is sealed by the apparition of Helen. The fight is over now and the movement rushes down to the catastrophe of the last scene in which there is only suffering and no action.

In the first part of the play, then, Faustus's mind reaches out eagerly to the new worlds before him, in spite of an occasional check from the suggestions of the good angel. In the second part, his tendency is to react from this and to repent, but he is checked and dragged back unwillingly to ruinous courses by the same spirit that had urged him on in the first part.

Thus the battle is in two parts, with the triumph of evil sealed in each case by the signing (or confirming) of a bond. In the first, Faustus is brought at length to throw in his lot with the evil forces and loosen his hold on the good; in the second, he is brought to despair of the good /83/ and so give himself over wholly to the evil. When the first has been accomplished the downward action sets in; the catastrophe follows immediately upon the second.

It is futile to conjecture too closely with a fragment like this as to the form of the original, two-thirds of which may have been lost. But these salient episodes have survived and may have been the main scenes of the original as they are of the present play. In any event, they make it clear that it is upon the figure of Faustus that such action as there is immediately depends.

The character of Faustus, it cannot be too often repeated, is not that of one man, but of man himself, of Everyman. There are no details, no personal traits, no eccentricities or habits, nothing that is intimate or individual. Marlowe could not have told us where, or in what way, Faustus differed from any other man. He was concerned only with that part of him which was common to all men, yet in virtue of which he exceeded all men, his mind. And that mind—we have met it already in an earlier play—is Marlowe's. The limitless desire, the unbridled passion for the infinite, a certain reckless, high confidence in the will and spirit of man are all there as before. Throughout the earlier scenes the mind of Faustus is still "lift upward and divine," still "climbing after knowledge infinite." There are in Faustus digni-ty, patience, tenacity and a certain profundity of thought that are not to be found in Tamburlaine:

> Faustus: What, is great *Mephastophilis* so passionate,
> For being deprivd of the joyes of heaven?
> Learne thou of *Faustus* manly fortitude,
> And scorne those joyes thou never shalt possesse.
> Go beare those tidings to great *Lucifer*,
> Seeing *Faustus* hath incurrd eternall death,
> By desprate thoughts against *Joves* deitie:
> Say, he surrenders up to him his soule,[16]

[16] *Ll.* 319–26. [I, iii, 83–90]

> Had I as many soules as there be starres,
> Ide give them al for Mephastophilis: /84/
> By him Ile be great Emprour of the world,
> And make a bridge through the mooving ayre,
> To passe the *Ocean* with a band of men,
> Ile joyne the hils that binde the *Affricke* shore,
> And make that country continent to *Spaine,*
> And both contributory to my crowne:
> The Emprour shal not live but by my leave,
> Nor any Potentate of *Germany:*[17]

But these are only the attributes of Marlowe grown older.

This rare power of abstracting the nature of man, of revealing only the universal and the general, yet so revealing it that it comes home to the heart of every individual man, reaches its height at the end of the play.

The broken prose speeches that pass between Faustus and the scholars before he is left alone, do indeed, for a moment, show more of normal human feeling than has been contained in all the preceding scenes, but they are eclipsed by the passions of the last scene so that they seem only the foil to it. For a while an unsuspected humanity and tenderness appear in Faustus, side by side with the resoluteness which never deserts him until his personality itself begins to disintegrate:

Faustus: Gentlemen away, lest you perish with me.
2nd Scholar: O, what shal we do to save Faustus?
Faustus: Talke not of me, but save your selves, and depart . . .
1st Scholar: . . . let us into the next roome, and there pray for him.
Faustus: I, pray for me, pray for me, and what noyse soever yee heare, come not unto me, for nothing can rescue me.
2nd Scholar: Pray thou, and we wil pray that God may have mercy upon thee.
Faustus: Gentlemen, farewel, if I live til morning, Ile visite you: if not, Faustus is gone to hel.[18]

But this is only a fitful gleam, a momentary illumination of the world of common affections and loyalties, serving to throw into greater relief the isolation and the horror of /85/ Faustus's position. It has the same value as the homely words spoken a few

---

[17] *Ll.* 338–47. [I, iii, 102–11]
[18] *Ll.* 1405–17. [V, ii, 70–82]

minutes before the murder of Duncan, when Macbeth, nerved to the deed with the horror of which the very air seems fraught, dismisses the servant in attendance:

> "Go, bid thy mistress when my drink is ready
> She strike upon the bell. Get thee to bed."

It is the last glance thrown back upon the normal world from the edge of hell.

Then Faustus is left alone in the room and he is reduced to the mere essence of man—to pure mind freed from all colour derived from human life. There are none of these objects, persons, or habits of life upon which the spirits of great tragic figures are allowed, in the hands of other dramatists, to cast strange, lingering illuminations in the very moment of death. Where Faustus stands, character and individuality no longer exist; there are no distinctions between man and man. In the final and all but inconceivable agony he becomes a sentient nucleus of nerves at the mercy of that terror which leaves him only the power to suffer and to exclaim against his suffering. There is no question any longer of self-reliance or of the preservation of any of the barriers that hold the personality together. For personality is dissolving under "a touch more rare" than has ever been portrayed in art, and we have only absolute and isolated passion, unmodified and uncontaminated by the influences which must confuse all others. The mind, upon the verge of dissolution, is given over to pure fear, absorbed by the inexpressible horror of the doom before it. A strange spiritual alchemy is at work; the soul itself disintegrates under our eyes. Marlowe follows Faustus further across the border line between consciousness and dissolution than do any of his contemporaries. With Shakespeare, with Webster, death is a sudden severing of life; their men die, conscious to the /86/ last of some part at least of their surroundings, influenced, even upheld, by that consciousness and preserving the personality and characteristics they have possessed through life. Macbeth dies fighting; Hamlet, commending the Danish Kingdom to Fortinbras; Mark Antony, though alone and more cut off than either of these, looks on towards the moment when he will again join Cleopatra. Webster's villains in *The White Devil* are steadfast and consistent; both Flamineo and Vittoria survey and comment upon the past in the light of approaching death. In Marlowe's *Faustus* alone is all this set aside. He penetrates deeply into the experience of a mind isolated from the past, absorbed in the realisation of its own destruction.

In Marlowe's great tragic fragment the conflict is not between man and man for the domination of one character over another, or in the interaction of a group of characters. But, as in Æschylus's *Eumenides,* the protagonists are man and the spiritual powers that surround him, the scene is set in no spot upon the physical earth, but in the limitless regions of the mind, and the battle is fought, not for kingdoms or crowns, but upon the question of man's ultimate fate. Before him lies the possibility of escape to spiritual freedom or a doom of slavery to demoniac powers. Thus and in such terms is staged the greatest conflict that drama has ever undertaken to present. /87/

Marlowe's Faustus: A Reconsideration

LEO KIRSCHBAUM

I

If, as E. E. Stoll cogently reiterates, it is true of Shakespeare, that it is not he but the critics who are misleading, it is equally true of Marlowe. As one reads *Doctor Faustus,* the play itself, after having perused modern appreciations of it, one is almost shocked. There seems to be *so little* relation between the artifact itself and the comment upon it. The reason for this false criticism is not far to seek. There are elementary principles without which neither Shakespeare nor Marlowe—nor any competent dramatist, we may add—can be dealt with justly. What these principles are cannot be too often repeated.

The Elizabethan dramatists themselves knew what they were doing. They knew that they were writing *plays.* They recognized and utilized the peculiar opportunities which the form allowed them. They knew what the special relationship in the theatre between the play and the audience allowed and demanded. *We* constantly forget that a play is a play. Thus, we search for recondite understanding when the dramatist himself by means of soliloquy or comment by other characters has given us a clear understanding which it is perverse not to accept. But though we are often over-subtle concerning the obvious, we are often not subtle enough when the dramatist legitimately uses dramatic irony or when he carefully complements an action or speech by a later action or speech. Basic in our confusion is an inability to absorb the consequences of the forgotten truth that drama is primarily action, progressive action—not poetry, not characterization, not

Reprinted from *The Review of English Studies,* XIX (1943), 225–41.

message. (True, these latter are all members of a tight family group, the organism which is the entirety, but none can be the /225/ leader if the audience is to remain interested in what is occurring on the stage. *That* condition is the *sine qua non* of the theatre. If the dramatist fails in *that,* he fails utterly—all other justification is beside the point. Action is the soul of drama.)

It is dangerous to discuss a passage in an Elizabethan play out of its context. The context conditions the interpretation of the passage. The 'Tomorrow and tomorrow and tomorrow' lines, so frequently found in bare isolation, are not a universal statement expressing Shakespeare's comment on life: they are the words of a particular character at a particular time and are dramatically revelatory of that character: they represent life as Macbeth sees it at the very end of his career of crime: they are the product of a twisted, tortured mind. Would any serious film director, today, snip forty seconds from a film and send it to a serious film critic in order that the latter might make serious talk about the fragment? The analogy is especially sound in a condition frequently overlooked. Informing the Elizabethan dramatist's technique is a knowledge that the forward movement of his play negates prolonged scrutiny of any particular part.

Hence, too, we prate about psychological integrity of characters in Shakespeare but do not seem to realize the issues involved. Drama is an imitation of men-in-action. We say that the closer to life the drama is the better it is. But a drama is not life. It is a construct using raw life as its material; and it is a construct through selection, omission, emphasis. It is a construct which gives the illusion of life. The immediate (though not the whole) test of a drama is not allegiance to the textbook or experience, to anything which we know of life when we are out of the theatre. The immediate test is whether when we are in the theatre what is on the stage is a successful illusion. And the audience's capacity for illusion is immense. Your Shakespeare understood that a character's being easily identifiable (i.e. by costume) was sometimes enough to make the audience accept as probable a series of actions by that character which in real life could not normally emanate from one character. Psychological inconsistency could be used by the dramatist for expedience or for greater effect. It might be maintained that such a combination of conscience and villainy as Macbeth could exist. When, however, Shakespeare has Lucio, the cheap sensualist in *Measure for Measure,* go completely out of character to praise the chaste Isabella (I. iv. 30–8), Shakespeare is employing the divergence between life and art to great effect. This device of disjunct character, of having a character not in sympathy with a group of values used, for the nonce, to praise these superior values, is not uncommon in Shakespeare. It is a dramatic device. And the audience's capacity for such dramatic device is also immense. One might think that expressionistic technique would not be understandable to an average audience. Yet *Beggar on Horseback* was a /226/ very successful Broadway play, and the expressionistic dream scenes of Garson Kanin's superb movie, *Tom, Dick, and Harry,* were mightily appreciated. That Shakespeare presupposes and utilizes the normal audience's capacity for dramatic illusion and dramatic device is clearly indicated in the Prologue to *Henry V.*

There are signs that we are beginning to understand Elizabethan drama in its own terms, in terms of the theatre. What is really happening is that we are beginning to slough off the æsthetic of naturalism, the prime purpose of which was to assert that such æsthetic was unnecessary, that art and life were the same. Today, it is admitted that the greatness of an E. M. Forster, of an André Gide, lies in utilizing the artistic techniques which the author of *A Winter's Tale* employed. The artist creates the impossible to reveal the eternal.

If the dramatist says we are in Lapland, we believe that the location of the action is Lapland. But what troubles critics of the early drama is that the play's continent of values—of *mores,* of customs, even of psychology—is also deemed to be foreign and unfamiliar to us. Now, it is probably true that the ethical, religious, and metaphysical concepts inherent in Shakespeare's great tragedies and comedies are, by and large, concepts which were predominant in Elizabethan civilization. It does not follow that we must study that civilization in order to understand Shakespeare. The best the historical critic can discover is something in Shakespeare's England which is already indicated in the play itself. A play, like any other work of art, tends to be complete in itself. But it always possesses a limited perspective. A drama presents only a part of life and that from a limited moral perspective. Though the concepts of Shakespeare's plays are the viable concepts of Shakespeare's environment, no one play gives all these concepts. Variation in ethical patterns was possible. The moral standards by which Iago, Shylock, Malvolio are to be judged are within the plays in which they appear. But note that the non-idealistic standards of Petruchio concerning dowry (I. ii. 50ff.) are similar to the material standards of Launce, the servant in *The Two Gentlemen of Verona* (III. i. 361ff.): in the former play they are apparently socially acceptable; in the latter, they are deliberately inferior to the values of Valentine, Sylvia, Julia, and Sir Eglamour. An Elizabethan drama's prevalent ethical system could be violently private, as in John Ford's *'Tis Pity She's A Whore*. Or it could be socially radical, as in Middleton's pro-feminine *The Roaring Girl*. It could be middle-class, as in *The Shoemakers' Holiday*. It could be aristocratic, as in *The Knight of the Burning Pestle*.

The particular glory of Shakespeare is that the psychology of his creatures, the ethics of their world, the universe which they inhabit *are more than merely plausible*. For the critics of the seventeenth and eighteenth /227/ centuries—Samuel Johnson is especially worthy of citation on this count—Shakespeare imitated not Elizabethan man but essential man. Essential man does not change. To imitate fundamental man is to imitate basic action-patterns of great moral and spiritual significance. To most of his audience Shakespeare's imitation *seems* right. To some of his audience, it *is* right.

Each Elizabethan play, therefore, has a particular world-view, a hierarchy of values and beliefs which may or may not possess the added quality of universality. A drama needs to be judged on a kind of double basis. Shakespeare is quite successful in *The Two Gentlemen of Verona* in getting us for the moment to believe in a fantastic world—a world in which artificial values of courtly love are not merely custom but nature. To be eternally true to one's beloved and to one's friend is the gravest consideration of the superior beings of this world; all else is dross—care for food or money, respect for parents, one's own comfort. The play is a Petrarchan sonnet put into speech and action. Are we to praise the play because it is close to life? Nonsense! We praise it because the inhabitants of its artificial world are constantly consistent in their remoteness from life. Of course, such praise is limited. Later on, Shakespeare learned to give touches of nature to the non-comic creatures of his artificial world. Luciana and Adriana of *The Comedy of Errors*, Biron of *Love's Labour's Lost*, Julia of *The Two Gentlemen of Verona* represent his first attempts in this direction. It is in the great comedies and the great tragedies that the basic nature of his beings and the morality which encompasses their actions become universal—that is, come close to life as the audience apprehends life. One finally judges a play, therefore, as a successful illusion in the theatre *and* as a successful mirror of life. We can *temporarily believe* that goats are blue, but we *know* that they are not. The æsthetic principle has been well put by the poet, Marianne Moore: the artist puts real toads into imaginary gardens.

In all the hurly-burly of understanding Shakespeare, we seem to forget that the Elizabethans, Shakespeare, and we ourselves are in the same stream of civilization; that even though we, today, may not sympathize with certain aspects of this civilization, we do *understand* those aspects; and that while we are in the theatre, the dramatist can get us to accept a scale of values which is different from our normal scale of values, the temporary suspension of disbelief operating. Thus, Shakespeare's men and Shakespeare's world are immediately understandable in New York City or London because the audience is prepared for and/or accepts the values which Shakespeare explicitly or implicitly presents in his plays. The audience at an Evans or Gielgud *Macbeth* accepts Shakespeare's premises. /228/

II

What I have written applies (with, of course, a recognition of inferior artistry) to Marlowe. *Outside* the theatre, we may mightily agree or disagree with the eschatology inherent in *Doctor Faustus*. But *in* the theatre, as we watch the play, we understand and accept (if only for the nonce) that man's most precious possession is his immortal soul and that he gains Heaven or Hell by his professions and actions on earth. *In* the theatre, we accept Marlowe's premises. That these premises were inherent in his first audience is of incidental interest to us as students and appreciators of the drama. The premises are instinct in every word, line, passage, speech, action of the play. The Christian view of the world informs *Doctor Faustus* throughout—not the pagan view. If we do not accept that Faustus's selling his soul to the devil for earthly power and pleasure is a serious business, we simply are not hearing what Marlowe wrote.

Critics confound Marlowe the man and Marlowe the playwright. They consider that the man was an atheist and so interpret *Doctor Faustus*. What if the play were anonymous? What has biography to do with a play which we are presumably watching in the theatre? Whatever Marlowe was himself, there is no more obvious Christian document in all Elizabethan drama than *Doctor Faustus*. Or critics will consider the protagonist as a representative of the Renaissance superman. Whatever their feelings and thoughts on the revival of learning and the Reformation are, let them open-mindedly look at the play unfolding on the stage before them. For earthly learning, earthly power, earthly satisfaction, Faustus goes down to horrible and everlasting perdition. It does not matter what *you* think of Hell or what Marlowe privately thought of Hell. What does matter is that in terms of the play, Faustus is a wretched creature who for lower values gives up higher values—that the devil and Hell are omnipresent, potent, and terrifying realities. These are the values which govern the play. You must temporarily accept them while you watch the play. You need not ultimately accept them. But you should not interpret the play in the light of *your* philosophy or religion or absence of religion. You cannot do so if you hear it properly— as a play, as an entity, as a progressive action, as a quasi-morality in which is clearly set forth the hierarchy of moral values which enforces and encloses the play, which the characters in the play accept, which the playwright advances and accepts in his prologue and epilogue, which—hence—the audience must understand and accept.

III

Now I want to apply what has been said above to the following famous speech from Doctor Faustus [V. i. 99–118]: /229/

> Was this the face that launch'd a thousand ships,
> And burnt the topless towers of Ilium?—
> Sweet Helen, make me immortal with a kiss.—

Her lips suck forth my soul; see where it flies!—
Come, Helen, come, give me my soul again.
Here will I dwell, for heaven is in these lips,
And all is dross that is not Helena.   *Enter old man*
I will be Paris, and for love of thee,
Instead of Troy, shall Wittenberg be sack'd;
And I will combat with weak Menelaus,
And wear thy colours on my plumed crest:
Yea, I will wound Achilles in the heel,
And then return to Helen for a kiss.
O, thou art fairer than the evening's air
Clad in the beauty of a thousand stars;
Brighter art thou than flaming Jupiter
When he appear'd to hapless Semele;
More lovely than the monarch of the sky
In wanton Arethusa's azured arms;
And none but thou shalt be my paramour!   *Exeunt.*[1]

This passage has again and again been presented in appreciation of Marlowe. 'What a marvellous pæan to beauty!' say the critics. Is it? Let us examine it in its context.

The reader will forgive a rapid survey of the play—which is necessary because of prevalent misunderstanding of Marlowe's artistic purpose in the drama. Necessarily, over-simplification must result, but major inaccuracy will not, I hope, be present.

The playwright immediately tells us in the Prologue:

> So much he profits in divinity,
> That shortly he was grac'd with Doctor's name,
> Excelling all and sweetly can dispute
> In th' heavenly matters of theology;
> Till swoln with cunning, of a self-conceit,
> His waxen wings did mount above his reach,
> And, melting, heavens conspir'd his over-throw;
> For, falling to a devilish exercise,
> And glutted now with learning's golden gifts,
> He surfeits upon cursed necromancy;
> Nothing so sweet as magic is to him,

---

[1] I employ the 1616 (B) text but have availed myself of the act, scene, line numbering; normalized spelling; lineation; stage-directions; and speech prefixes of F. S. Boas's edition. Since his is an eclectic text, I have had to make a few changes here and there—none material. I follow the 1604 (A) text in five places: II. ii. 20–2 and 100–2 which are not in B; the second half-line of V. i. 78; the entrance of the Old Man in the midst of the Helen eulogy, V. i. 113; and the Old Man's speech V. i. 127–9. The Old Man does not reappear in B after his exhortation.

Which he prefers before his chiefest bliss:
And this the man that in his study sits. /230/

We *must* trust Marlowe's *ex cathedra* description of his protagonist—a man who, swollen with pride in his attainments, comes to
a deserved end because he has preferred forbidden pursuits to
'his chiefest bliss'. (Certainly Marlowe guides us deftly by the
analogy with Icarus—who, of course, equates with Lucifer; see
below [I. iii. 65–9]). The Faustus whom Marlowe gives us in
the ensuing action is both more complex and less radiant than
the utterances of scholars would lead us to expect.

That thus and so the world is constituted, that given a certain
act of moral and spiritual significance such a consequence will
follow, is indicated implicitly not only by the occurrences of the
play but also explicitly by the choruses (as we have seen); by
Faustus's own recognition; by Mephistophilis; by the Scholars;
by the Old Man (perhaps, the most important guide Marlowe
supplies us), etc. A chief device of such exposition is the Good
Angel, the voice of God, the expounder of things as they are—
who always appears in concert with the Bad Angel, the emissary
of the Devil. Thus, at the very beginning of Faustus's temptation, the Good Angel says (I. i. 71–4):

> O, Faustus, lay that damned book aside,
> And gaze not on it, lest it tempt thy soul,
> And heap God's heavy wrath upon thy head!
> Read, read the Scriptures:—that is blasphemy.

But Faustus hearkens to the Bad Angel. And note what he expects as a reward for practising the forbidden black magic. Before the Good Angel enters, he gloats (I. i. 54–6):

> O, what a world of profit and delight,
> Of power, of honour, and omnipotence,
> Is promised to the studious artizan!

After this entrance, he further reveals his expectations. He will
not only get knowledge and power: his mind dwells longingly on
satisfaction of material appetite. The spirits will bring him
'gold', 'orient pearl', 'pleasant fruits', 'princely delicates', 'silk' (I.
i. 83–92).

Not only has Faustus intellectual pride to an odious degree,
but he is also avid for more vainglory (I. i. 113–9):

> And I, that have with subtle syllogisms
> Gravell'd the pastors of the German church,
> And made the flowering pride of Wittenberg
> Swarm to my problems, as the infernal spirits
> On sweet Musæus when he came to hell,
> Will be as cunning as Agrippa was,
> Whose shadows made all Europe honour him.

Faustus is wholly egocentric. To himself, he is either the greatest
of men or the greatest of abject sinners. He underrates his oppo-
nents, and relishes his inflated sense of his own abilities. Thus,
after Mephistophilis has left /231/ the stage at the behest of the
magician that he reappear in the more pleasant guise of a Franciscan (Marlowe is indeed subtle: Faustus will not and can not
accept things as they are: the truth must be side-stepped some
way, the bitter pill must be coated with sugar), Faustus wallows
in a delusion of self-importance [I. iii. 29–31]:

> How pliant is this Mephistophilis,
> Full of obedience and humility!
> Such is the force of magic and my spells. . . .

But Mephistophilis quickly disillusions him [I. iii. 45–54]:

> Faust. Did not my conjuring raise thee? speak?
> Meph. That was the cause, but yet *per accidens;*
> For, when we hear one rack the name of God,
> Abjure the Scriptures and his Saviour Christ,
> We fly, in hope to get his glorious soul;
> Nor will we come, unless he use such means
> Whereby he is in danger to be damn'd.
> Therefore the shortest cut for conjuring
> Is stoutly to abjure all godliness,
> And pray devoutly to the prince of hell.

Faustus agrees to worship Belzebub [I. iii. 59–63]:

> This word 'damnation' terrifies not me,
> For I confound hell in Elysium:
> My ghost be with the old philosophers!
> But, leaving these vain trifles of men's souls
> Tell me what is that Lucifer thy lord?

But note how Marlowe immediately shows up the vanity and foolhardiness of this last speech. In order to set forth that damnation and soul are not mere trifles, the playwright has the enemy of man strip Faustus of those very delusions which the enemy of man wants Faustus to possess in order that the enemy of man may destroy Faustus. This dramatic device is similar to that of disjunct character which I discussed earlier: the enemy of the truth supports the truth so that the audience will be absolutely clear as to what the truth is. And note that Mephistophilis foreshadows Faustus's fall in Lucifer's, and that insolence and pride are the instigators in both cases [I. iii. 65–82]:

> *Faust.* Was not that Lucifer an angel once?
> *Meph.* Yes, Faustus, and most dearly lov'd of God.
> *Faust.* How comes it then that he is prince of devils?
> *Meph.* O, by aspiring pride and insolence;
> For which God threw him from the face of heaven.
> *Faust.* And what are you that live with Lucifer?
> *Meph.* Unhappy spirits that fell with Lucifer,
> Conspir'd against our God with Lucifer,
> And are for ever damn'd with Lucifer. /232/
> *Faust.* Where are you damn'd?
> *Meph.*   In hell.
> *Faust.* How comes it then that thou art out of hell?
> *Meph.* Why this is hell, nor am I out of it:
> Think'st thou that I, that saw the face of God,
> And tasted the eternal joys of heaven,
> Am not tormented with ten thousand hells,
> In being depriv'd of everlasting bliss?
> O, Faustus, leave these frivolous demands,
> Which strikes a terror to my fainting soul!

But the foolhardy Faustus, having been warned by the Devil himself, reprimands the latter for cowardliness! He boasts [I. iii. 83–6]:

> What, is great Mephistophilis so passionate
> For being deprived of the joys of heaven?
> Learn thou of Faustus manly fortitude,
> And scorn those joys thou never shalt possess.

How can any one read the scene and call the self-deluded, foolishly boastful Faustus a superman?

Note carefully what Faustus wants in return for selling his soul to the devil [I. iii. 90–7]:

> Say, he surrenders up to him his soul,
> So he will spare him four-and-twenty years,
> Letting him live in all voluptuousness;
> Having thee ever to attend on me,
> To give me whatsoever I shall ask,
> To tell me whatsoever I demand,
> To slay mine enemies, and to aid my friends,
> And always be obedient to my will.

Utter satisfaction of the will and utter satisfaction of the senses are what Faustus desires. And how he prates [I. iii. 102–3]—who a little later will be quaking!

> Had I as many souls as there be stars,
> I'd give them all for Mephistophilis.

The next time we see Faustus, midnight of the same day, his emotional and intellectual instability is fully revealed. He veers between God and the Devil. At first, he is conscience-stricken. All his cocky effrontery is gone. But in a moment he is once more the user of egocentric hyperbole (II. i. 1–14):

> Now, Faustus, must
> Thou needs be damn'd. Canst thou not be sav'd?
> What boots it, then, to think on God or heaven?
> Away with such vain fancies, and despair;
> Despair in God, and trust in Belzebub:
> Now go not backward; Faustus, be resolute:
> Why waver'st thou? O, something soundeth in mine ear,
> 'Abjure this magic, turn to God again!'
> Ay, and Faustus will turn to God again. /233/
> Why, he loves thee not;
> The God thou serv'st is thine own appetite,
> Wherein is fix'd the love of Belzebub:
> To him I'll build an altar and a church,
> And offer lukewarm blood of new-born babes.

A weakling, he must cover his fears with megalomaniacal fantasy. Two points should be made. We must understand that Faustus' conclusion as to the impossibility of God's mercy is the mark of a diseased ego—a lack of humility. And also, we must particularly remark Faustus' self-recognition of his driving passion: 'The God thou serv'st is thine own appetite'.

The struggle between Faustus' uncontrolled appetite and the powers of Heaven continues (II. i. 15–26):

Enter the two Angels.

Bad Ang.   Go forward, Faustus, in that famous art,
Good Ang.   Sweet Faustus, leave that execrable art.
Faust.   Contrition, prayer, repentance—what of these?
Good Ang.   O, they are means to bring thee unto heaven!
Bad Ang.   Rather illusions, fruits of lunacy,
That make them foolish that do use them most.
Good Ang.   Sweet Faustus, think of heaven and heavenly things.
Bad Ang.   No, Faustus; think of honour and of wealth.
[Exeunt Angels.
Faust.   Wealth!   Why, the signiory of Embden shall be mine.
When Mephistophilis shall stand by me,
What power can hurt me?   Faustus, thou art safe:
Cast no more doubts—

He thus deludes himself. But again Faustus is warned by the emissary of Hell what awaits him if he sells his soul to the Devil [II. i. 38–43]:

Faust.   Stay, Mephistophilis, and tell me what good
Will my soul do thy lord?
Meph.   Enlarge his kingdom.
Faust.   Is that the reason why he tempts us thus?
Meph.   *Solamen miseris socios habuisse doloris.*
Faust.   Why, have you any pain that torture others?
Meph.   As great as have the human souls of men.

And that Faustus has free will, free choice, ability to affirm or deny God if he so wishes; that he cannot (as he does later) blame anyone but himself for his act and its consequences, Faustus himself makes clear when, after his blood has congealed so that he cannot sign the document and give his soul to Hell, he says [II. i. 65–8]:

Why streams it not, that I may write afresh?
Faustus gives to thee his soul: oh, there it stay'd!
Why shouldst thou not? is not thy soul thine own?
Then write again, *Faustus gives to thee his soul.* /234/

Marlowe's powers of compressed dramatic irony can be tremendous. As soon as Faustus has signed, he says 'Consummatum est' [II. i. 73], the last words of Christ on earth according to St.

John. What an insight into the twisted mind of the magician!
And what blasphemy! Jesus died that Faustus' soul might live;
Faustus flings away this priceless gift for a mess of earthly pot-
tage! But the words are also true in a more literal sense: the
good life, the possibility of reaching Heaven, are indeed finished
for Faustus.

When, immediately afterward, God's warning 'Homo, fuge!'
appears on Faustus' arm, he—characteristically—affirms the God
whom he has just denied and gets into a turmoil of conflicting
impulses [II. i. 76–80]:

> Homo, fuge!   Whither should I fly?
> If unto God, he'll throw me down to hell.
> My senses are deceiv'd: here's nothing writ:—
> O yes, I see it plain; even here is writ,
> Homo, fuge!   Yet shall not Faustus fly.

Hence, Faustus consciously and deliberately sets his will against
God's. But as he is in this state, Mephistophilis, knowing his victim, says in an aside, 'I'll fetch him somewhat to delight his
mind' [II. i. 81]. And then to the voluptuary [II. i. 82–8],

> *Enter Devils, giving crowns and rich apparel to Faustus.*
> *They dance, and then depart.*
>
> *Enter Mephistophilis.*
>
> Faust.   What means this show? Speak, Mephistophilis.
> Meph.   Nothing, Faustus, but to delight thy mind,
>   And let thee see what magic can perform.
> Faust.   But may I raise such spirits when I please?
> Meph.   Ay, Faustus, and do greater things than these.
> Faust.   Then, Mephistophilis, receive this scroll,
>   A deed of gift of body and of soul . . .

Thus, Mephistophilis deliberately offers Faustus sensual satisfaction in order to distract his mind from spiritual concern—which
might, of course, lead to repentance. This pattern is a basic one
in the play, and an understanding of it will eventually enable us
to interpret truly the Helen of Troy apostrophe. Whenever there
is danger (from the Devil's viewpoint) that Faustus will turn to
God's mercy, the powers of Hell will deaden their victim's conscience by providing him with some great satisfaction of the
senses. But sometimes Faustus will ask for the opiate himself.

In the same scene, Faustus receives a true description of his condition, but cheaply flaunts his disbelief—as though one should deny gravity! Once more it is Mephistophilis who forcefully establishes the eschatology and values [II. i. 125–35]: /235/

Faust.   I think hell's a fable.
Meph.   Ay, think so, till experience change thy mind.
Faust.   Why, dost thou think that Faustus shall be damn'd?
Meph.   Ay, of necessity, for here's the scroll
           In which thou hast given thy soul to Lucifer.
Faust.   Ay, and body too: but what of that?
           Think'st thou that Faustus is so fond to imagine
           That, after this life, there is any pain?
           No, these are trifles and mere old wives' tales.
Meph.   But I am instance to prove the contrary;
           For I tell thee I am damn'd, and now in hell.

And here, again, Marlowe shows the constitution of Faustus' mind. As soon as Mephistophilis has stated that hell with its tortures and damnation do exist, Faustus asks for his customary anodyne for uncomfortable conscience [II. i. 136–56]:

Faust.   Nay, and this be hell, I'll willingly be damn'd:
           What! sleeping, eating, walking, and disputing!
           But, leaving this, let me have a wife,
           The fairest maid in Germany, for I
           Am wanton and lascivious
           And cannot live without a wife.
Meph.   Well, Faustus, thou shalt have a wife.
             He fetches in a woman-devil.
Faust.   What sight is this?
Meph.   Now, Faustus, wilt thou have a wife?
Faust.   Here's a hot whore indeed!   No, I'll no wife.
Meph.   Marriage is but a ceremonial toy:
           And if thou lovest me, think no more of it.
           I'll call thee out the fairest courtesans,
           And bring them ev'ry morning to thy bed:
           She whom thine eye shall like, thy heart shall have,
           Were she as chaste as was Penelope,
           As wise as Saba, or as beautiful
           As was bright Lucifer before his fall.

See again Marlowe's compressed irony—Faustus shall have his appetite satisfied by women as beautiful 'as was bright Lucifer before his fall'.

In the next scene (II. ii.), the Devil's agent and Faustus are

again together. Faustus is going through another of his struggles
between repentance and non-repentance. He blames Mephistophilis for his misery (2–3), but the latter points out that the magician made his choice of his own free-will: "Twas thine own
seeking, Faustus thank thyself' (4). When Faustus says that he
'will renounce this magic and repent' (11), he himself in a lucid
moment recognizes that repentance is still possible. And the
Good Angel at once announces also that a true act of contrition
followed by God's forgiveness can still occur (12). But continued
exercise in sin is robbing Faustus of volition—'My heart is hardened, I cannot /236/ repent' (18). However, this too must be
taken as an egocentric conclusion. No sooner does he think of
holy things, than the assertion 'Faustus, thou art damn'd' thunders in his ears (19–21). And all kinds of instruments for self-destruction are placed before him (21–3). Then in self-revelation he
gives us another sharp insight into his essential make-up (24–5):

> And long ere this I should have done the deed,
> Had not sweet pleasure conquer'd deep despair.

As I have pointed out, sensuous pleasure is always Faustus' rem-
edy for spiritual despair. He has had Homer and Orpheus sing
for him (25–9). And now the very thought of former pleasure
drugs his conscience (31–2):

> Why should I die, then, or basely despair?
> I am resolv'd; Faustus shall not repent.

It is instructive to compare Macbeth with Faustus. The former is
tremendous in his spiritual agony. But the Faustus who, here
and elsewhere, goes through such rapid mental and emotional
gyrations is surely conceived of by his creator as of infinitely small-
er dimension.

In the latter part of this scene (II. ii.) there is almost a replica
of the pattern of the first part of the scene. Mephistophilis tells
Faustus: 'thou art damn'd; think thou of hell' [73]. And the
latter once more characteristically blames Lucifer's servant for
his plight: "Tis thou hast damn'd distressed Faustus' soul' [77].
And so once more the protagonist is in spiritual distress. The
Good Angel tells him there is still time to repent [80]. But the
Bad Angel promises, 'If thou repent, devils will tear thee in
pieces' [81]. (We must remember that the obverse of love of

pleasure is fear of pain.) Just as Faustus calls upon his Saviour for help [83–4], Lucifer, Beelzebub, and Mephistophilis enter. Lucifer appears menacing and frightening [87]:

> *Faust.*   O, what art thou that look'st so terribly?

And after a few lines of prodding [85–95], the wretchedly irresolute hedonist once more veers and blatantly boasts [97–100]:

> never to look to heaven,
> Never to name God, or to pray to him,
> To burn his Scriptures, slay his ministers,
> And make my spirits pull his churches down.

Once again the Devil gets Faustus out of his melancholy by providing him with some satisfaction of the senses—the show of the Seven Deadly Sins. Note again Marlowe's dramatic irony [106–7]:

> That sight will be as pleasant to me,
> As Paradise was to Adam, the first day
> Of his creation.

And after the show, the deluded magician in unconscious irony says [163], 'O, how this sight doth delight my soul.' /237/

In III. i. at the beginning of the anti-papist scene, we have another statement by Faustus of his motivating passion [58–62]:

> Sweet Mephistophilis, thou pleasest me,
> Whilst I am here on earth, let me be cloy'd
> With all things that delight the heart of man.
> My four-and-twenty years of liberty
> I'll spend in pleasure and in dalliance,

And in IV. v. the Horse-Courser scene, Marlowe shows the protagonist still tormented—but still capable of rapid self-delusion [33–8]:

> What are thou, Faustus, but a man condemn'd to die?
> Thy fatal time draws to a final end,
> Despair doth drive distrust into my thoughts.
> Confound these passions with a quiet sleep.
> Tush!   Christ did call the thief upon the Cross;
> Then rest thee, Faustus, quiet in conceit.

IV

In the last act, Marlowe once more returns us forcefully to the serious business of his play. At the very beginning Wagner is

struck by the inconsistency of his master's character. The latter
has made his will and hence 'means to die shortly' [V. i. 1]. But
says the puzzled servant [5–8]:

> if death were nigh
> He would not frolic thus. He's now at supper
> With the scholars, where there's such belly-cheer
> As Wagner in his life ne'er saw the like.

Thus, through the mouth of another character, the playwright
shows us Faustus as still the incorrigible hedonist. The Scholars
wish him to show them Helen of Troy. Mephistophilis brings in
the peerless dame, and the scholars are ravished. The latter leave
—and 'Enter an Old Man'. The latter movingly begs Faustus to
give up his wicked life [38–64]. Here we have explicit statement that Faustus is still a man (and not a spirit); that he still
has 'an amiable soul'; that he is still capable of repentance; that
if he does not change his wicked ways, his nature will become incapable of contrition; that by 'checking [his] body' 'he may
amend [his] soul'. Faustus's reaction to the Old Man's speech is
typical. He utterly despairs, is positive of his damnation, and is
about to kill himself with a dagger which Mephistophilis provides [59]. Thus, in the reverse kind of egotism in which Faustus indulges when he is conscience-stricken, he completely misses
the burden of the Old Man's message: no man's sins are too great
for God to forgive. But the Old Man cries out for him to stop,
tells him that 'precious grace' waits only upon prayer for mercy
[60–4]. Faustus thanks the Old Man for words that 'comfort
my distressed soul' /238/ and asks to be left alone to ponder his
sins [67]. But the Old Man knows how weak the magician is
[68–9]:

> Faustus, I leave thee; but with grief of heart,
> Fearing the enemy of thy hapless soul.

We soon see that the Old Man was right in his apprehensions. As
soon as he has left the stage, Faustus is in the toils [70–3]:

> Accursed Faustus, where is mercy now?
> I do repent; and yet I do despair:
> Hell strives with grace for conquest in my breast:
> What shall I do to shun the snares of death?

Hell strives against Heaven: despair against repentance. But as

soon as Mephistophilis arrests him for disobedience, commands
him to deny God, threatens physical pain—'Or I'll in piecemeal
tear they flesh' [74–6]—the weak-willed voluptuary caves in. He
'repents' (*sic!*) that he has offended Lucifer [77], offers of his
own volition to confirm with blood his former vow to Lucifer
and does so [78–81], and—characteristically blaming another for
his treason—brutally begs Mephistophilis to torture the Old Man
'With greatest torments that our (*sic!*) hell affords' [84–6]. Is
this the superman whom devotees of the Renaissance paint?

Once more we see the familiar pattern operating. Faustus requests the moly which will deaden his spiritual apprehension
[90–6]:

> One thing, good servant, let me crave of thee,
> To glut the longing of my heart's desire,—
> That I may have unto my paramour
> That heavenly Helen which I saw of late,
> Whose sweet embraces may extinguish clean
> Those thoughts that do dissuade me from my vow,
> And keep my oath I made to Lucifer.

Helen appears. Faustus delivers the famous apostrophe, 'Was this
the face . . .' and leaves the stage with her. How are we to take
these lines? The Old Man has appeared in the midst of them and
seen and heard Faustus. He recognizes what is happening, and so
should we. For the sake of bodily pleasure, Faustus has given up
the last possibility of redemption and embraced Hell. We do not
even have to recognize that Helen is a succuba, the devil in fe-
male guise, to know what Marlowe wants us to know. That there
should be no doubt, the Old Man tells us as soon as Faustus and
Helen have left the stage together [119–21]:

> Accursed Faustus, miserable man,
> That from thy soul exclud'st the grace of Heaven,
> And fliest the throne of his tribunal-seat!

(In the next six lines, Marlowe establishes a strong contrast between the hedonist and the Old Man. The devils come in to torture the latter, but he, strong in his faith, defies their torments.)
/239/

The next scene is that of Faustus's going down to Hell [V. 11].
The comment of Mephistophilis at its beginning is sharply de-
scriptive [12–16]:

> Fond worlding, now his heart-blood dries with grief,
> His conscience kills it and his labouring brain
> Begets a world of idle fantasies,
> To over-reach the Devil; but all in vain,
> His store of pleasures must be sauc'd with pain.

And note how admirably Marlowe shows us the kernel of this unstable, foolish worldling. The Second Scholar has asked him to repent, 'God's mercies are infinite' [40]. Faustus replies [41-51]:

> But Faustus' offence can ne'er be pardoned: the serpent that tempted Eve may be saved, but not Faustus. O, gentlemen, hear me with patience, and tremble not at my speeches! Though my heart pant and quiver to remember that I have been a student here these thirty years, O, would I had never seen Wittenberg, never read book! and what wonders I have done, all Germany can witness, yea, all the world; for which Faustus hath lost both Germany and the world; yea, heaven itself, heaven, the seat of God, the throne of the blessed, the kingdom of joy; and must remain in hell for ever—hell, oh, hell for ever! Sweet friends, what shall become of Faustus, being in hell for ever?

One should not pass over lightly the exceedingly dramatic nature of this speech. The quaking Faustus is still the blatant egotist. He *knows* that God cannot pardon him! And in the midst of his self-reproach, lo! the basic vanity leaps forth—'and what wonders I have done, all Germany can witness, yea, all the world'. Critics tend to consider Marlowe capable only of broad effects—erroneously, I believe.

Faustus sums up his situation succinctly: 'for the vain pleasure of four and twenty years hath Faustus lost eternal joy and felicity' [63-4]. He gave up higher values for lower. And the burden of the Good and Bad Angels who come on is that for small pleasure the voluptuary has given up great pleasures, for small pleasures he must now endure all the horrible sensory tortures of Hell [103-27]. The Bad Angel concludes, 'He that loves pleasure, must for pleasure fall.' Such is the ironic outcome.

But the most trenchant stroke of Marlowe's pervading irony is in the famous last soliloquy. Faustus, too late, begs for time to repent, and in his agony cries out [139], '*O lente, lente currite, noctis equi!*' This is Ovid, *Amores*, I. xiii. 40. Habituated to sensual pleasure, Faustus—begging now for time to save his soul—must perforce use the words of Ovid in his mistress's arms!

My main story is done. I hope I have made my major point,

that the Helen of Troy speech is hardly what critics take it to be, an unencumbered pagan pæan. I hope I have shown that in the pattern of the play Helen is a temporary pleasure that costs the protagonist eternal pain. It is worthwhile to examine the lines to Helen more carefully, for they are fraught /**240**/ with dramatic irony. Faustus himself points out the danger in Helen's beauty. It caused the great Trojan war—and the destruction of man's greatest edifices. Faustus' request, 'Sweet Helen, make me immortal with a kiss', is, of course, blasphemous. On the contrary, it will mean eternal torment; and it will rob him of immortal bliss. When he says, 'Her lips suck forth my soul', he is being literally true. And as he once more kisses her, what an ironic confusion of values there is!

> Here will I dwell, for heaven is in these lips
> And all is dross that is not Helena.

Rather, Hell lies in her lips—for the sake of which he has given up Heaven: and Helen is the 'dross' for which he is giving up the 'all'. In the rest of the passage, Marlowe's irony persists—but not so near the surface. There is still a reversal of the normal. Faustus will be Paris (who was defeated) and fight 'Weak Menelaus' (who was stronger, actually). Furthermore, Faustus will be like the violator of order (Paris), whereas his opponent (the husband, the symbol of order) will be weak; but in *The Iliad* order wins— and it is bound to win in the play, too. Faustus will wear the colours of Hell on his crest. He will ignominiously fight a weak opponent—and he will wound another in his foot! Helen's beauty is like the night and stars. One remembers:

> Had I as many souls as there be stars,
> I'd give them all for Mephistophilis [I. iii. 102–3]

and

> as beautiful
> As was bright Lucifer before his fall. [II. i. 155–6]

'Brighter art thou than flaming Jupiter' suggests the ever-burning flames of Hell—of which we hear much in the next scene. And note the proportion—Helen : Jupiter :: Faustus : 'hapless Semele'. Helen indeed overcomes the hapless Faustus. And note the next proportion—Helen : Jupiter :: Faustus : 'wanton Arethusa'. Wanton Faustus! /**241**/

From *Marlowe's Heroes*

M. M. MAHOOD

One disastrous result of the humanist disintegration was that man's refusal to understand or accept his 'middle state', by depriving his nature of its equilibrium, left him helpless between the extremes of rationalism and fatalism. At first, in the stage of thought represented by *Tamburlaine,* man asserts his self-sufficiency with a pride which is loth to allow God any part in his existence. But we have already seen, in that play, how the insatiable mind, 'Still climbing after knowledge infinite', seeks a superhuman virtue even in terrestrial power. Natural man, growing aware of his insufficiency, likewise begins to crave the completion of his experience in the knowledge of spiritual worlds. Here he runs his head against a wall erected by himself; his vaunted self-sufficiency prevents him from putting any faith in that interpenetration of the natural and spiritual worlds which is implicit in Christian doctrine. Deprived of his self-esteem, he swings rapidly from his assertion of man's greatness independent of God to the other blasphemy of denying human greatness altogether. The titanic hero shrinks to the plaything of malignant powers which are more capricious than just. Some of the greatest Elizabethan and Jacobean tragedies depict this ebb and flow of exultant individualism and despairing fatalism in the minds of their heroes.

No play isolates this conflict more clearly than *Doctor Faustus.*

Reprinted from *Poetry and Humanism* (London: Jonathan Cape, 1950).

That this is the main theme of the play becomes even more apparent if we strip the action of its playhouse accretions.[1] There then remain six episodes in which the tragedy of Renaissance humanism is told with a swift simplicity paralleled only in Greek tragedy and in *Samson Agonistes*. Of course, what remains after these textual prunings is not the play as Marlowe wrote it. /64/ The Wagner scenes suggest that he intended the work to be a typical Elizabethan blend of high tragedy and ironic fooling; one must regret the loss of Wagner, who has the making of a real Shakespearean clown. He might have been the little man shrewdly commenting on the vagaries of the great, *l'homme moyen sensuel* always at hand to deflate the bombast of fanatics. But Wagner disappears early in the printed play, and the comic scenes are botched by less skilful pens. So this tragedy of the Renaissance mind survives as a play of almost Hellenic intensity, unrelieved by that Shakespearean comedy which relaxes the tragic tension only to increase it the next instant.

While Faustus's character is complex by contrast with Tamburlaine's, it is evolved from it, since Marlowe continues to draw on his and his contemporaries' experience of the humanist fallacy. The opening speech by the Chorus, although it contrasts Tamburlaine's 'prowd audacious deedes' with Faustus's retired life, suggests many points of similarity between the two heroes. Like Tamburlaine, Faustus is low-born, but endowed with the natural gift of a brilliant mind. The mention of Icarus, a prey like Phaethon and the Titans to a fatal ambition, prepares us for the appearance of a second Promethean hero:

> . . . swolne with cunning, of a selfe conceit,
> His waxen wings did mount aboue his reach,
> And melting heauens conspirde his ouerthrow,
>
> 20-2   [Prologue]

and the speech ends with the clear statement that once again we are to hear the story of misdirected desire:

<hr>

[1] See P. Simpson, 'The 1604 Text of Marlowe's *Doctor Faustus*', *Essays and Studies*, Vol. VII. P. Kocher (*M.L.Q.*, III (1942) makes out a very strong case for 'Nashe's Authorship of the Prose Scenes in *Faustus*'. [Miss Mahood bases her essay upon the 1604 text of *Faustus* on the assumption that the additional elements in the 1616 text represent "playhouse accretions." Her perpetuation of this presently discredited notion does not greatly affect the interest or validity of her criticism of the play.—Ed.]

Nothing so sweete as magicke is to him
Which he preferres before his chiefest blisse.

                                        26–7   [Prologue]

It is worth noting that the Titan *motif* appears in Marlowe's source, the *English Faust Book,* where the magician is stated to be 'worse than the Giants whom the Poets feign to climb the hills to make war with the Gods: not unlike that enemy of God and his Christ that for his pride was cast into Hell'.[2] /65/

This theme of misdirected desire is sustained all through Faustus's opening soliloquy. His ambition to become a great physician is directed only by the craving for present wealth and posthumous fame:

> Be a physition *Faustus,* heape vp golde,
> And be eternizde for some wondrous cure.
>
>   42–3   [I, i, 14–5]

But neither wealth nor fame can satisfy an aspiration which transcends mortal limits. Like Tamburlaine, Faustus desires a godlike power over life and death:

> Yet art thou still but *Faustus,* and a man.
> Wouldst thou make man to liue eternally?
> Or being dead, raise them to life againe?
> Then this profession were to be esteemd.
>
>   51–4   [I, i, 23–6]

'But a man': in this phrase the self-contradiction of a false humanism is already seen at work. Pride in man's potentialities is swiftly reversed to despair at his limitations. The cave of Despair lies at no great distance from the castle of Orgoglio; and in the absence of conclusive evidence for a late date of *Doctor Faustus,* this natural kinship of the two states of mind suggests that the play was successor to *Tamburlaine.*[3] Here again Marlowe found in the *English Faust Book* a parallel to the humanist experience: 'Dr. Faustus was ever pondering with himself how he might get loose from so damnable an end as he had given himself unto,

---

[2] *The Historie of the damnable life, and deserued death of Doctor John Faustus,* ed. W. Rose, p. 75.

[3] F. S. Boas, in the introduction to his edition of *Doctor Faustus,* argues for a much later date for the play, which he considers to be Marlowe's most mature work. But see P. Kocher, 'The Early Date for Marlowe's *Faustus*' (*M.L.N.,* XVI (1941).

both of body and soul: but his repentance was like to that of Cain and Judas, he thought his sins greater than God could forgive and here upon rested his mind.'4 Already in this opening soliloquy Faustus is a prey to such spiritual despondency, and it proves his undoing when, with the words 'When all is done, Diuinitie is best', he turns to the one learning which might slake his thirst of mind. Faced by the barrier which a false humanism has erected between God and man, he discovers as the sum of all theology nothing but the threat of doom. With the superstitious fatalism of the High Renaissance, he flings /66/ open the Vulgate in order to force two random texts—*Stipendium peccati mors est* and *Si peccasse negamus, fallimur et nulla est in nobis veritas*—into a syllogism which, if it did in fact comprise all divinity, would undoubtedly make it 'Vnpleasant, harsh, contemptible and vilde'. The action represents both contemptuous pride and credulous despair—the extreme swings of the pendulum.

The main crisis of the drama is reached in this first soliloquy when Faustus bids 'Diuinitie, adieu'. Divinity to God—and Faustus to the devil. Despair deflects Faustus's natural and rightful thirst for knowledge from divinity to magic, which alone seems to offer a way of escape from human insignificance:

> But his dominion that exceeds in this,
> Stretcheth as farre as doth the minde of man.
>
> 88-9   [I, i, 61-2]

This theme of despair dominates the play, and the word itself recurs with a gloomy, tolling insistence. Faustus, at the beginning of the third episode, his conveyance of his soul to the devil by deed of gift, soliloquises upon 'Despaire in God, and trust in Belsabub'; and his words

> I [Ay] and Faustus wil turne to God againe.
> To God? he loues thee not,
>
> 441-2   [II, i, 9-10]

voice a despondency which is deepened by the Evil Angel's insistence that 'God cannot pitty thee'. The intervention of the Old Man in the fifth episode suggests that Faustus's soul might be regained if only his despair could be overcome. As Mephistophilis gives Faustus a dagger that he may confirm his desperation by

4 *Ed. cit.*, pp. 92-3.

killing himself, the Old Man pleads with him to 'call for mercie and auoyd dispaire', and leaves him

> with heauy cheare,
> Fearing the ruine of thy hopelesse soule.
>
> 1298-9   [V, i, 68-9]

The ill-success of the Old Man's mission is clear from Faustus's next words: 'I do repent, and yet I do dispaire'. In this despondent /67/ state he is easily made to cower under Mephistophilis's threats. He summons Helen to help him to forget the heritage he has lost; but his tongue betrays him into a pathetic reminder of the price he has paid—'Sweete *Helen, make* me immortall with a kisse'.

All through the play, the triumphs of Faustus's magic are accompanied by such chilling undertones; the delights he seems to enjoy serve only as drugs to alleviate the pain of loss. Wrenched from their setting, the famous lines upon Greek poetry and legend appear to express the heady excitement of the humanists over the New Learning. In their context, they have a querulous tone, as if Faustus were struggling hard and painfully to justify his choice:

> And long ere this I should haue slaine my selfe,
> Had not sweete pleasure conquerd deepe dispaire.
> Haue not I made blinde *Homer* sing to me
> Of *Alexanders* loue and *Enons* death,
> And hath not he that built the walles of *Thebes,*
> With rauishing sound of his melodious harp
> Made musicke with my *Mephastophilis?*
> Why should I dye then, or basely dispaire?
>
> 635-42   [II, ii, 24-31]

The questionings of a brilliant mind cannot long be silenced by such diversions. Faustus's intellectual vigour drives him on to seek some resolution of the conflicting views of man as god and as nonentity, some balance between pride and despair.

After a fashion, he solves the problem; but his solution is yet another tragic error. Like the heroes of Chapman and Webster, he makes a virtue of his despair, turning it into a stoical indifference to his fate and confounding Hell in Elysium, since there he may be with the old philosophers who have led him to this view of life. In his pride at finding such a solution, he even dares to lecture Mephistophilis on the attainment of a stoical detachment: 'Learne thou of *Faustus* manly fortitude'.[5] There is not only a grim humour here in the choice of epithet, but characteristic irony as well; this flimsy philosophy of self-reliance is /68/ destined to final collapse, and he is to meet death with none of the stoicism which distinguishes the Jacobean tragic heroes.

The main crisis of *Doctor Faustus* comes at the forty-seventh line of the opening speech. Thus the end of the play is made inevitable before it is well begun. Marlowe hereby sets himself a difficult problem which he solves in a manner that not only preserves the dramatic tension of the play, but also deepens its philosophical meaning. In this opening speech, Faustus has turned from God; God has not turned from him. In the ensuing scenes we are continually made aware of the presence of a Divine Mercy which Faustus will not allow himself to trust. Just as Tamburlaine's pride blinds him to the Divine Justice whose existence is kept before the audience throughout the earlier play, so Faustus's stoical despair renders him insensible to the Divine Mercy which surrounds him—whose presence, indeed, is felt even at the moment he makes his disastrous choice. For there is a clear message of hope in the two texts which appear to Faustus to counsel despair. '*Stipendium enim peccati mors*' has as its corollary '*Gratia autem Dei, vita aeterna, in Christo Jesu, Domino nostro*': while the sorrow of St. John's words is dispelled by those which follow: '*Si confiteamur peccata nostra, fidelis est et justus, ut remittat nobis peccata nostra, et emundet nos ab omni iniquitate*'.[6] The Good Angel, in his first appearance, reproaches Faustus for this wilful blindness when he begs him to 'Reade, reade the scriptures'. But his appeal is overborne by the Evil Angel's words:

> Go forward *Faustus* in that famous art
> Wherein all natures treasury is containd:
> Be thou on eath as *Ioue* is in the skie,
> Lord and commaunder of these Elements.
>
> 102–5   [I, i, 75–8]

No longer is the hero to scale the crystal battlements and usurp divine authority. There is now to be a division of power, and

[5] L. 321. [I, iii, 85]
[6] Rom. vi. 23; I John i.8.

provided man is absolute lord of everything beneath the sun, God may keep whatever is beyond it. Such is the arrangement in this second stage of the humanist revolt; that in which a /69/ dividing wall has been built between the two worlds, and built by man alone.

Throughout the tragedy, the obstacles to Faustus's salvation are raised only by him. He is always at liberty to repent and return, since Marlowe softens and almost erases the idea found in the *English Faust Book,* that the devils withhold him by brute strength from such a course. On the contrary, when Faustus has rejected both revelation and reason—the words of Scripture and the Good Angel's warnings—the speeches of Mephistophilis himself begin to contain warnings which would be clear to any ears less deafened by a stoical pride. At his first conjuration of the fiend, Faustus questions Mephistophilis about his master, Lucifer. The replies which he receives point a clear likeness between his own case and that of the rebel angel. It is a comparison implied all through the play, by many seemingly chance references such as Mephistophilis's promise to bring Faustus a courtesan 'as beautiful As was bright *Lucifer* before his fall.'[7] Mephistophilis's powerful words upon the Hell that encompasses him should likewise remind Faustus of the existence of worlds other than the visible. But these warnings go unheeded, and the hero sells his soul.

Even at this juncture, the idea of Divine Mercy is presented to the unresponsive Faustus by the fact that the deed of gift has to be signed in blood: for another deed of blood—the Crucifixion—is the crowning pledge of that Mercy. The words '*Consummatum est*' with which Faustus hands the parchment back to Mephistophilis imply that the comparison is there, in some recess of that 'perplexed, labyrinthicall soule'. But the bargain is made; the words which were perhaps prompted by some stirrings of remorse, are spoken as a satanic parody.

The deed once sealed and delivered, Mephistophilis's task is to confirm Faustus in his despair. He is not wholly successful; sometimes he finds himself acting as God's advocate in his own despite. At the beginning of the next episode, Faustus cries, 'When

[7] L. 589. [II, i, 156]

I behold the heauens, then I repent'. The fiend tries to dissuade
him from such thoughts, with the question, /70/

> Thinkst thou heauen is such a glorious thing?
> I tel thee tis not halfe so faire as thou,
> Or any man that breathes on earth.
>
> 616–18   [II, ii, 5–7]

The words are intended as a bait at which the humanist pride of
Faustus may rise. But they do not quite repeat Tamburlaine's
claim that heavenly joys cannot compare with those of kings on
earth. For when Mephistophilis replies to Faustus's quick challenge, 'How proouest thou that?' with 'It was made for man,
therefore is man more excellent', Faustus for the first time com-
prehends the full dignity of man which previously his despair
had forced him to deny; and his logician's mind leaps to the only
possible conclusion:

> If it were made for man, twas made for me:
> I wil renounce this magicke, and repent.
>
> 621–2   [II, ii, 10–11]

This moment of inner crisis is externalised by a contention between the Good and the Bad Angels. The Bad Angel wins and
Faustus seeks to escape from his uneasy thoughts by disputing of
astronomy with Mephistophilis. The replies to his questions do
not satisfy his thirsty intellect; they are all 'slender trifles *Wagner* can decide'. Besides which, they bring his thoughts back to
the 'heavens'—to the magnificent order in the universe which at
the beginning of the scene prompted his desire for repentance—
and he faces Mephistophilis with the defiant question: 'tell me
who made the world?'[8]

He gives the answer himself. At this critical moment of the
play, Faustus comes near to understanding that the one thing
which can overcome his despair is the love of God who made the
heavens for man, made the earth for man, and at last sent His
Son to redeem man fallen, like Faustus, through the misdirection
of his desire for knowledge. At the first faint recognition of this
truth, Mephistophilis vanishes, a brief contest gives the Good
Angel the victory over the Bad Angel, and Faustus is on the
verge of recovery in his cry /71/

---

[8] L. 678. [II, ii, 67]

Ah Christ my Sauiour,
Seeke to saue distressed Faustus soule.

                              695-6   [II, ii, 83-4]

But the moment represents a true peripeteia; no divine messenger, but the Arch-fiend Lucifer, appears to drive all thought of
salvation out of the hero's mind. One last effort is made to reclaim Faustus. The Old Man is moved to the attempt by a share
of the love of which Faustus has become dimly conscious in the
preceding episode. The theme of redemption is made explicit as
the Old Man pleads with the conjuror to trust in—

   ... mercie Faustus of thy Sauiour sweete,
   Whose bloud alone must wash away thy guilt.

                              1283-4   [V, i, 61-4]

This last effort also fails. Faustus even seeks the destruction of
this one remaining means whereby grace might reach him;
henceforth he is lost. The utter finality of his despair is conveyed
by the flat tone of his prose conversation with the scholars, which
also forms an area of neutral colour to isolate the sharp brilliance of the last soliloquy. In this final hour, the fact of redemption to which Faustus has closed his eyes for so many years becomes apparent to him with a terrifying clarity, since now it is a
vision of the unattainable: 'See see where Christs blood streames
in the firmament.'

   Thus, despite the confusion of the extant texts, the philosophical structure of the play is perfect and more than justifies
Goethe's exclamation: 'How greatly it is all planned!' As James
Smith has shown, far from this last soliloquy being a *volte face*
to appease the pious, it is an integral part of the play.[9] Themes
taken from earlier scenes recur in almost every line, but all are
transposed into an ironic key. It has long been acknowledged a
master-stroke of irony that this Renaissance Everyman should
quote Ovid's '*Lente currite, noctis equi*' in the hour of his downfall; nothing could be more aptly bitter than the contrast between Faustus's present position and that of the contented lover
who first spoke the words. There is a further irony in Faustus's
dread of an inescap-/72/able anger, to escape which the once

   [9] Marlowe's *Dr. Faustus*', *Scrutiny*, June, 1939.

titanic hero would heap Pelion and Ossa upon himself; it is in
forcible contrast with his earlier indifference to an after-life:

> Thinkst thou that Faustus is so fond, to imagine,
> That after this life there is any paine?
>
> 565-6   [II, i, 131-2]

It is supremely ironic that the interpretation of two worlds,
made possible by the Divine Mercy which Faustus has repudia-
ted, is now at last effected by the Divine Justice. In the closing
phrases of the soliloquy, the crowning irony is achieved. It is not
just the indomitable strain of speculation in Faustus's nature
which makes him babble of metempsychosis at such a moment;
Marlowe is drawing a deliberate contrast between his hero's present envy of 'brutish beasts', whose 'soules are soone dissolud in
elements', and his earlier pride in an individuality which could
not be destroyed. As the clock strikes, this craving for annihila-
tion becomes frantic:

> O it strikes, it strikes: now body turne to ayre,
> Or *Lucifer* wil beare thee quicke to hel:
> O soule, be changde into little water drops,
> And fal into the *Ocean,* nere be found.
>
> 1470-3   [V, ii, 180-3]

Such irony is not limited to the last scene, but is found
throughout the play. It shows itself in the way Faustus gains
nothing whatever from his bargains with the devils. The information they give him is trifling, mere 'freshmens suppositions'.
The material pleasures are undistinguished and even trivial; a
soul is a high price to pay for admission to a conventional
masque of the Seven Deadly Sins. But Faustus did not sell his
soul for such diversions; he turns to them for consolation or escape when he is disappointed in the replies given to his questions by Mephistophilis. All these questions he could himself
have answered—this is the central irony of the play—without selling his soul at all, but by attaining his 'chiefest bliss' in the study
of that divinity from which he turned aside in the opening scene.
/73/

Doctor Faustus is Marlowe's one complete tragedy. *Tamburlaine* had little dramatic conflict and was more a chronicle play
than a tragedy—the chronicle, not only of external events, but

also of the Renaissance discovery that human nature, cut off from its divine source, was not emancipated, but impoverished. In Faustus we see man struggling against this sense of impoverishment, but himself blocking the only way of return, and consequently driven to despair. The experience of despair in itself gives the opportunity for recovery, and the play's suspense consists in this; but Faustus's despair is pagan and stoical rather than Christian. With Renaissance man, he asserts his self-sufficiency and rejects the grace which is offered him. The separation of the natural from the spiritual man is hereby completed, and in *The Jew of Malta* Marlowe portrayed this third stage in the humanist dialectic. /74/

Science Without Conscience

HARRY LEVIN

Knowledge is power. The realization was Bacon's: *Nam et ipsa scientia potestas est.* But power corrupts, and Bacon—the Cambridge alumnus taking all knowledge for his province, the Lord Chancellor found guilty of corruption—demonstrated the incompatibility of the serpent and the dove. Hence the parable of Baldock in *Edward II,* the prodigal scholar corrupted by worldliness, was not uniquely applicable to Marlowe; given full scope, it could and did become an allegory for his century. Earlier in that century, Rabelais had voiced its self-conscious expansiveness in the famous letter purporting to have been written by the allegorical giant, Gargantua, to his even more gigantic son, Pantagruel. More than a father's thoughtful advice to a student, this was a medieval salute to the great instauration of humanism. Hailing the revival of the classics and the investigations into nature, it was charged with awareness of their potentialities for good—and likewise for evil. If the late invention of printing was an angelic inspiration, obviously gunpowder had been invented by diabolical suggestion. And Gargantua's eulogy is tempered with the warning that *science sans conscience*—science without conscience, or perhaps we should say "without consciousness"—is but the ruin of the soul (II, viii). There were lurking dangers, as well as enriching adventures, in this brave new world which was opening up before the European imagination. Yet we justifiably stress the excitement, the exploration, the experience, which no man has more fully personified than Leonardo da Vinci. The secret of power, for that powerful genius, was a desire for flight: *La po-*

Reprinted from *The Overreacher: A Study of Christopher Marowe* (Cambridge, Mass.: Harvard University Press, 1952).

tenza è solo un desiderio di fuga. Along with his vision of a flying machine, his paintings and anatomical researches and projects of military engineering, his city planning and stage designing and endlessly fascinating notations, the artist-engineer momentarily considered the possibility of necromancy. That was a delusion, he duly noted; but if only it were possible, how much it could so easily obtain! Riches, conquest, ability to fly, everything, except escape from death.

Magic was originally the appurtenance of religion; and when religion cast it off, it subsisted in the outer darkness, along with appetites and curiosities which religion proscribed. Between magic and science, as we have more recently come to know it, the lines were not yet sharply drawn. Magicians, however, were rigorously distinguished on the basis of whether they practiced white or black /108/ magic: whether they sought to control the elements, through natural philosophy and supernatural wisdom, as Prospero does in *The Tempest,* or whether they trafficked with the devil and conjured up the dead, through witchcraft and particularly necromancy, as does Marlowe's ultimate protagonist. The legendary Faust was neither a creature of folklore, such as Pantagruel, nor a figure from history, such as Leonardo. His legend emerged from the flickering limbo between the admonitions of the Middle Ages and the aspirations of the Renaissance. More precisely, he was begotten by the Reformation out of the Teutonic north, like his fellow-unbeliever, the Wandering Jew, and quite unlike his Mediterranean contemporary, Don Juan, whose destiny ran so strangely parallel. That Faustus meant "well-omened" in Latin was a paradox which did not pass unobserved. The disreputable name and vagabond career of an actual Georg Faust can be traced from one German university to another, skeptically pursued by accusations of charlatanism and suspicions of pederasty. It is rumored that he enlivened the pedagogical technique of his classical lectures by the necromantic practice of bringing Homeric shades to life. Marlowe, to whom this feat had its perspicuous appeal, seems to class it with the so-called shadows of Cornelius Agrippa, and glories in having resurrected blind Homer to sing for his hero. More remotely Simon Magus, a charlatan hovering on the fringes of early Christianity, who was

accompanied by a certain Helen and was killed in a desperate
effort to fly, seems to have some bearing upon this story; and
there was the Greek precedent of Empedocles, the philosopher
who disappeared into Ætna. Dr. Faust lost his original Christian
name and got another by being confounded with Johann Fust,
one of the earliest printers and therefore the practitioner of an
art still held by many to be ambiguous. The sinister repute of
the prototype, thereby enhanced with an aura of Titanism, pro-
jected the shadowy image of a latter-day Prometheus, bearing
gifts which were dangerous for mankind.

It is not clear how Faust gained his reputation as a god-defier,
unless it be through his pretensions as a necromancer. He seems
to have ended by mysteriously disappearing, leaving behind him
a cloud of sensational rumors as to his "damnable life, and deserued death," his "Epicurish" habits and Atheistical blasphemies.
These were gathered together a generation later, in 1587, and
widely cir-/109/culated by a pious printer, Johann Spies through
the solemnly edifying and crudely jocular redaction known as
his *Faustbuch*. In 1592 it was published in the free English
translation that Marlowe so closely depends upon for his
play. The translator, who seems to have been more of a humanist
than was the didactic Lutheran author of the chapbook, takes advantage of Faust's travels to expatiate upon Italian topography.
Marlowe follows his guidance through the ruins of Rome, and
the guide is responsible for such atmospheric details as the mention of Vergil's tomb. Moreover, he contributed an epithet
which, though Marlowe makes no use of it, cannot have failed to
affect his impression: at the University of Padua Faust registers
as "the vnsatiable Speculator." The English *Faustbook* is at once
a cautionary tale and a book of marvels, a jestbook and a theological tract. Its chapters, anecdotal and homilectic, are roughly
grouped in three sections. The first deals, extensively and system-
atically, with the diabolical pact; the second, rather more discur-
sively, with Faust's speculations and journeys; and the third,
after a series of miscellaneous jests, with "his fearfull and pitiful
ende." Here, amid much that was not germane to his purpose,
was a vehicle for the highest and purest expression of Marlowe's
libido sciendi, a speculative sublimation of Tamburlaine's or the
Guise's insatiable thirst—a hero who, "taking to him the wings of

an Eagle, thought to flie ouer the whole world, and to know the secrets of heauen and earth."

This desire for flight transcended the pomp and dalliance of those preceding plays which Marlowe all but repudiates at the outset of *The Tragicall History of Doctor Faustus*. Yet, although intellectual curiosity is now the activating force, it cannot finally be detached from the secondary motives that entrammel it, the will to power and the appetite for sensation. The interrelationship of thought and action is the major problem for Dr. Faustus, as it can become for Shakespeare's heroes. It is not just a historical coincidence that Hamlet and Faustus were both alumni of Martin Luther's university, Wittenberg; in other words, their consciences had been disciplined within the *feste Burg* of Protestantism. There, were Luther threw his inkstand at the devil, Faustus comes to terms with the adversary; yet, when Faustus laments his devil's bargain, he blames his alma mater: "O would I had never seen Wittenberg, never read book [V. ii. 45]. When he appears at court /110/ and is scoffed at by a courtier, he displays his professional pride by humbling the scoffer and bidding him thereafter "speak well of scholars" [IV, ii, 110.] The cry of the triumphant scholastic disputant, *sic probo*, must ring through a wider arena than the schools [I, ii, 2]; the intellect must prove itself by mastering life at large. Scholarship is rewarded by no greater satisfactions for Faustus than sovereignty is for Edward and Tamburlaine, or conspiracy for Barabas and the Guise. What is worse, the notorious alternative to that straight and narrow path is the primrose path to the everlasting bonfire. The formal pattern of Marlovian drama tends to be increasingly traditional. Having created the tragedy of ambition with *Tamburlaine* and put his stamp on the tragedy of revenge with *The Jew of Malta* and tried his hand at the chronicle with *Edward II*, Marlowe reverts to the morality play with *Doctor Faustus*. But within the latter, the most general of forms, he elaborates the most personal of themes—an Atheist's tragedy, an Epicurean's testament, a mirror for University Wits.

The prologue, after its apology for not presenting matters of love and war, presents character in biographical synopsis and plot in ethical perspective. The universal hero of this morality will not be Everyman; he will be a particular private individual;

and Marlowe highlights his attainment, as usual, by emphasizing the lowness of his birth. Nevertheless, the Muse intends to "vaunt his heavenly verse" upon this theme [6]; and, passing over the unexpected gender of the personal pronoun, our attention is directed by the adjective to the vertical scale of the drama. Its coördinates will be nothing less than heaven and hell; while on the horizontal plane, at opposite sides of the stage, the conflict of conscience will be externalized by the debate between Good and Evil Angels; and, even as the heroes of the moralities traverse a circle of symbolic mansions, so Faustus will pay his respects to personifications of the World, the Flesh, and the Devil. As his academic career proceeds, it is metaphorically described. Literally, a scholar's name was registered in the Cambridge Grace-Book when he took a degree, and the quibble on the word "grace" serves to bring out its nontheological overtones:

> So much he profits in divinity,
> The fruitful plot of scholarism graced,
> That shortly he was graced with doctor's name, /111/
> Excelling all whose sweet delight disputes
> In th'heavenly matters of theology,
> Till swoll'n with cunning of a self-conceit,
> His waxen wings did mount above his reach,
> And melting, heavens conspired his overthrow.
>
> [15–22]   [Prologue]

The last three words, a Marlovian idiom for the counteraction of antagonistic forces, recur in *Tamburlaine*. In *Tamburlaine* the emblem of tragic pride is Phaëthon, rashly attempting to drive the fiery chariot of the sun. In *Doctor Faustus* it is Icarus, whose "wings of wax" had already figured as an omen portending the tragedy of Dido. In each instance it is a question of flying too high, of falling from the loftiest height imaginable, of seeking illumination and finding more heat than light. Faustus prefers, like the Guise, to seek what flies beyond his reach; he is accused of trying "to over-reach the devil" [V, ii, 15]. After the prologue speaks of overreaching, the emphasis shifts from the heavenly to the hellish—and the phrase "devilish exercise" is borrowed straight from the *Faustbook*. With this shift, the rising verse subsides toward a dying fall, and the ethereal image of flight gives way to grosser images of appetite. These were anticipated by "swoll'n with cunning" and will be continued by allusions to *hu-bris* in terms of overeating. "Necromancy" is given unwonted stress by its overhanging monosyllable, and "bliss" reminds us that magic is to Faustus what a crown was to Tamburlaine, gold to Barabas, or companionship to Edward:

> For, falling to a devilish exercise
> And glutted now with learning's golden gifts,
> He surfeits upon cursed necromancy.
> Nothing so sweet as magic is to him,
> Which he prefers before his chiefest bliss;
> And this the man that in his study sits.
>
> [23–28]   [Prologue]

The speaker of these lines may well be Wagner, the famulus, half-servant and half-disciple, since it is indicated that he reappears to speak the later choruses. It is a long way from his moral earnestness to the cynical tone of Machiavel introducing Barabas. But, as with *The Jew of Malta*, this introduction is completed by drawing aside the curtain to the inner stage—which, in Elizabethan theatrical usage, was appropriately called "the study." The protagonist is then discovered in his literal study, the little room, the monkish cell /112/ that comprises his library and laboratory. His profession is not usury but divinity, which subsumes all the others, permitting him to "level at the end of every art" [I, i, 4]. Thus his introductory soliloquy is no mere reckoning of accounts but an inventory of the Renaissance mind. Cornelius Agrippa, that disillusioned experimentalist, whose namesake plays an appropriate role in Marlowe's tragedy, had latterly made such a survey in his treatise *Of the Vanity and Uncertainty of Arts and Sciences*. Goethe's nineteenth-century Faust could do no better than bring up to date those *Fakultätswissenschaften*, those categories of learning which Marlowe now passes in review: *Philosophie, Juristerei, Medizin, Theologie*. Whatever the contemplative life can teach, his Dr. Faustus has learned. He has mastered the liberal arts, the learned professions, and the experimental sciences of his day. To be or not to be, *"on cay mae on"* [I, i, 12]—the existential dilemma seems to him insoluble; consequently, he is ready to take his leave of philosophy. Against Aristotle he quotes the axiom of Ramus that the end of logic is "to dispute well" [I, i, 8]; and, since rhetoric itself is a means toward some further end, it does not gratify Faustus' *libido sciendi*. As for jurisprudence and medicine, though they help man to exist, they do not justify his existence. The "body's health" is scarcely a fulfillment of *libido sentiendi;* whereas *libido dominandi* requires more than a "case of paltry legacies" [I, i, 30]. Yet the Roman statute that Faustus cites at random does not seem to be wholly irrelevant; it has to do with the ways and means whereby a father may disinherit a son.

Saying farewell to the other discipline, he turns again for a moment to theology, picks up Saint Jerome's Bible, reads from the Vulgate, and comments upon two texts:

> *Stipendium peccati mors est:* Ha! *Stipendium, &c.*
> The reward of sin is death. That's hard.
> *Si peccasse negamus, fallimur*
> *Et nulla est in nobis veritas.*
> If we say that we have no sin,
> We deceive ourselves, and there's no truth in us.
>
> [I. i. 39–44]

This latter text, quoted from the very epistle of Saint John (I, i, 8) that goes on to warn against worldly lust and vainglory, gives Faustus an ominous pause. Tentatively he balances it against the stern quotation from Saint Paul's epistle to the Romans (vi, 23). All men are sinners, ergo all men are mortal, he syllogizes with a /113/ sophistical shrug: *"Che serà, serà"* [I, i, 48]. Such was Edward's sentiment, spoken in English rather than Italian, when he accepted his fate: "What shall be, shall be." Faustus, whether in Calvinistic or Epicurean fatalism, is anxious to say "Divinity, adieu," to embrace the "metaphysics of magicians," and to replace the Scriptures with "necromatic books" [I, i, 50–1] which, by the subversion of an adjective heretofore consecrated to religious objects, now seem "heavenly." Faustus' references to his magical art, like Prospero's, sustain the additional ambiguity of referring us back to the author's literary artistry, to the "lines" and "signs," the "letters, and characters" in which Marlowe himself set the end of scholarism. As a scholar-poet, Marlowe had been taught that the aim of poetry was profit and delight. Is it the scholar, the conjurer, or the artist who can make good this boast?

O what a world of profit and delight,
Of power, of honor, of omnipotence
Is promised to the studious artisan!
All things that move between the quiet poles
Shall be at my command, Emperors and kings
Are but obeyed in their several provinces,
Nor can they raise the wind or rend the clouds,
But his dominion that exceeds in this
Stretcheth as far as doth the mind of man.
A sound magician is a demi-god.   [I, i, 54–63]

Marlowe's protagonists do not simply out-Herod their fellow
mortals; they act out their invidious self-comparisons with the
gods; and, from Æneas to Faustus, they see themselves deified in
one manner or another. Faustus' Evil Angel holds out the hope
that he will be "on earth as Jove is in the sky"[I, i, 77.] Ignoring his Good Angel and the threat of "God's heavy wrath" [I, i,
73], Faustus readily amplifies the enticement, which far outdoes
all other Marlovian seductions. He envisages a hierarchy of spirits, answering his queries and serving his whims:

I'll have them fly to India for gold,
Ransack the ocean for orient pearl,
And search all corners of the new-found world
For pleasant fruits and princely delicates.   [I, i, 83–6] /114/

The panorama extends across the western hemisphere, where
they are subsequently pictured as Indians, obeying their Spanish
masters and conveying

. . from America the golden fleece,
That yearly stuffs old Philip's treasury.   [I, i, 132–3]

But Marlowe's wandering fantasy comes home with an anticlima-
tic suggestion, which incidentally reveals the Canterbury boy
who was sent to Corpus Christi on a scholarship:

I'll have them fill the public schools with silk,
Wherewith the students shall be bravely clad.   [I, i, 91–2]

Faustus has his own Rosencrantz and Guildenstern in the two
adepts of the black art, Valdes and Cornelius. Abetted by their
instructions, he repairs at midnight to a solitary grove, where he

draws a magic circle and abjures the Trinity. Just as Sir Walter
Ralegh's friends were alleged to have spelled the name of God
backwards, so here the name of Jehovah is

> Forward and backward anagrammatized.   [I, iii, 9]

Blasphemy has its irreligious observances, and this is the dread
ceremonial of the Black Mass. The play itself is almost macaron-
ic in its frequent scholarly lapses into Latinity, and the incantation is deliberately heightened by what Faustus calls "heavenly
words" [I, ii, 27] and the Clown will call "Dutch fustian."*
Though the demon makes his due appearance, first as a dragon
and then in the garb of a friar, he does not appear as the devil's
plenipotentiary; he has responded to the conjuration, so he explains in scholastic terminology, because Faustus has jeopardized
his soul. It is the first of Faustus' disappointments, and is immediately solaced by the delight that he takes in his personal relation with Mephostophilis. Again, even more emphatically than
with Gaveston, the name itself is something to conjure with, all
the more potent because it accounts for half a line of blank
verse:

> Had I as many souls as there be stars,
> I'd give them all for Mephistophilis.   [I, iii, 102–3]

Marlowe's protagonists tend to isolate themselves; yet they also
tend, as we have seen, to ally themselves with some deuteragon-
ist. Ed-/115/ward had his evil genius in Gaveston, Barabas his
demonic familiar in Ithamore; and Faustus has in Mephostophilis an alter ego who is both a demon and a Damon. The man has
an extraordinary affection for the spirit, the spirit a mysterious
attraction to the man. Mephostophilis should not be confused
with Goethe's sardonic nay-sayer; neither is he an operatic villian
nor a Satanic tempter. He proffers no tempting speeches and
dangles no enticements; Faustus tempts himself, and succumbs to
temptations which he alone has conjured up. What Mephostophilis really approximates, with his subtle insight and his profound sympathy, is the characterization of Porfiry, the examining
magistrate in Dostoevsky's *Crime and Punishment*.

The dialogues between Faustus and Mephostophilis resemble

---

* [In the A-text only (line 431, ed. Tucker Brooke).—Ed.]

those cat-and-mouse interrogations in which Porfiry teaches the
would-be criminal, Raskolnikov, to accuse and convict himself.
Faustus is especially curious about the prince of darkness, whose
name once proclaimed him the bearer of light; who was once an
angel "most dearly loved of God," as Mephostophilis points out,
but was thrown from heaven for his "aspiring pride," the
primordial tragic fault.

> And what are you that live with Lucifer?   [I, iii, 70]

Faustus asks. And Mephostophilis answers:

> Unhappy spirits that fell with Lucifer,
> Conspired against our God with Lucifer,
> And are for ever damned with Lucifer.   [I, iii, 71–3] ·

The reiteration reminds us that Faustus' plight, or any other
human predicament, is the outcome of that Miltonic struggle,
that fall of the angels, that tragedy of tragedies which brought
original sin and consequent suffering into the world. It is ironic,
of course, that Faustus should be asking to be admitted into the
company of the damned. But misery loves company, and Mephostophilis will warrant his own role by quoting the proverb in
Latin. The special poignance of the relationship lies in his fore-
knowledge and his foresuffering. Once the sin is committed, he
cannot but hold the sinner to his unholy covenant. Faustus, with
a blithe humanistic pantheism, "confounds hell in Elysium" [I,
iii, 60]. He has no ear for Mephostophilis' heart-cry, /116/

> Why this is hell, nor am I out of it,   [I, iii, 76]

nor for his painfully explicit amplification,

> Hell hath no limits, nor is circumscribed
> In one self place, but where we are is hell . . .
> All places shall be hell that is not heaven.   [II, i, 119–24]

Orcanes, the noble infidel in the second part of *Tamburlaine,*
used a similar expression to affirm a belief in a god who is not
circumscriptible. Nothing like this Marlovian conception is hin-
ted among the fundamentalist tenets of the *Faustbook,* although
Marlowe might have learned from Lucretius that during our lifetime we undergo what is fabled to happen afterwards in Acheron (III, 978–9). Faustus is quite as unconcerned with "heaven

and heavenly things" [II, i, 21], when his Good Angel commends them to him; and when his Evil Angel bids him "think of
honor and wealth" [II, i, 22], he has no compunction in choos-
ing the pomps of Satan. On condition that he be enabled to "live
in all voluptuousness" for twenty-four years [I, iii, 91], and that
Mephostophilis obey his commands and reply to his inquiries,
Faustus is willing to sign a legal deed empowering Mephostophilis and Lucifer "to fetch or carry the said John Faustus, body
and soul, flesh, blood, or goods, into their habitation wheresoever" [II, i, 107–8]. When his blood congeals, after he has stabbed
his arm, he ignores the portent; and when it streams again, having
been heated with coals, it warns him to escape while there is
time: *"Homo, fuge"* [II, i, 76]. Instead, he affixes his bloody
signature with a blasphemous mockery of the last words of Jesus,
according to the gospel of Saint John (xix, 30): *"Consummatum
est."*

Mephostophilis does nothing to lure Faustus on; he suffers for
him, he sympathizes with him, above all he understands him;
and, through this understanding, we participate in the dramatic
irony. Faustus persists in regarding his fiendish attendant as a
sort of oriental slave of the lamp, and Mephostophilis ironically
promises more than his temporary master has wit to ask. Some
day, after one fashion or another, Faustus will be "as great as
Lucifer" [II, i, 51]—he will arrive at the kind of ambiguous
greatness that Fielding would attribute to Jonathan Wild. In the
interim he shrugs:

I think hell's a fable.   [II, i, 125] /117/

To which the suffering spirit replies with the bitterest of all his
ironies:

Ay, think so still, till experience change thy mind.   [II, i, 126]

For Faustus, even more than for Edward or Barabas, the fruit of
experience is disillusionment. As soon as the contract is signed
and sealed, he is eager to resolve ambiguities, to satisfy the cosmic questions that teem in his brain. He is keenly aware that
there are more things in heaven and earth than the trivium and
the quadrivium; but his discussions with Mephostophilis scarcely
proceed beyond the elementary data of natural history and the
unquestioned assumptions of Ptolemaic astronomy. Faustus cries

impatiently, "These are freshmen's suppositions" [II, ii, 55].
To the more searching inquiry, "Who made the world?" [II, ii,
67] his interlocutor must perforce be silent, since fiends are in-
terdicted from naming God. When various books of occult and
pseudo-scientific lore are provided, Faustus nervously thumbs
through the black-letter pages, only to realize that he has ex-
changed his soul for little more than the quiddities of Wittenberg: "O thou art deceived."* In his undeception he listens to
the conflicting angels again, and again the Evil Angel outargues
the Good. Faustus, at all events, is beginning to respect the grim
silences of Mephostophilis. Now it becomes the latter's task to
divert him, but each diversion turns out to be a snare and a delusion. Faustus, being "wanton and lascivious, . . . cannot live
without a wife" [II, i, 140–41]. This demand is frustrated, as
the *Faustbook* emphasizes, because marriage is a sacrament;
whereas, for Mephostophilis, it is "a ceremonial toy" [II, i,
149]. The best that Mephostophilis can provide is equivocally di-
verting: *"a devil dressed like a woman, with fire works."*

There are more and more of these ghoulish antics, which always seem to end by intensifying the actual harshness of the situation. Faustus, prompted by the Good Angel for the nonce, inevitably breaks down and calls upon Christ. Thereupon—most
terrifying shock of all—it is Lucifer who rises with Beelzebub,
presumably through the trap from below the stage, to hold Faustus to the letter of their agreement. As a pastime and a
confirmation of his unregenerate state, they witness together Lucifer's pageant of the Seven Deadly Sins, the *Walpurgisnacht* in-
terlude at the midpoint of the play, a sight as pleasing to Faustus
as Paradise was to Adam before /118/ the fall [II, ii, 106–7].
Marlowe, interpolating this quaint procession of gargoyles, harked
back to a more deeply rooted medieval tradition than the
"hellish pastimes" of the *Faustbook*—to the earliest subject of the
moralities, as well as the homilies of Chaucer and Langland.
Marlowe's treatment, curiously enough, bears a closer resem-
blance to theirs than it does to the Renaissance triumph of Luci-
fera in *The Faerie Queene*. Pride is the inevitable leader, and
the others follow as the night the day, parading the principal
weaknesses of the flesh, brandishing their respective perquisities,

---

* [In A-text only (line 610. ed. Tucker Brooke).—Ed.]

and speaking their pieces in highly seasoned prose. Faustus must indeed be a hardened sinner to contemplate their grossness without revulsion. Though he has a greeting for each of them, it seems to be Gluttony that inspires his· reaction: "O, how this sight doth delight my soul!" [II, ii, 163.] This has been heralded when the prologue touched upon the theme of satiety, is resumed when Faustus is "glutted" with a foretaste of what lies ahead [I, i, 79], and will be rounded out in the final scene where he diagnoses his illness as "a surfeit of deadly sin that hath damned both body and soul" [V, ii, 37]. Perdition is the more awful for Mephostophilis because he has "tasted the eternal joys of heaven" [I, iii, 78]. As for Faustus, he has candidly dedicated himself to carnal egoism:

> The God thou serv'st is thine own appetite.   [II, i, 11]

His quest for knowledge leads him to taste the fruit of the tree that shaded Adam and Eve, to savor the distinction between good and evil. From that point he abandons his disinterested pursuit— or, rather, he abandons himself to the distractions that Mephostophilis scatters along his ever more far-flung itinerary. His further adventures are calculated less to fulfill his boundless ambition than to palliate his disappointment, to make the most of a bad bargain.

The rest is hedonism. It is conveniently preluded by Wagner, as expository chorus, describing how Faustus, like Phaëthon and other reckless adventurers,

> Did mount him up to scale Olympus' top,
> Where, sitting in a chariot burning bright.   [III, Prologue, 4–5]

A characteristic accomplishment of the legendary Faust was aeromancy, the magical power of flight. Unlike his resurrections and pyrotechnics, this does not lend itself very effectively to theatrical /119/ presentation. Wagner narrates his aerial voyages "to prove cosmography" [III, Prologue, 20], and Faustus himself discusses geography with Mephostophilis, pausing· significantly over that Venetian temple which "threats the stars with her aspiring top" [III, i, 18], and ultimately alighting at papal Rome. There the slapstick banquet at the Vatican, where they snatch food and drink away from the Pope and the Cardinal of

Lorraine, is at best a satirical comment upon the blind mouths
of the clergy, and at worst a callow manifestation of Elizabethan
Catholic-baiting. But the pith of the episode is the ceremony of
anathema, which definitively places Faustus under the most solemn ban of the Church. The dirge of malediction, the curse with
bell, book, and candle, "forward and backward" [III, ii, 96] , is
the religious counterpart of the sacrilegious rite he performed by
anagrammatizing the name of God. He and Mephostophilis re-
tort by beating the Friars and scattering firecrackers. The episode
has been considerably augmented along these lines by Marlowe's
presumptive collaborator, who introduces an antipope named
Bruno—possibly in honor of Giordano Bruno—condemned to the
stake and rescued by Faustus and Mephostophilis in the guise of
cardinals. But it is a peculiarly Marlovian twist, an antireligious
fascination with ceremonial, which animates Tamburlaine's
burning of the Koran as well as Faustus' celebration of the Black
Mass, and culminates in the ritual of excommunication. Faustus
is pledged, as was Barabas, to pull down Christian churches.
From the negative commitment of his Atheism he moves on to
the positive exploit of his Epicureanism, when we next see him
at the court of the Holy Roman Emperor. There we first behold
him exercising his distinctive gift of sciomancy, and raising—in a
more or less elaborated dumb show—the shades of Alexander and
his paramour, evidently the fabulous Thaïs.

It must be admitted that Faustus is more impressive as an
Atheist than as an Epicurean. We might have expected more
for the price he is paying, after his terrible renunciation, than the
jaunty hocus-pocus that produces grapes out of season for a preg-
nant duchess or defrauds a horse dealer and fobs him off with a
leg-pulling practical joke. Such conjuring tricks may be mildly
amusing, but are they worthy of the inspiration or worth the
sacrifice? Certainly not; and we ought to feel some incongruity
between the monologues and the gestures, between the seemingly
unlimited /120/ possibilities envisioned by Faustus' speeches
and their all too concretely vulgar realization in the stage business. Putting ourselves in his position, we protest with Browning's
Paracelsus, "Had we means / Answering to our mind!" We
probably feel the incongruity more than the Elizabethans did,
for a number of reasons: and first of all, because we have lost

their habit of accepting the limitations of the stage as the conventions of the theater, of taking the word for the deed and the
part for the whole. Suspending disbelief, in short, we ought to be
more impressed than we usually are. Still, if we remain skeptical,
we may remember that so was Marlowe; he is on record asserting
that the prophets and saints of the Bible were so many jugglers.
His refusal to believe in miracles may well have hindered him
from making sorcery altogether credible in his plays—wherein,
contrary to the custom of Shakespeare and his other contemporaries, there are no ghosts; except in *Doctor Faustus*, there are
naturalistic explanations for seemingly supernatural interven-
tions. This second consideration is neutralized by a third: whatever our doubts or Marlowe's, his audiences were convinced. His
talent for lurid spectacle, supported by Henslowe's most elabo-
rate properties, and by the intermittent discharge of squibs and
crackers, undoubtedly graveled the groundlings. A supernatural
atmosphere was devised and sustained with such effectiveness
that a veritable body of legends grew up around the performance
of the play, most of them involving a personal appearance of the
devil himself, who is temporarily mistaken for one of the caper-
ing devils of the tiring house.

Large allowances should be made for the mangled and encrus-
ted form in which *Doctor Faustus* has survived. Its very popularity seems to have subjected it to an inordinate amount of cutting
and gagging and all the other indignities that dramatic texts are
heir to. It was not published until 1604, more than a decade
after Marlowe's death; this first quarto and later editions based
on it seem to represent an unauthorized abridgment. The quarto
of 1616 and others deriving from it seem to stem independently
from a fuller and more authoritative manuscript, upon which
editors are inclined to place increasing weight. Unfortunately,
neither one—nor the combination of both—is satisfactory. The
1616 text contains about half again as much material, and preserves the play in clearer and firmer structure; yet much of that
construction is filled in by an inferior hand, /121/ and several
important passages are omitted. These we know from the 1604
text, which is the one most frequently reprinted; and since it is
so terse a condensation, it can be very handily performed; yet it
is not devoid of extraneous matter, while some of its scenes are

misplaced or unduly telescoped. The recent parallel edition of Sir Walter Greg does justice, at least, to the complexity of the problem. Moreover Sir Walter confirms, with his considerable authority, the tendency to push the dating ahead to the latest period in Marlowe's career. The argument for 1592, after the publication of the *Faustbook,* seems cogent—though it carries the surprising consequence of making *Doctor Faustus* the follower rather than the forerunner of Greene's *Friar Bacon and Friar Bungay.* Even more perplexing is the enigma of Marlowe's collaboration. Not that there seems to be much disagreement about the identity of his collaborator, Samuel Rowley. But why should Rowley's clumsy journeywork eke out the greatest masterwork the English theater had thus far seen? It seems unlikely, from what Kyd tells us, that Marlowe could have worked in harness with Rowley. Was his *Doctor Faustus,* then, a fragment like *Hero and Leander?* If so, was it left unfinished at his death, or had he dropped it somewhere along the wayside? All too understandably, he might have found his task an uncomfortable one. Was he inhibited from finishing it by some psychological complication, or by some more instrumental reason equally inscrutable at this date?

In spite of its uneven texture, we must view the play as a whole, since its total design is not less meaningful than its purple passages, and textual disintegration will not improve its fragmentary condition. Critics have questioned the authenticity of the comic scenes, on the grounds that Marlowe lacked a sense of humor—a premise which they support by begging the question, and denying his authorship whenever they are confronted with a humorous speech. Marlowe's laughter, to be sure, is not Shakespeare's; yet, as *The Jew of Malta* must have shown us, his wit has a salt of its own. Furthermore, Elizabethan tragedy delegates a conventional function to comedy, and *Doctor Faustus* need be no exception to that rule. Thus Wagner, the clever servant, mimics his master in chopping logic with the other students. He remarks, immediately after the scene in which Faustus has bargained with Mephostophilis, that the Clown "would give his soul to the devil for a shoulder of mutton" [I, iv, 8]. /122/ Similarly, the hostlers, Rafe and Robin, burlesque the conjuration of Dr. Faustus; their scene, which is out of place in the 1604 text, should come after the scene in which Mephostophilis provides Faustus with conjuring books; for Robin, it appears, has just stolen one of those potent volumes; and Rafe, with its help, expects to seduce Nan Spit the kitchenmaid, even as Faustus' necromancy will capture the love of Helen of Troy. Before this comedy team joined Marlowe's dramatis personæ, Rafe and Robin had parts in Lyly's *Galatea,* where they played their pranks with alchemist's equipment; but there they had little connection with the main plot, while their roles are intrinsic—if not essential—to *Doctor Faustus.* And while the comic underplot reduces the main plot of Marlowe's drama to absurdity, the overplot is luminously adumbrated—sketched, as it were, in lightning against a black sky. It is the adumbration of Faustus' downfall, glimpsed in the aboriginal tragedy of the fallen archangel. Victor Hugo's formulation for western art, the intermixture of grotesque and sublime, could not adduce a more pertinent example.

How grandly all is planned! (*Wie gross ist alles angelegt!*) Goethe's appreciation of *Doctor Faustus,* as recorded by Crabb Robinson, must refer primarily to its conception. In its execution, it adheres somewhat too faithfully to the undramatic sequence of the *Faustbook.* The opening scenes are necessarily explicit in underlining the conditions of the pact; but, as a result, the play is half over before the document is ratified and Faustus can start out upon his adventures. Out of the 1,485 lines in the 1604 Quarto, 791 have gone by before he leaves Wittenberg for Rome. The 1616 Quarto augments the ensuing scenes and links them loosely together with allusions to the papal-imperial struggle, which Rowley apparently gathered from Foxe's *Book of Martyrs.* But both versions move anticlimactically from the Pope and the Emperor to the Duchess of Vanholt and the trivial incident of the grapes. This, in the text of 1604, concludes a scene which commences at the Emperor's court and includes midway the buffooneries of the Horse-Courser. Faustus is well advised to pause for an instant and meditate on the restless course of time. Such drastic telescoping seems to indicate an acting version constrained by the narrow resources of a touring company. It is divided into fourteen continuous scenes, whereas the text of 1616 is subdivided into twenty scenes which /123/ editors distribute among five acts. Viewed in outline, the plot is perfectly classical in its climactic ascent: the conjuration of Mephostophilis, the compact with Lucifer, the travels to Rome and elsewhere, the necromantic evocations, and the catastrophe. Faustus' rise is harder to triangulate than the careers of Marlowe's other heroes, because each worldly step is a spiritual lapse. Examined more technically, the play has a strong beginning and an even stronger end; but its middle section, whether we abridge it or bombast it out with Rowley's hack-work, is unquestionably weak. The structural weakness, however, corresponds to the anticlimax of the parable; it lays bare the gap between promise and fruition, between the bright hopes of the initial scene and the abysmal consequences of the last. "As the outline of the character is grand and daring," William Hazlitt has said, "the execution is abrupt and fearful."

At the request of the Emperor, Faustus has evoked no less a shade than Alexander the Great, archetype of *libido dominandi*. For the edification and pleasure of the scholars, when he returns to the university, he evokes the archetype of *libido sentiendi*. Among all the beautiful women who ever lived, they have agreed that Helen of Troy is peerless, "the pride of nature's works," the "only paragon of excellence" [V, i, 33–4]. Disputation is silenced when she makes her fugitive appearance in their incongruous quarters. Since the days when Marlowe studied the classics at Cambridge, Helen had been his cynosure of comparison—comparison with Zenocrate in *Tamburlaine* and even with Gaveston in *Edward II*. But metaphor is never enough for Marlowe; he must have the real thing, beauty in person; in *The Jew of Malta* policy was personified by Machiavelli himself; and the consummation of Faustus' desire—or the consolation, at any rate, for his regret—is to have Helen as his paramour. Mephostophilis produces her "in twinkling of an eye" [V, i, 98]; and the glamor of the subsequent lines has obscured this interesting verbal coinage of Marlowe's, an apt phrase for a magician's assistant engaged in bringing off his employer's most spectacular trick. This, of all occasions, is the one to which language must rise; and, in so doing, it brilliantly redeems the shortcomings of previous episodes. The apostrophe to Helen stands out from its context, not because anthologists excerpt it, but because Marlowe carefully designed it to be a set piece, a purple passage, a supreme invitation /124/

to love. Its lyrical formality, its practiced handling of stylistic
and prosodic devices from his established repertory, set it off
from the pithy prose, the sharp dialectic, the nervous colloquies
and rhythmic variations of his maturing style. Characteristically,
it does not offer any physical description of the heroine. It esti-
mates, as Homer did, her impact. How should Faustus react to
the sight that had stirred the elders of Troy to forget their argu-
ments in admiration? Chapman would render their winged
words in his *Iliad:*

> What man can blame
> The Greekes and Trojans to endure, for so Admir'd a Dame,
> So many miseries, and so long? In her sweet countenance shine
> Lookes like the Goddesses.　　　　　　　　　(III, 167–70)

That could be a marginal gloss for Marlowe's twenty lines,
which constitute three fairly symmetrical strophes. The starting
point for the first, the invocation, is the most rhetorical of questions. Though it is Marlowe's culminating hyperbole, it may not
strike us with the fullest impact, precisely because it has struck so
often before, because it has been echoed and reëchoed as one of
the striking exaggerations of poetry—like the tower of ivory in the
Song of Songs. The thousand ships are not exaggerated; they are
specified by Ovid's matter-of-fact account of the Trojan War in
the *Metamorphoses* (XII, 7); but here poetic audacity intervenes
to transpose a lover's emotion into a large-scale naval operation.
The topless towers are recurrent symbols for illimitable aspiration, and Marlowe habitually juxtaposes them to the all-consum-
ing element of fire. Cavalierly he poses a moral issue, and the alternative is absolute: the destruction of a city, the calamities of
war, the world well lost, all for love.

> Was this the face that launched a thousand ships
> And burnt the topless towers of Ilium?
> Sweet Helen, make me immortal with a kiss.　　　[V, i, 99–101]

The third line is an implicit stage direction, leading on to the
enactment of a metaphysical conceit; whereupon Faustus claims
that Helen's lips suck forth his soul, and then reclaims it with
another kiss. Underneath their amorous byplay runs the disturb-
ing hint that she may be a succuba; this may not be the only
world that is at stake for him. When Dido wooed Æneas and spoke

of becoming "immortal with a kiss," it seemed to be little more
than a figure of speech. For Faustus immortality means vastly
more /125/ than that, in one way if not in another, although
he may actually get no closer to heaven than Helen's embrace.
No wonder he changes his evaluation from other worldly to mercenary terms:

> Here will I dwell, for heaven is in these lips,
> And all is dross that is not Helena.   [V, i, 104–5]

The second strophe is in the active mode of *Tamburlaine,* and
the phrase "I will" resounds through it. Since Helen is notorious-
ly a *casus belli,* Faustus proposes to reënact the Trojan War
through the sack of Wittenberg. He will be Paris as, in parody,
Ithamore would be Jason, with Bellamira for his golden fleece.
Faustus challenges the Greek heroes to a tournament, imagined
as medieval tapestry rather than a classical frieze, a colorful but
two-dimensional representation of the basic conflict between
pagan and Christian values. In the third strophe the knight, returning to the lady he has championed, salutes her with a gallant
array of invidious comparisons and mythological superlatives. He
modulates from the threat to the persuasion, the more passive
mode of *Edward II.* If he cannot visualize Helen distinctly, it is
because she bedazzles him. Her fairness, outshining the starlight,
surpasses the goddesses—or is it the gods?

> Brighter art thou than flaming Jupiter
> When he appeared to hapless Semele,
> More lovely than the monarch of the sky
> In wanton Arethusa's azured arms.   [V, i, 114–17]

It is not to these nymphs, but to Jupiter himself, that Helen is
being compared. Strange as this may seem, it is not inconsistent
with the prologue's allusion to a masculine muse. It throws some
light back on the offer of Mephostophilis to procure the fairest
of women for Faustus, be they as chaste as Penelope, as wise as
the Queen of Sheba,

>   or as beautiful
> As was bright Lucifer before his fall.   [II, i, 155–6]

Helen, whatever she is, whoever she was, says nothing. Her
part is purely visual, entirely mute. Faustus might almost be

talking to himself, and when we notice how many of his speeches are addressed to himself, the play becomes a kind of interior monologue. Whatever satisfaction he obtains from Helen is bound to be illusory; /126/ as a necromancer he knows in advance that the shadow is not substantial, that the apparition he has materialized will vanish sooner or later. The *Faustbook* reports that she bore him a child, which disappeared—along with its mother—on the day of Faustus' death. Was it a vision or a waking dream, or does the fair exterior disguise some hideous monster like Keats's Lamia? Lucian, in his *Dialogues of the Dead*, pictures Menippus descending into the underworld, inquiring after Helen, and being shown a skeleton. Yes, Hermes assures him, this was the skull that caused the Greeks to launch a thousand ships. And the refrain is the timeless *Ubi sunt?* Where are they now—Helen, Thaïs, Dido, Zenocrate? Marlowe cannot have been insensitive to the traditional mood so poignantly expressed by his sometime collaborator, Thomas Nashe:

> Brightnesse falls from the ayre,
> Queenes have died yong and faire,
> Dust hath closde Helens eye . . .

It is not for nothing that Faustus characterizes Helen by her face, with the connotation of skin-deep beauty as opposed to harsh truth. His rhetoric is an ornate façade, an esthetic surface masking an ethical reality. A third dimension is given to the speech by the entrance—after the first strophe—of a third character, who is indubitably real. This is the Old Man, whom the *Faustbook* identifies as a neighbor, the exemplary figure whom Marlowe employs as a spokesman for Christianity and a counterweight for the ideal of paganism. It is he who penetrates Faustus' conscience:

> Break heart, drop blood, and mingle it with tears.*

Faustus admits his sinfulness and might be moved to repent, were it not for the threatening Mephostophilis and the enticing Helen. When Faustus sweeps her off the stage, it is the Old Man who stays to pronounce the moral; and while Faustus enjoys her elusive favors, the Old Man is "sifted" and tried by devils; but his faith triumphs over Satan's pride, and he ascends to heaven

---

* [In A-text only (line 1277, ed. Tucker Brooke).—Ed.]

while the fiends sink back into hell. The absence of this crucial speech is a reason for continuing to distrust the 1616 Quarto.†

With every scene the pace of the drama accelerates, reaching a climax with the final monologue, which syncopates an hour into fifty-nine lines. This is much too fast, and we share the suspense /127/ with Faustus, whose contract expires at midnight; and yet, in a sense, it is slow enough to fathom—as it were—the thoughts of a drowning man. It is a soliloquy in the profoundest sense, since it isolates the speaker; at the end, as at the beginning, we find him alone in his study. Tragedy is an isolating experience. To each of us, as to Proust on the death of his grandmother, it conveys the realization that we are truly alone. When the time comes, each tragic protagonist must say, with Shakespeare's Juliet:

> My dismal scene, I needs must act alone.   (IV, iii, 19)

So with Faustus, whose fellow scholars rally him for becoming "over-solitary" [V, ii, 33]. They must leave him to his solitude, just as the friends of Everyman desert him on his way to the grave. In contradistinction to the specious grandeur of Faustus' apostrophe to Helen, his last words are an inner revelation, the excruciated agony of a lost soul. It is now too late for vaunting or pleading; it is Marlowe's occasion to develop the less characteristic mode of lamentation; and he does so with the utmost resourcefulness, timing and complicating his flexible rhythms to catch the agitations of Faustus' tortured mind. It is hard to think of another single speech, even in Shakespeare, which demands more from the actor or offers him more. Edward Alleyn, in a surplice with a cross upon it, was famed for his portrayal of the part and may well have left some marks upon these lines. They begin, with a portentous sound effect, at the stroke of eleven:

> Ah Faustus,
> Now hast thou but one bare hour to live,
> And then thou must be damned perpetually.   [V, ii, 130–32]

Time is the essence, and also the substance, of the soliloquy. Its underlying contrast between eternity and transience is heavily enforced, in this distich, by a slow succession of monosyllables

---

† [The B-text actually presents the speech in an entirely different form. See V, i, 38–54.—Ed.]

leading up to the rapid adverb, with the hypermetrical syllable,
"perpetually." Words of comparable significance—"ever," "still,"
"forever," "everlasting"—abound throughout. Where Edward im-
plored the sun to gallop apace and hasten events, Faustus now
bids the planetary system stand still. A humanist to the last, he
recalls a line from Ovid's *Elegies:*

> *O lente, lente currite noctis equi!*   [V, ii, 139] /128/

The utterance falls ironically, but not inappropriately, from the
lips of the scholar turned sensualist, the erstwhile lover of Helen
of Troy. The difference is vast between his motive for wanting
the dawn to be postponed and the classical lover's plea to Auro-
ra. As Marlowe himself had rendered it:

> Now in her tender armes I sweetly bide,
> If euer, now well lies she by my side.
> The aire is cold, and sleepe is sweetest now
> And birdes send forth shrill notes from euery bough:
> Whither runst thou, that men, and women loue not?
> Hold in thy rosy horses that they moue not . . .
> But heldst thou in thine armes some *Cephalus,*
> Then wouldst thou cry, stay night and runne not thus.
>   [I, xiii, 5–40]*

Such a miracle might be accomplished at the behest of the
gods, as Jupiter boasted in *Dido;* but for Faustus, all too human,
the spheres go on revolving. Soon it will be his turn to be tormented; and he is not armed, as the Old Man was, with faith.
Suddenly he seems to witness an epiphany. "See see," he exclaims, "where Christ's blood streams in the firmament." [V, ii,
143] The line echoes and answers Tamburlaine's final challenge,
when he threatened to march against the powers of heaven and
"set black streamers in the firmament." The change of colors is
emblematic of two opposing attitudes toward death: massacre for
the man of war, sacrifice for the man of peace. When Faustus excommunicated himself by signing the deed, his own blood was
ominously reluctant to flow. He asked, "Why streams it not?"
[II, i, 65] and coals were brought to warm it—more omens.
Blood, for the Guise, was the only fluid that could extinguish the

---

* [While still a student at Cambridge, Marlowe had translated Ovid's *Amores.*
—Ed.]

flames of lawless ambition; but Faustus is denied the blood of
Christ, the only thing that could save him, because of his own
denial. "The heavy wrath of God" [V, ii, 150], as the Good
Angel admonished, is now on his head; and his diction grows
scriptural, echoing the Prophets and the Apocalypse, as he vainly
thinks of hiding from the "ireful brows" of Jehovah. The striking of the half-hour alerts him again to temporal considerations,
both relative and absolute.

O, no end is limited to damnèd souls.   [V. ii, 168]

Damnation is an unlooked-for way of transcending limits and
approaching infinity; it is immortality with a vengeance; and
Faustus /129/ would rather be a soulless beast and look forward
to oblivion. Marlowe elsewhere uses the trope of "water drops"
when he reckons innumerable quantities. Here, with fire in the
offing, they are a welcome mirage of dissolution; now, from the
combining elements, a vapor ascends. If time oscillates between
swiftness and slowness, space is measured by the span between
heaven and hell. Although those two words are paired off against
each other in this speech and through the play, somehow "hell"
and its cognates occur fifty-eight times to forty-nine occurrences
for "heaven"—the proportion is forty-five to twenty-seven in the
shorter edition. Faustus is accorded a glimpse of paradise in the
Faustbook; the 1616 Quarto directs the "throne," the Elizabethan god-in-the-machine, briefly to descend from the "heavens," the roof of the stage; while hell, which is also conveniently
adjacent to the localities of the play, yawns in a discovery scene.
The denouement is a foregone conclusion: "for the vain pleasure
of four and twenty years hath Faustus lost eternal joy and felicity" [V, ii, 62–4].

As the clock strikes twelve, with thunder and lightning, the
leaping demons enter to carry him off; in terror he makes his last
offer to burn his books, and his very last word is the shriek,
"Mephistophilis!" He makes his definitive exit through the mon-
struous jaws of the hell-mouth. That popular but obsolete prop-
erty, which Marlowe resurrected from the mysteries, symbolizes
pain and punishment more terribly than the sordid details of
Edward's murder and more pitifully than the crude melodrama
of Barabas' caldron. There is one more scene in the 1616 version,

where the scholars interchange proper moral sentiments; like the sextet at the end of *Don Giovanni*, it seems unduly sententious after what has just happened; and, with some justification, it is not printed in the Quarto of 1604. The Chorus, or Wagner, draws the arras across the inner stage, and the black curtain prevails over the smoking red grotesquerie. If the classical imagery of the epilogue is at odds with its medieval purport, this reflects the tension of the play. If the branch is cut, if Apollo's laurel is burnt, let it be an object lesson for those "forward wits" who are so enticed by "deepness." The celestial-infernal antithesis is conclusively asserted, and the workings of "heavenly power" are discerned in the "hellish fall" of Dr. Faustus. Thus the tragedy is framed by the fundamental dogmas of Christian morality. How far, then, should they be taken literally? How far do they merely furnish /130/ Marlowe with expressionistic scenery? How far was he utilizing theology as a modern playwright might utilize psychology? Faustus has maintained that hell is a fable, and Mephostophilis has declared—in an unexpected burst of humanistic fervor—that man is more excellent than heaven. Dr. Faustus' worst mistake has been to confound hell with Elysium. Between the classic shades and the quenchless flames, even in *Tamburlaine*, Marlowe had discriminated. If heaven was placed in hell, or hell in heaven, the inversion had to be reversed; and the reversal is all the more decisive in *Doctor Faustus* because it comes as a recognition, and because the movement of Marlowe's imagination—at its uppermost—turns and takes a plunge into the abyss.

Unless, with the credulous members of his audience, we regard his fireworks as sparks of hellfire, we must assume that Marlowe's Inferno is a genuine but unlocalized phenomenon. In the same spirit, Paracelsus repeatedly averred that there is a heaven in each of us, and Milton's Satan announces: "My self am Hell" (IV, 75). There is a god infused through the universe, so it was affirmed in *Tamburlaine;* and there is a hell which has no limits, Faustus is informed by Mephostophilis. Every man, according to his lights and through his own endeavors, has a chance to know both; and Milton is not being paradoxical when Satan announces in *Paradise Lost:*

> The mind is its own place, and in itself
> Can make a Heav'n of Hell, a Hell of Heav'n.   (I, 254-5)

The Seven Deadly Sins, the Good and Evil Angels, Mephostophilis himself, upon this level, may be regarded as materializations like Helen of Troy. "Hell strives with grace" in a *psychomachia,* a spiritual battle within the breast of Faustus [V, i, 72]. Pointedly the Old Man rebukes him for excluding "the grace of heaven" from his soul [V, i, 120]. It is plainly lacking, but has he excluded it? Before his blood was dry on the parchment, he was thoroughly remorseful; and his remorse, increasing over his pleasure, gradually deepens into the hopeless despair of his concluding soliloquy.

> Contrition, prayer, repentance—what of these?   [II, i, 17]

he has wondered; he has resolved to renounce his magic, and been distracted by his Evil Angel. Later, when his Good Angel all but persuades him to repent, he tries; but his heart is so hardened that /131/ he can scarcely utter such words as "salvation, faith, or heaven" [II, ii, 19]. Yet he does so, with no little eloquence; and, by uttering the name of God, he prays—albeit no more effecutally than Claudius in *Hamlet.* As between the "Never too late" of the Good Angel and the "Too late" of the Evil Angel, the latter prevails with a Manichæan fatality [II, ii, 79-80]. Christian doctrine vouchsafes mercy to repentant sinners:

> Tush! Christ did call the thief upon the cross.   [IV, v, 37]

Even "the serpent that tempted Eve may be saved" [V, ii, 41-2]. Then why not Faustus? Having become a spirit in form and substance, has he ceased to be a man? Why, when the Old Man all but converts him, should Faustus accept the dagger of Mephostophilis? Why, when he calls upon Christ, is it Lucifer who emerges? George Santayana, acting as devil's advocate, and felicitously stating the case for Faustus as a martyr to the ideals of the Renaissance, would argue that he "is damned by accident or by predestination; he is browbeaten by the devil and forbidden to repent when he has really repented." The pedestrian counterargument would be based on the *Faustbook*'s account of

Faustus, "never falling to repentance truly" but "in all his opin-
ions doubtful, without faith or hope." Luther, followed by such
English theologians as Richard Hooker, in his revolt against
Catholicism had made contrition so difficult that at times it
seemed virtually unattainable. What was worse for Faustus, he
was no ordinary sinner; he was, like Marlowe himself, that im-
penitent and willful miscreant whom Elizabethan preachers
termed a scorner. Far from denying sin or its wages, death, his
course of action was premised on their inevitability: *Che serà, serà.*
This led him, not to fatalism, but to an extreme act of the will—
namely, the commission of an unpardonable sin, a sin against the
Holy Ghost. Casuistry could have found theological loopholes,
had a penitent Faustus been conceivable. But that would have
presupposed an orthodox Marlowe.

As a measure of his heterodoxy, it has proved suggestive to
compare *Doctor Faustus* with *El Mágico Prodigioso*, the sacra-
mental drama at Calderón, grounded upon the analogous legend
of Saint Cyprian. There the magician repents, forswears his magic,
is converted to Christianity, and undergoes martyrdom—to be reu-
nited /132/ in heaven with his lady, who also dies a Christian
martyr. Death is a happy ending in the next world, after the
uncertainties and horrors of life here below. Tragedy is intercep-
ted by eschatology. Extremes meet, when we glance away from
that simple and reassuring cosmos toward the chaos of modernity, and to the magistral exploration of it that Goethe achieved in
his *Faust*. Goethe's Faust is a man of affirmations, bedeviled by a
spirit of denial, whom he overreaches in the end by what—to
sterner moralists—might well seem a legalistic ruse. He is free to
stray so long as he strives; the forfeit need only be paid when he
is satisfied with the passing moment. Though he is momentarily
tempted to express such satisfaction, it is not occasioned by the
present but by the prospect of a better world in the future.
Hence his soul remains his own, on condition that he persist in
his strivings toward the infinite, aided and comforted by eternal
womanhood. Tragedy is here defeated by optimism. Enlightenment and humanitarianism absolve and regenerate Faust, just as
salvation cancels out sin in that unworldly world of the Middle
Ages which is still reflected by Calderón. Balancing precariously
between those two worlds, Marlowe achieves his tragic equilibri-

um: the conviction of sin without the belief in salvation. That is sheer damnation; but damnation is man's unmitigated lot; this is hell, nor are we out of it. Such a pessimistic view is woefully incomplete; but tragedy is an intensive rather than a comprehensive inquiry, which concentrates upon the problem of evil and the nature of suffering. When Marlowe swerved from his predilection for the good things of life, he concentrated upon the evils with unflinching—not to say unbearable—intensity.

Doctor Faustus does not have the coherence of Calderón's ethos or the stature of Goethe's protagonist; yet, contrasted with the English play, the Spanish seems naïve and the German sentimental. We need not push these contrasts invidiously, given the differences in time and place, in poetic language and dramatic convention. Given the unchallengeable greatness of Goethe's achievement, it is noteworthy that certain readers have preferred Marlowe's treatment of the legend—notably Scott and Coleridge, Lamb and Hazlitt, all of them conceivably biased by their cultural leanings, and by their unfamiliarity with the second part of *Faust*. The first part, the romantic and domestic drama of Gretchen, admittedly belongs to /133/ Goethe's little world; it may have been in emulation of Marlowe that Goethe went on to investigate the macrocosm. It may well be that Faustus has less in common with Faust than with Euphorion, the hybrid offspring of Faust and Goethe's Helena, who meets a premature death by attempting to fly. It may well be, in spite of Marlowe's narrower range and less philosophical outlook, that he grasped the core of his subject more objectively and with a keener awareness of its implications; that, because his background was nearer to obscurantism than to enlightenment, he appreciated the hazards and pangs of free-thinking. A later epoch than Goethe's, with less faith in progress or hope for individualism, may feel itself in closer accord with the earlier poet. It cannot dream about flying, with Leonardo, since the dream has not only come true but turned into a nightmare. It can add very little, except for amen, to the admonition of Rabelais that science is ruinous without conscience. It cannot but discern its culture-hero in the ancient myth of Icarus, in Cervantes' twice-told tale of the curious impertinent, above all in Marlowe's tragedy of the scientific libertine who gained control over nature while losing control of himself.

"The reason Milton wrote in fetters when he wrote of Angels
& God, and at liberty when of Devils & Hell, is because he was a
true Poet and of the Devil's party without knowing it." Blake's
problematic note to *The Marriage of Heaven and Hell*, like
most paradoxes, stresses a neglected facet of a complicated truth
at the expense of what is more obvious. Marlowe, much more obviously than Milton, is committed to this kind of poetic dia-
bolism; and, conversely, Marlowe can write with genuine yearning of paradise lost. No doubt he yearns all the more avidly with
Faustus, but with Faustus he condemns himself; the Good Angel
and the Old man are at liberty, while Mephostophilis is in perpetual fetters. Yet, it is just at this point that Marlowe abandons
his preoccupation with unfettered soaring, and seems to submit
himself to ideas of durance, torment, and constraint. If he is imag-
inatively identified with any character, it is no longer Faustus;
it is Mephostophilis, who suffers with Faustus like a second self,
yet also plays the cosmic ironist, wise in his guilty knowledge and
powerful in his defeated rebellion. Through his agency Marlowe
succeeds in setting the parable of intelligence and experience
within a Christian framework, even while hinting that the
framework is arbitrary and occasionally glancing beyond it. /134/
Such is the attitude of ambivalent supplication that Hart
Crane rephrases in his poem "For the Marriage of Faustus and
Helen":

> Distinctly praise the years, whose volatile
> Blamed bleeding hands extend and thresh the height
> The imagination spans beyond despair,
> Outpacing bargain, vocable, and prayer.

Such is the way in which Goethe's Faust eluded his devil's bargain, and it applies to Marlowe if not to Faustus. If hell is destruction, it follows that heaven is creation; and perhaps the
highest form of creation is that engendered out of the very forces
of destruction, the imagination spanning beyond despair. Perhaps we may say of Marlowe what the Florentines said of Dante:
this man has been in hell. As we broadly interpret that concept,
many men have been there; but few have mastered their terrors
and returned to communicate that mastery. /135/

The Comic Synthesis in *Doctor Faustus*

ROBERT ORNSTEIN

I do not propose in this article to argue Marlowe's authorship of the prose comedy in *Doctor Faustus,* though for convenience I will follow tradition in attributing to him those scenes under discussion. Actually, the problem of authorship is irrelevant here, for my concern is with the integrity of the play as a work of dramatic art, not with the integrity of the text as a literary document. . . . I intend no apology for the crude buffoonery in *Doctor Faustus.* I would suggest, however, that there is more than one level of comedy in the play—that the slapstick scenes which tickled groundling fancies unite with the seemingly fragmented main action to form a subtly ironic tragic design.

To begin with, let us admit that Sir Philip Sidney's criticism of the Elizabethan stage was well taken though somewhat aca-/165/demic. Marlowe's contemporaries did mingle kings and clowns "not because the matter so carrieth," but because an Elizabethan audience expected variety and comedy. After all, high seriousness and buffoonery had long before joined hands in the Miracles and Moralities, and popular taste weighed more heavily than critical theory in the public theatres. But the custom of mingling kings and clowns could not remain a naive literary practice as Elizabethan drama matured. Like all literary practices, it was sophisticated for better and for worse. When imagination faltered, clowns—the musicians in *Romeo and Juliet,* for instance—made purely routine appearances in tragedy. But when inspiration mounted, the Elizabethan comedians found themselves in more significant roles: as the grave diggers in *Hamlet* or

Reprinted from ELH: *A Journal of English Literary History,* XXII (1955), 165-172.

as the drunken Porter in *Macbeth* (a character rejected by Coleridge, ironically enough, as a "disgusting" interpolation by the
actors).

It was inevitable too that incongruous mixtures of kings and
clowns should have developed into formalized contrasts used to
enhance the beauty and substance of a main dramatic action.
The highly stylized device of the antimasque merely refined the
once indiscriminate jostle of coarse and courtly elements in the
masque. The popular drama produced less formalized, more sa-
tiric "antimasques" of clownish servants who aped the manners
and pretensions of their betters. In Shakespeare's romantic comedies a pair of rustic sweethearts stumble through the arabesques
of courtship, naturalizing by their improbable amour the
artificial languors and melancholies of courtly heroes and her-
oines. In Ford's tragedies we find comic foils remarkably similar
in one respect to the clowns in *Doctor Faustus*. Like Rafe and
Robin, they are not very amusing. The best are innocuous, the
majority unattractive, and the rest simply offensive. Ford, lacking
a sense of humor, and at times a sense of decency, tried to use
comic lewdness to set off more delicate and consuming passions.[1]
His was the last and least successful attempt to subtilize the
comic contrasts of Elizabethan drama. Marlowe's was an imper-
fect but brilliant innovation.

Comparing Marlowe's clowns to those in Ford's tragedies,
however, merely underlines the unique function of the comic
/166/ contrasts in *Doctor Faustus*. Obviously Marlowe does not
enhance the main action of his tragedy by reducing it to absurdity scene by scene. He does not magnify Faustus' achievements by
having clowns parody them immediately afterwards. (By analogy,
no Elizabethan would try to heighten the beauty of a masque by
closing it with grotesque dances. The antimasque must come
first; it must prepare the audience for the familiar contrast, for
the metamorphosis of antic into courtly elegance.) Yet the pattern of *Doctor Faustus* is consistently "wrong." In the first scene
Faustus announces his intellectual supremacy and his decision to
gain a deity through magic. In the second scene Wagner apes his
master's display of learning by chopping logic with two scholars.
In the third scene Faustus agrees to sell his soul for power and

---

[1] See, for instance, *Love's Sacrifice*, in which the witty lecheries of Ferentes contrast with the nobler passions of Fernando and Bianca.

voluptuousness. Immediately afterwards the Clown considers bartering his soul for a shoulder of mutton and a taste of wenching. In the following scenes Faustus makes his compact with the Devil, discusses astronomy with Mephistophilis, and is entertained by the Seven Deadly Sins. He then launches his career as a magician by snatching away the Pope's food and drink. Next Rafe and Robin burlesque Faustus' conjurations and try to steal a goblet from a Vintner.

Judging by their enthusiasm for the play, however, Marlowe's contemporaries did not find the pattern of *Doctor Faustus* "wrong." Perhaps because parody is its own excuse for being when its target is the heroic stance. Is there not something infinitely reassuring in the clown who apes the manner and the mannerism of the superman? And the ironic comedy in *Doctor Faustus* is more than reassuring. Its intention, I think, is both didactic and comic. Simultaneously nonsensical and profound, it clarifies our perception of moral values.

We see the world through the lenses of custom: when false values pass current, even elemental truths appear distorted, naive, or absurd. The ironist often deals in elemental absurdities —the absurdity of eating children to cure poverty or of mortgaging one's immortal soul for a piece of mutton (if it be well roasted). We smile at such absurdities because we have a more sensible and realistic appraisal of the world. We know that society does not and would not eat children. We know that no man, however foolish, would damn his soul to satisfy /167/ his belly —to gain infinite power, yes, but we consider such aspiration heroic. We smile, however, only until we discover beneath the surface of our sensible view of life the grim absurdity depicted by the ironist—only until sensible or grandiose appearance and absurd reality melt into one. Because the ironist (like the Shakespearean Fool) is licensed to reveal "absurd" truths only when he amuses his audience, Marlowe entertains us with Clowns and with the ancient but eternally successful comedy of futility. It is hardly accidental that in the crucial scene when Faustus first repents Lucifer appears, impressario-like, with the Seven Deadly Sins. Faustus "feeds" on the spectacle and jests with these harmless bogies of the superstitious mind. Entranced by Lucifer's vaudeville show he forgets salvation. Lucifer is also entertained but on a more intellectual plane. The consummate cynic, he diverts his victim with a picture gallery that suggests Faustus' own futility.

Professor Harry Levin describes Marlowe's Deadly Sins as a "quaint procession of gargoyles" and interprets Faustus' unalloyed amusement as a sign of moral decay.[2] I would agree but also add that the Deadly Sins are supposed to be amusing in *Doctor Faustus* as they are in much of medieval literature. The fourteenth century artist took sin seriously enough and yet caricatured it even as he caricatured Satan, arch-enemy of God, who appears in the Miracles and Moralities as a comic villain beaten off the stage to the accompaniment of divine and human laughter. The medieval playwright gave the Devil his due; he showed the human soul caught in a satanic web of pleasure and deceit. But he showed also the inevitable triumph of God's love which made the efforts of satanic evil vain and risible. In short, the medieval mind understood the ludicrousness of insatiable desire. It knew that vice (to use Santayana's definition) is "human nature strangled by the suicide of attempting the impossible."[3] /168/

Of course Faustus is never ludicrous; he is no fustian villain ranting of his powers. But from the beginning there is casuistic self-deception in his speeches. Blind to the ever-present possibility of grace, he facilely reduces theology to the dogma of pitiless damnation. Misunderstanding his relationship with God, he completely mistakes his rapport with the Devil. He thinks that through magic he has gained control of the spirit world and of Mephistophilis, who appears at his command and changes shape to please him. Faustus finds Mephistophilis "pliant . . . full of obedience and humility." Mephistophilis, a scrupulous corrupter, insists that he has only one master—Lucifer—but Faustus will not believe him. When Mephistophilis shudders at the terrors of damnation, Faustus sets himself up as an example of fortitude to the angel who openly warred against God. Later he argues with Mephistophilis about the reality of hell even though indisputable evidence of its reality stands before him.

[2] Harry Levin, *The Overreacher: A Study of Christopher Marlowe* (Cambridge, Mass., 1952), p. 119.

[3] In his essay on Dickens (from *Soliloquies in England and Later Soliloquies*), Santayana argues that we do not connect Dickens' caricatures with real personalities because we cannot face the honesty of his comic realism. Our failure to connect Marlowe's clowns, caricatures of the tragic hero, with Faustus is perhaps due to a comparable failure to recognize that Marlowe was also, in a sense, a comic and moral realist.

Fleeing his own Master, Faustus contracts with the Devil for the services of Mephistophilis, who, like the cunning slave of Roman comedy, quickly gains the upper hand. Frightening and distracting Faustus from salvation, he caters to his sensuality and diverts his creative energies into court performances and .practical jokes. Though at times compassionate, Mephistophilis has his joke with Faustus on the subject of lechery. Lucifer toys with his dupe on a grander scale. He assures Faustus that "in hell is all manner of delight" and promises an excursion through it:

> At midnight I will send for thee. Meanwhile peruse this book
> and view it thoroughly, and thou shalt turn thyself into
> what shape thou wilt.   [II, ii, 167–69]

The Devil is as good as his word. He does send for Faustus at midnight. And he does help Faustus to change his shape. But the transformation is from aspiring hero to despairing libertine.

At the beginning of the play Faustus' plans, though egocentric and grandiose, are constructive. He wants pleasure, riches, and power, but he also intends to make all learning his province, better the lot of students, improve geography, and defeat tyranny. Faustus' dreams of creativity, however, are /169/ only dreams; indeed, the measure of his tragic fall is the increasing disparity between his aspirations and his achievements. He travels at first, takes in the wonders of the world, and wins fame as a magician. But on the stage itself Faustus' accomplishments grow increasingly petty: he discomforts the Pope, horns a Knight, entertains an Emperor, cheats a Horse-Courser, and delights a Duchess with grapes out of season. Here is travesty of a high order! In the latter half of the play, the mighty Faustus parodies his own high-vaulting thoughts and ambitions even as Wagner and the Clown had parodied them earlier. Or more correctly, as Faustus changes shape the tragic comic contrast begins to coalesce. Scene by scene the apposing images approach one another until at last we discover beneath the exalted appearance of the fearless rebel the figure of the fool. When Faustus steals the Pope's cup and Robin steals the Vintner's goblet the tragic and comic images nearly merge. The difference between hero and clown is one of degree, not of kind.

We need no acquaintance with Elizabethan ethical psychology to appreciate the ironic fate of a hero who in striving to be a god

becomes less than a man. Only a dimwitted Clown would sell his
soul for a mutton roast and a bit of lechery. Yet Faustus ends his
days in "belly cheer," carousing and swilling with the students.
The scholar who pursued knowledge beyond the utmost bound
of human thought finally takes Helen for his paramour to drown
vexatious thought in wantonness.[4] Actually it does not matter
whether one sells one's soul for infinite power or for belly cheer.
Both transactions are ridiculous, the first even more than the second because it is far less realistic. Faustus, who dreamed of commanding the powers of heaven and earth, finds that he cannot
check the movement of the stars when death threatens. In his
vain rebellion there is comedy; in his fall from grace irrevocable
tragedy.[5] /170/

I do not mean to suggest any ambiguity or ambivalence in
Marlowe's attitude towards his tragic hero. Despite persistent ar-
guments,[6] it is difficult to believe that Marlowe secretly identified himself with Faustus and that Faustus' catastrophe is a sop
to Nemesis or to conventional morality. For Marlowe gives an
almost Dostoievskian sense of damnation as an earthly as well as
spiritual fact; he depicts the corruption of the mind that destroys
the soul. Like Mephistophilis (and like Ivan Karamazov)[7] Faustus makes his own personal hell of negation, a hell that "hath no

---

[4] The ecstatic poetry of Faustus' apostrophe to Helen [V, i, 99–118] does not
mask the corruption of his genius. Once before in despair he had summoned
Homer, the "maker," who sang of Troy. In the lines to Helen, however, he identifies himself with an effeminate Paris whose sensuality destroyed the topless towers
of Ilium. As the comparison to Jupiter and Semele suggests, Faustus does not take
Helen—he abandons himself to her.

[5] The balance of tragic and comic elements in *Faustus* is somewhat comparable
to that in *Paradise Lost*. C. S. Lewis has suggested that Satan might have been
a comic figure had Milton chosen to emphasize, more than he does, the absurdity
of diabolical ambition (*A Preface to Paradise Lost* [Oxford, 1952], pp. 92–93).
Like Faustus, Satan changes his shape; the brightest of angels becomes the scarred
fallen leader who, reaching toward heaven, transforms himself into cormorant,
toad, and "monstrous Serpent." Satan, however, is the unwitting fool of God,
the brilliant schemer whose victory turns to ashes and whose evil will produces
good, the "fortunate" fall of man. Faustus' destiny is more obscure and pathetic;
he is Lucifer's fool, not God's.

[6] See, for example, Paul H. Kocher, *Christopher Marlowe: A Study of His
Thought, Learning, and Character* (Chapel Hill, 1946), pp. 118–19.

[7] Compare the two intellectuals, Faustus and Ivan Karamazov. Both rebel against
God because they cannot believe in His redeeming love; and they cannot believe because they are detached, superior beings incapable of ordinary human sympathies.
Both reject intellectually what they cannot emotionally "conceive of" and accept.
Spiritually isolated, trapped by their own dialectical subtleties, they dissipate their
creative gifts. They escape the restrictive bonds of morality only to discover too late
that they have cut themselves off from the humanity of those who would save them.

limits, nor is circumscrib'd/In one self place." But he attempts
to escape it in death by losing himself in the natural forces that
were to have been his agents of creation:

> Mountains and hills, come, come and fall on me,
> And hide me from the heavy wrath of God.
> No! no!
> Then will I headlong run into the earth;
>
> . . . .
>
> O, it strikes, it strikes! Now, body, turn to air,
> Or Lucifer will bear thee quick to hell.
> O soul, be chang'd into little water-drops,
> And fall into the ocean, ne'er be found!
>> *Thunder, and enter the Devils.*
>> [V, ii, 149–83] /171/

Here is the ultimate irony; Faustus would escape the negation of
hell by annihilating body and soul. The diseased creative will
succumbs at last to frenzied desire for self-destruction—for noth-
ingness. *Consummatum est!*

To say that *Doctor Faustus* can be read as the tragedy of a
creative mind destroying itself in fascination with the esoteric is
not to make of the play a secularized Christian allegory. Marlowe adds new dimension to the Morality framework; he does
not use it as a literary, "mythical" apparatus. Hell is a reality in
Doctor Faustus whether experienced in an earthly nihilistic despair or in the horror of an eternal void. Marlowe's religious
thought may be heterodox in some respects, but his ethics are
sound. We are always aware that Faustus the aspiring titan is
also the self-deluded fool of Lucifer. The emancipated intellectual who confounds hell in Elysium spends his last hours as a
lonely, terrified penitent.

Doctor Faustus, then, is not the tragical history of a glorious
rebellion. For Marlowe shared with his admiring contemporary,
George Chapman, the disenchanted vision of the aspiring mind—
the knowledge that the Comic Spirit hovers over the Icarian
flight of the self-announced superman. /172/

Doctor Faustus:
The Vision of Tragedy

RICHARD BENSON SEWALL

W. H. Auden observed that at the end of a Greek tragedy we say, "What a pity it had to be this way"; at the end of a Christian tragedy, "What a pity it had to be this way when it might have been otherwise."[1] If there is more freedom in Greek tragedy and more of a sense of fate in Christian tragedy than this statement suggests, still it points to the true tragic locus and tone of Marlowe's *Doctor Faustus,* the first major Elizabethan tragedy and the first to explore the tragic possibilities of the head-on clash of the Renaissance compulsions with the Hebraic-Christian tradition. His *Tamburlaine,* presumably written in the previous year (1587), for all its scenes of violence and pathos, was more of a single-voiced statement of the outward Renaissance thrust, a reckless flouting, without much inner concern, of all that Greeks knew as *hubris* and fate and all that Christians knew as sin, guilt, and damnation. Marlowe viewed it as "tragic," perhaps, in its picture of suffering and destruction and in the spectacle of

Reprinted from *The Vision of Tragedy* (New Haven: Yale University Press, 1959), pp. 57–67, notes pp. 159–60.

[1] "The Christian Tragic Hero," *New York Times Book Review,* Dec. 16, 1945. I agree with Laurence Michel [. . .] that tragedy is not Christian and never can be, and that such terms as "Christian tragedy" involve dangerous ambiguities. But (to repeat): the term is permissible and, I think, useful, to indicate the new dimensions and tensions introduced into human life by Christianity and which perforce entered into the Elizabethan tragic synthesis. Tragedy puts to the test *all* the formulations of a culture and comes out committed to none. What Auden describes as the Greek "tragedy of necessity" actually shows the extent to which man is free in the midst of fate; and what he calls the Christian "tragedy of possibility" shows the old sense of fate in the midst of the new freedom. I use this much-quoted remark from his *New York /159/ Times* essay merely to point to the central stress (not new but more exigent) of Elizabethan tragedy:

death overtaking in the end even this mightiest of worldly con-
querors.[2] Although there are spiritual reaches and broodings in
Tamburlaine that Marlowe never got from the Greeks, it was in
Faustus that he turned the focus inward, saw the soul as the tragic battlefield, and wrote the first "Christian tragedy." ‧

"Cut is the branch that might have grown full straight." So
says the Chorus in the final speech of *Faustus,* bringing the play
to a typical morality-play or *De Casibus*-story ending with a
warning against such fiendish practices as Faustus followed.
"What a pity it had to be this way when it might have /57/
been otherwise." The choice which would have made all the
difference belonged to Faustus, and he knew it. No god urged
him on, no oracle foretold his fate. He sinned, suffered remorse,
and was damned. The medieval predecessors of the play had told
the same story, with variations, again and again; and insofar as
Faustus merely repeats the old pattern it is anything but tragic.
There is no mystery in this kind of universe; it is all too predictable, and the moral issues are clear cut. The terror, had Faustus
only chosen differently, might have been avoided; and we are left
comfortable and secure in the knowledge of how to escape his
downfall.

But Marlowe did not merely repeat the old pattern, and his
universe is not comfortable or secure. The Elizabethan theater
invited something like the same kind of aesthetic interest in the
direful aspects of human experience that Greek tragedy had stim-
ulated in both artist and spectator. Indeed, knowledge of the
Greek form, to humanists like Marlowe, must have had a com-
pulsive force of its own, quite apart from personal predilections—
although in Marlowe's case, there is evidence that those predilec-

---

[2] Cf. Theodore Spencer, *Death and Elizabethan Tragedy* (Cambridge, Harvard University Press, 1936), p. 232. To the Elizabethans, "Death, indeed, *was* tragedy; a
tragedy was a play which ended in death." Death was feared as "the end of accomplishment"; it destroyed beauty, power, wealth—all the good things of life. Spencer
suggests (to anticipate for a moment) that the increasing number of tragedies during
the early years of the seventeenth century was due in part, at least, to a kind of
national preoccupation with death during Elizabeth's last years and following her
death. "There is more than merely biographical importance in the fact that Shakespeare stopped writing comedies in [these years]. He simply expressed better than
anyone else the trend of contemporary thought . . . He began to contemplate life
tragically" (p. 233). (One is reminded of Dr. Johnson's remark [19 Sept. 1777]: "Depend upon it, Sir, when a man knows he is to be hanged in a fortnight, it concentrates his mind wonderfully.") /160/

tions were many and strong. That the Greeks had once ordered
and presented human experience in such a way, and so powerfully, was an inescapable and compelling fact. Popular taste, which
had been nourished on the rudimentary action of the old religious (but increasingly secular) plays, asked to see the full story
acted out. With the dramatic treatment of action freed from ec-
clesiastical control, the way was open for the expression once
again of "tragic" truth—the truth of man in action as seen by the
free and inquiring artist. Marlowe had said enough in *Tamburlaine* to get himself excommunicated many times over, but he
had said it in a play, in a dramatic context, and he was not pre-
vented from writing more plays. If, in *Faustus,* he brings the play
to a pious conclusion, the "truth" of the play goes far beyond the
Chorus' final piety, just as the meaning of *Oedipus* transcends by
far the choric summing up of that play. The voice of the Chorus
is not the only voice in *Faustus.* For one thing, no figure of the
old moralities talks so much or takes us so deep into his own
being as does Faustus—or does so /58/ much and so boldly.
Faustus in thought and action, brooding, philosophizing, disputing, conjuring, defying God and risking all with a flourish, does
not suggest so much the lay figure of the moralities, Everyman,
as, (in one of his phases) Adam the knowledge-seeker and (in
others) the defiant hero of the Greek tradition—a Prometheus or
Tamburlaine.

Thus the "secret cause," the true source of the tragic terror of
the story of *Faustus* as Marlowe treated it, does not lie in the
Christian moral equation of which Faustus in the end finds himself an inevitable term. The "fearful echoes" that "thunder in
his ears" in the interludes between his conjuring exploits are
momentarily terrifying to him but not because of the mystery of
their origin, which is fifteen centuries of Christian teaching and
spiritual discipline. He tells the Scholars [V, ii, 37–8] that he
suffers from "a surfeit of deadly sin that hath damned both body
and soul." Such was the fate of the sixteenth-century German
magician whose story Marlowe dramatized. But like the Poet of
Job and the Greek tragedians, who found new and tragic meaning in old and orthodox stories, Marlowe interpolated into the
old medieval equation the new, mysterious, and terrifyingly ambiguous dynamic of the Renaissance, gave it a fascination and a

dignity never realized in previous treatments of the story, and made Faustus, rather than Hamlet, "the first modern man." The story of this twenty-four-year action, telescoped by Marlowe into a few vivid scenes, introduced the modern tragic theme of the divided soul—soon to become "the complicated modern soul" of Dostoevski's analysis—torn between the desire to exploit its new mastery and freedom and (on the other hand) the claims of the old teachings, which to defy meant guilt and a growing sense of alienation. Faustus is tragic because he recognized the dilemma as real. Even as he boasts that his soul is his own, to dispose of as he will, he hears the fearful echoes thundering in his ears.

As with Job and Oedipus, we first see Faustus at the peak of his worldly power and influence. He is master of the new knowledges and skills, a famous physician, honored by whole cities, and revered by his students. Why was he restless? Why /59/ was he unwilling to remain "but Faustus, and a man"? Why this urge to command "all things that move between the quiet poles"? The one fixed "star" of tragedy, writes Arthur Miller,[3] is the hero's urge to "realize himself" fully in the face of all that would rob him of his just deserts or repress what he feels to be his true nature; and the gauge of his heroism is the magnitude of the risk he is willing to take. In this sense the tragedy of Faustus is the tragedy of Adam, "goaded" (as Kierkegaard saw it) by the knowledge of his freedom into what seemed like the one possibility of self-realization his situation offered. Paradise was not enough. To the orthodox, Adam's action was not only sin but utter folly, just as to the Chorus who begins and ends the play Faustus' action was wholly devilish. This too is the sense of the opening soliloquy, in which Faustus brushes aside all studies but necromancy, the key to the self-realization he craves. Immediately the Good Angel tells him to "lay that damned book aside," and the Angel who bids him "go forward in that famous art" is "Evil."

But to Marlowe (judging from the way he presented it) the case was more complicated and more fascinating. He saw the en-

[3] "Tragedy and the Common Man," *New York Times Theater Section*, Feb. 27, 1949. Miller here stresses what I regard as only the first phase of the tragic hero's experience, the romantic or rebellious phase: Faustus, that is, as he embarks on his course. /160/

tire action not only as "Good" or "Evil" would see it but as the man of flesh and blood, the one who takes the risk, sees it and lives it out. What are the inner sources of such an action, what is the feel on the pulse, what is the discovery? The meaning of the play is not only that Faustus' act was sinful and foolish. The meaning is in all that Faustus says and does and becomes; it is the total yield of the "boundary-situation" into which Faustus walks of his own accord, acting out the mysterious tragic dynamic of his times.

If Job began in bitterness, and Oedipus in self-confidence too close to complacence, Faustus' first mood after seizing upon necromancy as his study is one of arrogant and impatient lust for power. It is redeemed, if at all, by the full imaginative run that gives even his petty wishes—"the pleasant fruits and princely delicates"—a kind of poetic validity. Marlowe sets his hero's mind completely free to range forbidden realms, and no voice save Tamburlaine's gives comparable expression to the outward Renaissance thrust. /60/

> All things that move between the quiet poles
> Shall be at my command. Emperors and kings
> Are but obeyed in their several provinces,
> Nor can they raise the wind or rend the clouds;
> But his dominion that exceeds in this
> Stretcheth as far as doth the mind of man.
> A sound magician is a mighty god:
> Here, Faustus, try thy brains to gain a deity!
>
> [I, i, 57–64]

"How am I glutted with conceit of this!" cries Faustus, as he relishes his promised power over all things great and little, temporal and spiritual. His whirling wishes at first have little pattern, no redeeming cause or ideal—no quest for justice or truth; and as his desires grow more fantastic and vainglorious the spectacle is not pretty. But the opening scenes do not wholly condemn him. His absurd egotisms are mixed with intellectual and humanitarian impulses. He would "resolve all ambiguities," read strange philosophy, clothe the schoolboys in silk, and rid his country of the foreign yoke. When Valdes warns him that he must be "resolute," his courage is tested and he responds like a hero. He is prepared (at the end of Scene 1) to take the ultimate risk: "This night I'll conjure though I die therefore." Later, in Scene 3, he rallies the spirits of the Devil's own messenger, Mephistophilis, whose heart faints as he foresees Faustus' awful future. Rising in his "manly fortitude," he scorns Mephistophilis' warning, rejects all hopes of heaven's joys, and offers his soul to Lucifer for twen-ty-four years of his heart's desires. With his decision come new energy, new power, new command. However "evil" his course, he has left the apathetic and cynical talk of the opening lines of the play and is now man "on the way."

It is said that the great tragedies deal with the great eccentrics and offenders, the God-defiers, the murderers, the adulterers. But it is not tragedy's primary concern to establish the moral truth or the sociological meaning of the hero's action. It is the orthodox world, and not the tragic artist, which judges (or prejudges) a Job or an Oedipus, a Faustus or a Hester Prynne. To bring his protagonist swiftly to the point of ultimate test, the artist imag-ines a deed which violently /61/ challenges the accepted social and (it may be) legal ways. Hence the fact that tragic heroes are often criminals in the eyes of society, and hence the frequency of the legal trial as a symbolic situation in tragedy from Aeschylus to Dostoevski and Kafka. It is the characteristic emphasis of trag-edy written in the Christian era that the "criminals" become "sinners" as well, so that the hero is ranged not only against his society but against God and his own soul. Starbuck could not see why Ahab should go whaling for anything but profit; he was ⁀ighast at Ahab's "sin" toward one of God's dumb creatures; and had the *Pequod* ever returned, Ahab would have had to stand trial for his criminal neglect of his charge, as before Starbuck's God he must stand trial for his immortal soul. But *Moby-Dick* is not primarily concerned with Ahab as a criminal or sinner, nor is Marlowe's play primarily concerned with Faustus as the Church or society would regard him. The moral qualities or the sociological aspects of the hero's initial choice are less important than the qualities he shows and the discoveries he makes in the subsequent action. Indeed, as Dostoevski was to show about the increasingly standardized society of his time, for purposes of moral discovery the "criminals and outcasts" provide the richest material for the inquiring artist. Judged in this scale, it was bet-ter for Faustus to sell his soul, for Hester to sin with Dimmes-dale, and for Raskolnikov to commit murder than that no action

at all be joined. Thus (as we have seen) the Greeks respected
pride and made it a heroic quality, though they saw its destruc-
tive side. Stripped of its eschatology, the Christian doctrine of
the *felix culpa*, the fortunate fall of Adam, is akin to the treatment in tragedy of the hero's initial crime or sin.[4] Precarious as
such an ethic is, tragedy holds aloof from moral judgment and
presents the action in such a way that moral judgment can be
only one element, and not the most important, in the total response. Marlowe asks us to view the entire action before judging
Faustus, and so presents him that unequivocal moral judgment is
impossible.

The strange course begins directly Faustus has made his
choice. In the upsurge of his arrogance he feels confident and secure. He ridicules such notions as "hell" and "damnation" and
"these vain trifles of men's souls." He is elated with the /62/
success of his first conjuring [I, iii], reproves the faint-hearted
Mephistophilis, and sends him to strike the twenty-four-year bargain with Lucifer. In a similar mood, after signing the contract
in blood, he calls hell a "fable" and the threat of eternal torment
an "old wives' tale." "Ay," says Mephistophilis, "think so, till experience change thy mind." It is Faustus' redeeming quality that
experience *could* change his mind and that he is sensitive to
every stage of the process. By the time of his second conjuring
[II, i], even before the signing, he confesses doubts. "Something
soundeth in mine ears," he says—a voice that calls upon him to
abjure his magic and turn to God again. "Why waverest thou?"
he asks himself. "Be resolute." As he comes ever closer to the
edge of the known and the tried, a glimpse into the abyss brings
a moment of intense self-realization:

> Ay, and Faustus will turn to God again.
> To God? He loves thee not;
> The God thou servest is thine own appetite.
>
> [II, i, 9–11]

---

[4] Indeed, as Herbert Weisinger suggests (*Tragedy and the Paradox of the Fortunate
Fall*, E. Lansing, Michigan State College Press, 1953, p. 10), the doctrine of the *felix
culpa* springs from the same archetypal experience. Just as the primitive king or hero
—and later, the Savior—taking upon himself the sins of the people, died sacrificially,
was reborn and brought new life, so the tragic hero in his pride "sins," dies, and
brings us "new life." Weisinger sees the secularization of the paradox of the fortunate
fall as "the substance out of which tragedy, and particularly Shakespearean tragedy,
is made." /160/

In the dialogue with the Good and Evil Angels, immediately following, the tone with which he speaks of "Contrition, prayer, repentance—what of them?" is hesitant and nostalgic. "Sweet Faustus—" pleads the Good Angel, and Faustus seems for a moment to yield, only to be drawn back to his arrogant ways by the Evil Angel's reminder of honor and of wealth that now lie within his power. "Of wealth!" cries Faustus,

> Why, the signiory of Emden shall be mine.
> When Mephistophilis shall stand by me
> What God can hurt me? Faustus, thou art safe:
> Cast no more doubts.
>
> [II, i, 23–6]

But the doubts will not vanish, and Faustus lives out his twenty-four-year gamble as the first modern tragic man, part believer, part unbeliever, vacillating between independence and dependence upon God, now arrogant and confident, now anxious and worried, justified yet horribly unjustified. He is forced constantly to renew his choice between two awesome alternatives, and in the opposite phases of the rhythm he sees greater and more glorious heights, and depths of greater /63/ terror. Soon the gentle voice that "sounded" in his ears, bidding him abjure his magic and return to God, becomes the fearful thundering echoes: "Faustus, thou are damned!" What he is learning is the truth of his own nature—a truth which it was his peculiar Renaissance compulsion to forget or deny: that he is creature as well as creator; a man and not a god; a dependent, responsible part of a greater whole. He learns that his soul is not a mere trifle of his own, to use as a commodity, and that "contrition, prayer, repentance," hell and damnation, are not (as the Evil Angel told him)

> . . . illusions, fruits of lunacy,
> That make men foolish that do trust them most.
>
> [II, i, 19–20]

Like Koestler's Rubashov (in *Darkness at Noon*) he had "forgotten the infinite" and the humbling terror with which it invests all the undertakings of man.

Pressing on in spite of the echoes and the doubts, he reaches levels of perception never gained by the less venturous. Like Job, he was not content with having "heard by the hearing of the ear"; he must see with his own eyes. He has frivolous moments (some of them surely not of Marlowe's conceiving), when he boxes the Pope's ears and gets grapes in January. But the random wishes of his early days of conjuring take a more salutary direction. He does not want so much what power will bring—he never takes the Signiory of Emden, never walls Germany with brass, never clothes the schoolboys in silk. He wants what all men, good and bad, have wanted; to conquer time, space, and ignorance. Above all he wants knowledge: what is hell? where is it? who made the world—"the plants, the herbs, the trees that grow upon the earth"? He cruises hither and yon in the world and above it, exploring all climes and the secrets of the heavens. He delves into the past, makes "blind Homer sing," Amphion play the harp, and Helen appear for a dazzling moment. What Marlowe dramatizes is not only the terror of the black art as the old story told about it and as we see it reflected (in the play) in the eyes of the lesser characters, The Old Man, Wagner, and The Scholars, but the wonder of it—the wonder of the man who dared use it and the wonder of the mysteries it unfolds.[5] /64/

But within the wonder is the terror of its fascination and compulsion, beckoning man into the peculiar dilemma of modern times. On the one hand is human limitation and finiteness, the necessary postulate and the first step in the Christian experience. On the other, with the old catechism wearing thin, it is the compulsion of modern man to deny his limitations, press ever further into the mysteries of a universe which appears steadily to yield more and more of its secrets to his inquiring mind. To rest content with his limitations seems to deny his own God-given powers; and yet to challenge the mystery is somehow evil and portends not only present suffering but, such are the echoes that thunder in his ears, the horrors of eternity.

[5] Paul H. Kocher, in his introduction to *Doctor Faustus* (Crofts Classics ed. New York, Appleton-Century-Crofts, 1950, p. viii), sees this, on whatever authority, as related directly to Marlowe's personal experiences: ". . . his imagination leaped to the wonder and terror of the deeds of magic, and the religious conflict drew powerfully on feelings which he was undergoing in his own life. It was for him the perfect theme." It is worth noting, now that we have reached in our study the era of modern drama when biographical information accumulates, that such suggestions—they can seldom be more than that—about the "involvement" of the artist in his fictions increase. Berdyaev, for instance, makes them repeatedly about Dostoevski: "The destiny of his characters is his own, their doubts and dualities are his, their iniquities are the sins hidden in his own soul." (*Dostoievsky*, p. 32) /160/

Why wert thou not a creature wanting soul?
Or why is this immortal that thou hast?

[V, ii, 169–70]

asks Faustus in his last despairing moments. To the medieval theology which held that man *is* because he believes, the Renaissance replied that man is because he thinks and acts and discovers. Neither one, as Marlowe presents Faustus' dilemma, is wholly right or wholly wrong. The world of certainties is no longer intact, and we are only a step from the riddles and the eternal questioning that harrassed the Karamazovs. In the world of tragedy, the hero can only take the road of experiment. He must follow his bent, take action, and live it through. By contrast, in Goethe's version of the story, Faust has divine sanction. "The Prologue in Heaven" dramatizes a quite different universe, as amidst its harmonies God specifically commends Faust's inquiring mind and authorizes the pact with the Devil. The Goethean Faust knows melancholy and frustration. He gets himself (and Gretchen) into a sad scrape. But he never experiences the terror of the Elizabethan hero's dilemma or takes so bold a risk or suffers his despair. He adjusts himself nicely to Gretchen's death, and in the end his actions are brought into harmony with good nineteenth-century humanitarianism.

The end of Marlowe's play shows, of course, that (like the tragic Karamazovs) Faustus could not live out his idea. But between the disillusioned scholar of the first scene and the /65/ agonizing, ecstatic figure of the final scene there is a notable difference. He enters, not alone this time, but with the Scholars; and for the first time in the play he has normal, compassionate discourse with his fellows. His role of demigod over, he is human once more, a friend and befriended. "Ah, gentlemen, hear me with patience," says he who has but recently lorded it over all creation. His friends now seem more "sweet" (as he thrice addresses them) than any princely delicate or Signiory of Emden. Although the thrill of his exploits still lingers— "And what wonders I have done all Germany can witness, yea all the world . . ." —he is humble and repentant. He longs to be able to weep and pray but imagines in his despair that devils draw in his tears and hold his hands as he would lift them up. He confesses to the Scholars the miserable source of his cunning. Knowing his doom is near, he refuses their intercession and bids them "Talk not of me, but save yourselves and depart." They retire, like Oedipus' children at Colonus, for the hero to meet his fate alone. "Gentlemen, farewell," he says as they go. "If I live till morning I'll visit you; if not, Faustus is gone to hell."

If to the orthodox it is more a sinner's fate than a hero's, there is something of the classic apotheosis in Faustus' final moments. He transcends the man he was. He goes out no craven sinner but violently, speaking the rage and despair of all mankind who would undo the past and stop the clock against the inevitable reckoning. The grandeur of conception of his earlier worldly imaginings gains a kind of sublimity.

> Stand still, you ever-moving spheres of heaven,
> That time may cease and midnight never come.
>
> [V, ii, 133–4]

Like Job in the agony of his suffering, he has visions never vouchsafed in his days of prosperity. The nearer to Hell, the closer he is to Heaven:

> O I'll leap up to my God! Who pulls me down?
> See, see, where Christ's blood streams in the firmament!—
> One drop would save my soul—half a drop! ah, my Christ!
>
> [V, ii, 142–4]

He asks no questions now; he sees with his own eyes: first the Christ of mercy, then the God of wrath as He "Stretcheth out /66/ his arm and bends his ireful brows." He longs to be hidden under hills, thence to be borne aloft to heaven in the volcano's breath; he would be dissolved into a cloud and thus ascend; he would be turned into a beast with no immortal soul: "All beasts are happy . . ." It is eternity that appals him, the consequence of his living, immortal soul. He curses the parents who engendered him, he curses Lucifer, and (most justly) himself. He does not hide his eyes. "My God, my God, look not so fierce on me!"

> Adders and serpents, let me breathe awhile!
> Ugly hell, gape not—come not, Lucifer—
> I'll burn my books—ah, Mephistophilis!
>
> [V, ii, 185–7]

The Devils lead him off, amidst thunder. If he is more sinning than sinned against, he yet has shown great capacities for good as well as evil, and we cannot feel that perfect justice has been done. Theologically, of course, Faustus in his extremity was mistaken: it is never too late to ask and receive God's mercy and pardon. Or, does Marlowe present him as still unpurged of his pride ("And what wonders I have done all Germany can witness, yea all the world . . ."), a sinner not wholly repentant? He does not completely abase himself in self-loathing (as a good Christian would) nor accept without demur a fate which he knows, according to the contract, is just. Rather, he resists his fate, imagines impossible evasions, clings to every precious second of remaining life. Perhaps Marlowe believed that Faustus was doomed no matter how humble his repentance; or he may have conceived him as so hardened in his rationalism as to believe faith a mere function of reason. But the final scene gives a sense, not so much of the justice and goodness of the universe as of the transcendent human individual, caught in the consequences of a dilemma which, granted the conditions of his times, it was impossible for any imaginative man wholly to avoid. /67/

Doctor Faustus

WOLFGANG CLEMEN

Marlowe's *Doctor Faustus*[1] signalizes a new stage in the history of English drama in so far as here for the first time a playwright embodied in dramatic form a symbolic representation of his own spiritual wrestlings. A spiritual conflict had, it is true, been dramatized in the Morality Plays—in *Everyman,* for example. There, however, it had been the universal human conflict between good and evil, entirely divorced from the individual standpoint of the playwright. In contrast to this, although to some extent he employs the same technique as the Moralities, Marlowe endows Faustus with his own personal problems, and dramatizes his own conflicting /147/ ideas about the fundamental issues of human life.[2] Thus *Doctor Faustus* develops into a spiritual tragedy, in the sense that the external circumstances and events of the play no longer have any intrinsic value, but are significant only in so far as they enable us to understand Faustus's spiritual state and to see what goes on inside his mind. In this context we may disregard the interpolated episodes, which were provided partly as comic relief and partly to pander to the audience's fondness for spectacle; Marlowe's authorship of these episodes is very questionable, and in any case they do not represent the core of the play.[3] *Doctor Faustus* is, like *Tamburlaine,* a single-character

Reprinted from *English Tragedy before Shakespeare,* trans. by T. S. Dorsch (London: Methuen & Co., 1961).

[1] Greg is followed in placing *Faustus* late in Marlowe's development, though not later than *Edward II.* /147/

[2] Here and later, cf. Ellis-Fermor, *Christoper Marlowe* (London, 1927), Chap. V.

[3] Even in the other parts the state of the text makes judgement of the play difficult; however, as far as the thesis of his book is concerned, the comments made above can be justified in the face of all textual uncertainties. Cf. Greg, *The Tragical History of the Life and Death of Dr. Faustus: A Conjectural Reconstruction,* Oxford, 1950; *Marlowe's Doctor Faustus, 1604–1616* (esp. pp. 97 ff. for detailed discussion of the problem); Wilson, *Marlowe and the Early Shakespeare* (Oxford, 1953).

play, in that the action proceeds entirely from the central figure and is entirely dependent on him; with the difference, however, that this action is not kept in motion, as in *Tamburlaine,* by the 'acting' and willing of the hero, but represents, as in *Everyman,* the temptations, conflicts, and inner struggles by which Faustus himself is beset. The other characters have therefore very little existence of their own; Faustus's antagonists are not human beings, but ultimately supernatural powers which ally themselves with the forces in his own soul.[4]

This specific pattern is responsible for some of the essential qualities in Faustus's speeches. Although his soliloquies and longer speeches do not by any means take up the greatest amount of space in the play, for it abounds in dialogue, they are nevertheless its lifeblood, and the most important part of what it has to say.

These speeches are the natural vehicle for the expression of the spiritual warfare and the conflicts of ideas that take place in Faustus himself, the successive stages of which also determine the external structure of the play. This no longer takes the form of parallel /148/ scenes presenting contrasts or variations on a theme,[5] but is a true sequence of scenes which have their basis entirely in Faustus's own development. Thus Marlowe in this play advances a further step towards dramatic unity, towards a full internal coherence in the dramatic structure.[6] Not only is Faustus himself on the stage during the greater part of the play, not only does he sustain its spirit from beginning to end, but his speeches and soliloquies open before us a path of spiritual experience the different stages of which are organically related to one another. This was not the case in *Tamburlaine.* There the longer speeches merely represented variously stated expressions of the same mental attitude and of the same determination on the protagonist's part to impose his will on others; they cannot be said to give us any feeling of development in him.

The internal conflict which we see going on through all of

[4] Cf. Poirier, *Christopher Marlowe* (London, 1951), p. 114. Fischer, *Zur Kunstentwicklung der englischen Tragödie* (Strassburg, 1893), p. 134, adopts a different standpoint.

[5] Cf. Schirmer, *Geschichte der englischen Literatur,* Vol. I 1954, p. 251.

[6] With the reservations applied to the text, however; see p. 148, note 2. Cf. also Wilson, op. cit., pp. 70 ff.

Faustus's speeches and soliloquies may affect their structure and diction. This is to be seen happening already in the opening soliloquy, with which Goethe's presentation of Faust has so often been compared. Here is a short excerpt:

> 'Stipendium peccati mors est.' Ha! 'Stipendium,' etc.
> The reward of sin is death: that's hard.   [Reads.
> 'Si pecasse negamus, fallimur
> Et nulla est in nobis veritas.'
> If we say that we have no sin,
> We deceive ourselves, and there is no truth in us.
> Why, then, belike we must sin,
> And so consequently die;
> Ay, we must die an everlasting death.
>
>   [I, i, 39–47][7]

In this, as in many other passages, Latin or English sayings in the form of moral maxims and *dicta* are introduced, and at first sight it might seem that the same thing is being done here as was done by Seneca and his direct imitators in England, namely, that epigrams /149/ and sententious maxims are being dragged in at every conceivable opportunity. But in *Faustus* these sayings have an entirely different function, both in the text of the play and in the train of thought. They are not just rhetorical adornments imposed on the speeches; they are judgments that Faustus arrives at for himself, truths that he lays out before himself for examination, and which call out in him new questions or contradictions. There is serious meaning in these maxims of his; they represent for him the heads round which his thoughts revolve.

Analysis of this soliloquy as a whole, as of the majority of Faustus's speeches and soliloquies, shows that in this play we have got away from the form of set speech which deals successively, according to a plan prescribed in advance, with stereotyped themes and motifs; in its place we have self-communion, which evolves according to the promptings of the moment. Up till this time the practice of systematizing the set speech and tricking it out with rhetorical devices had stifled and deadened the processes of real thought and feeling. Here, however, Faustus is actually thinking at the same time as he is speaking; the speech grows step by step, keeping pace with the progress of his thoughts, and this is a very

---

[7] This speech should probably be printed as prose; cf. Greg's *Conjectural Reconstruction*, p. 3.

significant fact for the future development of dramatic speech. The voicing of genuine doubt and irresolution has taken the place here of the old see-saw of argument and counter-argument, and instead of a character talking to himself, using his speech as a means of self-revelation for the benefit of the audience, we have true soliloquy; instead of quotations and maxims with a purely decorative function, we have personal judgements which the speaker has painfully arrived at by puzzling them out for himself.

There are some exceptions, of course. A few of Faustus's speeches follow the earlier method of providing internal directions for stage-business [e.g., I, iii, 1–15] or merely reporting action [e.g., III, i, 1–25]. Others again are reminiscent of the wishful thinking that was so characteristic of Tamburlaine's speeches, for Faustus shares with Tamburlaine his aspirations towards the remote, the fabulous, and the unattainable.[8] In a good many passages, however, it is evident that a new language has been created to express hesitation /150/ and irresolution and the fluctuations of a mind torn by changing moods—for the expression, in short, of spiritual conflict. Thus the handling of the soliloquy in such a way that for the first time in English drama it reproduces the actual inner experience of a soliloquy has led in this play to the development of a new type of speech, and one that is unmistakably different from anything that had been heard before. This is illustrated in the following two short soliloquies, neither of which expresses any particular 'point of view', and 'plan', any *ad hoc* form of self-revelation; on the other hand, they both mirror exactly what goes on in Faustus's mind in those moments when he is alone:

> Now, Faustus, must
> Thou needs be damn'd, and canst thou not be sav'd.
> What boots it, then, to think on God or heaven?
> Away with such vain fancies, and despair;
> Despair in God, and trust in Belzebub:
> Now go not backward; Faustus, be resolute:
> Why waver'st thou? O, something soundeth in mine ear,
> 'Abjure this magic, turn to God again!'
> Ay, and Faustus will turn to God again.
> To God? he loves thee not;

[8] Cf. I. i. 79–97; I, iii, 102–14.

The God thou serv'st is thine own appetite,
Wherein is fix'd the love of Belzebub:
To him I'll build an altar and a church,
And offer lukewarm blood of new-born babes.

[II, i, 1–14]

What might the staying of my blood portend?
Is it unwilling I should write this bill?
Why streams it not, that I may write afresh?
Faustus gives to thee his soul: oh, there it stay'd!
Why shouldst thou not? is not thy soul thine own?
Then write again, *Faustus gives to thee his soul.*

[II, i, 63–8]

It is not only in the soliloquies that we are made aware of these fluctuations and conflicts in Faustus's mind; this also happens in some of the speeches that he utters in the presence of others. These /151/ often have a passionate intensity which must suggest that Marlowe was translating into dramatic speech his own personal and most deeply experienced spiritual struggles (cf. II, ii, 18–32).[9] And this is a very remarkable, indeed astonishing, thing to find in the drama of this period, not excluding Shakespeare's.

Faustus's famous last soliloquy shows how these processes of thought and feeling may be given a setting in time, and here too the irrevocability of the fleeting time is emphasized by the stage-device of the clock that strikes the half-hours from eleven o'clock to midnight. This is one of the outstanding passages of pre-Shakespearian drama; W. W. Greg describes it as 'spiritual drama keyed to its highest pitch'.[10] Here are the first twenty lines or so;

[*The clock strikes eleven.*

Ah Faustus,
Now hast thou but one bare hour to live,
And then thou must be damn'd perpetually.
Stand still, you ever moving spheres of heaven,
That time may cease, and midnight never come;
Fair Nature's eye, rise, rise again, and make
Perpetual day; or let this hour be but
A year, a month, a week, a natural day,
That Faustus may repent and save his soul!

---

[9] In the same way Tamburlaine's self-obsessed monologues might be regarded as a reflection of Marlowe's own personal preoccupations. However, the consciousness of two souls within his breast, the need to grapple with two alternatives, makes Faustus's speeches a species of dialogue with himself, a theatre of conflict.

[10] *Marlowe's Doctor Faustus, 1604–1616,* p. 10.

O lente, lente currite, noctis equi!
The stars move still, time runs, the clock will strike,
The devil will come, and Faustus must be damn'd.
O, I'll leap up to my God!—Who pulls me down?—
See, see, where Christ's blood streams in the firmament!
One drop would save my soul, half a drop: ah, my Christ!—
Ah, rend not my heart for naming of my Christ! /152/
Yet will I call on him: O, spare me, Lucifer!—
Where is it now? 'tis gone: and see, where God
Stretcheth out his arm, and bends his ireful brows!
Mountains and hills, come, come, and fall on me,
And hide me from the heavy wrath of God!
No, no!
Then will I headlong run into the earth:
Earth, gape! O, no, it will not harbour me!

[V, ii, 130–53]

It is a very long way from this to the rhetorical rant of the common run of pre-Shakespearian tragic heroes when they are at the point of death. Here it is deep spiritual experience that is being transmuted into drama, reproduced with unexampled immediacy and verisimilitude in the diction and imagery, and, too, in the exclamatory character of the soliloquy.[11] This is a true soliloquy, the utterance of a tragic hero who is overcome by a sense of desertion in the agony of his returning self-knowledge and his realization that he must carry on his struggle completely unaided. The tendency towards abstract thinking which elsewhere marks Faustus's speeches has been replaced here by the capacity to see spiritual abstractions in concrete terms as visible figures and actions, so that the spiritual conflict is transformed into something that happens before our eyes. It impresses itself on us so strongly as 'happening' for the further reason that here, probably for the first time in pre-Shakespearian drama, time is made a part of the very substance of the speech; the swift and irresistable passing of that final hour before midnight is conveyed by the unrealistic but in the dramatic sense unusually effective compression of this period of time into a speech of fifty-eight lines.[12] It is true that the soliloquy opens with the conventional apostrophe to the heavenly spheres to stand still and the appeal to the sun to go on shining through the night. However, in this instance both ap-

[11] Cf. Ellis-Fermor, op-cit., p. 68.
[12] Cf. Levin, *The Overreacher* (Cambridge, Mass., 1952), p. 128.

peals have their rise in Faustus's horror at the unstayable passing
of time. They are not just dragged in from outside, and then immediately forgotten; the image is kept alive, so that a few lines
later we read, 'The stars move still . . .' The same is /153/ true
of the later invocation to the stars [ll. 160 ff.] and the images of
heaven and the clouds, which are instinct with the agonized im-
potence of the soul that is shut off from all hope of salvation and
is 'damn'd perpetually'. Desire and the frustration of desire, aspiration and its violent disappointment, here affect the character of
the language itself, down to the very movement of the sentence
and the choice of diction. The thrusting together within a single
line of two short statements, the second of which negatives the
first and despairingly acknowledges it as something impossible of
fulfilment, may be classed as a form of antithesis, but it is antithesis which has ceased to be a mere rhetorical trick, because in
this case it has been overlaid with reality. The tendency in the
language towards a lapidary conciseness and direct simplicity, already apparent in a few of the dialogue-passages, but also to the
fore in the present speech, suggests that a new type of subject-
matter and a remarkable intensification of experience have forced
the playwright to seek out new forms of expression and style.
In passages like this we find Marlowe's most mature dramatic
writing, and the power with which Faustus's spiritual experience
is conveyed in certain scenes of the play places *Doctor Faustus*,
for all its deficiencies, at the very summit of Marlowe's achievement. /154/

"The Form of Faustus' Fortunes Good or Bad"

C. L. BARBER

Doctor Faustus tends to come apart in paraphrase. It can be turned into a fable about a Modern Man who seeks to break out of Medieval limitations. On the other hand, when one retells the story in religious terms, it tends to come out as though it were Marlowe's source, *The History of the Damnable Life and Deserved Death of Doctor John Faustus*. The truth is that the play is irreducibly dramatic. Marlowe dramatizes blasphemy, but not with the single perspective of a religious point of view: he dramatizes blasphemy as heroic endeavor. The play is an expression of the Reformation; it is profoundly shaped by sixteenth-century religious thought and ritual. But in presenting a search for magical dominion, Marlowe makes blasphemy a Promethean enterprise, heroic and tragic, an expression of the Renaissance.[1]

The emergence of a new art form puts man in a new relation to his experience. Marlowe could present blasphemy as heroic endeavor, and the tragic ironies of such endeavor, because he had the new poetic drama, which put poetry in dynamic relation to action—indeed he himself had been the most important single pioneer in creating this form, in *Tamburlaine*. This creation, in turn, depended on the new professional repertory theatre to which, when he came down from Cambridge in 1587, he brought his talents, and his need to project possibilities of human omni-

Reprinted from *The Tulane Drama Review*, VIII (1964), 92–119.
[1] This essay is adapted from a study centering on *Tamburlaine* and *Doctor Faustus*, to be entitled *Marlowe and the Creation of Elizabethan Tragedy*.

potence. The London theatre was a "place apart" of a new kind,
where drama was not presented as part of a seasonal or other social occasion but in its own right. Its stage gave a special vantage
on experience: /92/

> Only this (Gentlemen) we must perform
> The form of Faustus' fortunes good or bad.
> To patient judgements we appeal our plaud . . .
>   (7–9)[2]   [Prologue]

Marlowe, with characteristic modernity, calls his play just what
we call it—a form. He has an audience which includes gentlemen,
to whose patient judgments he appeals. In this new situation,
blasphemy can be "good or bad."

.   .   .   .   .   .

Professor Lily B. Campbell has related *Doctor Faustus* to fundamental tensions in Reformation religious experience in an
essay which considers Marlowe's hero, against the background of
Protestant casuistry, as "a case of Conscience."[3] She focuses on
Faustus' sin of despair, his inability to believe in his own salvation, a sin to which Protestants, and particularly Calvinistic
Protestants, were especially subject. They had to cope with the
immense distance of Calvin's God from the worshipper, and with
God's terrifying, inclusive justice, just alike to the predestined
elect and the predestined reprobate. And they had to do without
much of the intercession provided by the Roman church, its
Holy Mother, its Saints, its Masses and other works of salvation.
Faustus' entrance into magic is grounded in despair. He quotes

---

[2] Line references for Marlowe's plays are to *The Works of Christopher Marlowe*,
edited by C. F. Tucker Brooke, 1946 (first edition, 1910). I have modernized the
spelling. The punctuation has been modernized with an exception, the use of the
colon to indicate a pause; this feature of Marlowe's punctuation is so effectively
and consistently used that to substitute full stop or comma often involves losing part
of the sense. Almost everything I find occasion to use is in the 1604 Quarto; and I
find its readings almost always superior to those of 1616. This experience inclines me
to regard most of the 1604 text (with some obvious interpolations) as Marlowe's, or
close to Marlowe's, whereas most of the additional matter in the 1616 version seems
to me to lack imaginative and stylistic relation to the core of the play. Thus my
experience as a reader runs counter to the conclusions in favor of the 1616 Quarto
which W. W. Greg arrives at from textual study and hypothesis.

[3] "*Doctor Faustus*: a Case of Conscience," PMLA, Vol. LXVII, No. 2 (March,
1952), pp. 219–39; for Spira, pp. 225–32.

crucial texts, regularly heard as part of the Anglican service: /**93**/

> Jerome's Bible, Faustus, view it well.
> *Stipendium peccati mors est:* ha, *Stipendium peccati mors est.*
> The reward of sin is death: that's hard.
> *Si peccasse negamus. fallimur, et nulla est in nobis veritas.*
> If we say that we have no sin,
> We deceive ourselves, and there's no truth in us.
> Why then belike
> We must sin, and so consequently die.
> Ay, we must die an everlasting death:
> What doctrine call you this, *che sera, sera,*
> What will be, shall be? Divinity, adieu,
> These metaphysics of magicians
> And necromantic books are heavenly: . . .
>
>   (65–78) [I, i, 38–51]

Faustus leaves out the promises of divine grace which in the service go with "the reward of sin is death"; here, as always, he is unable to believe in God's love for him. But he does believe, throughout, in God's justice.

Miss Campbell observes that it was peculiarly the God-fearing man who was vulnerable to despair, dragged down, like Spenser's Red Cross Knight in the Cave of Despair, by a sense of his sins. What Despair in his cave makes Spenser's knight forget, by insisting on his sinfulness, is God's love; as Una tells him in snatching away the dagger: "Where Justice grows, there grows eke greater Grace." Faustus forgets this too: vivid as is his sense of the lost joys of heaven, he never once expresses any sense that God could love him in spite of his sins. ". . . Faustus will turn to God again. / To God? He loves thee not" (440–441) [II, i, 9–10]. Lucifer himself points to divine justice: "Christ cannot save thy soul, for he is just" (697) [II, ii, 85].

Miss Campbell parallels Faustus as Marlowe presents him with the experience of Francis Spira, a historical case of conscience which became an exemplar of despair for Protestants. This Italian lawyer, who in 1548 died of no outward cause, surrounded by counseling Catholic doctors but miserably certain of his own damnation, had recanted Protestant views under Catholic pressure. Earlier he had been enthusiastic in his conviction of the truth of justification by faith. In his last weeks, Spira was tor-

mented by a burning physical sensation of thirst which no drink
could assuage.

Spira, dying in terror, could no longer believe in the efficacy of
the Roman rites. Faustus embraces magical rituals; they are
some-/94/thing he can *do*. It can help in understanding his
turning to magic—and, indirectly, Marlowe's turning to poetic
drama—if we consider the tensions which were involved, for the
Elizabethan church, in the use and understanding of Holy Communion. Faustus near the end expresses his longing for communion in imagery which reflects these tensions:

> O I'll leap up to my God: who pulls me down?
> See, see, where Christ's blood streams in the firmament.
> One drop would save my soul, half a drop, ah, my Christ.
> Ah, rend not my heart for naming of my Christ,
> Yet will I call on him: O, spare me, Lucifer!
> Where is it now? 'tis gone: and see, where God
> Stretcheth out his arm, and bends his ireful brows.
>
> (1431–1438)   [V, ii, 142–8]

The immense distance away that the blood is, streaming in the
sky like the Milky Way, embodies the helplessness of the Protestant who lacks faith in his own salvation. Calvin taught that
communion could come by the lifting up of the soul to heaven,
that it was not necessary that the essence of the flesh descend
from heaven. But Faustus must try to leap up by himself, without the aid of Grace. His focus on the one drop, half a drop, that
he feels would save his soul, expresses the Reformation's tendency to isolate the individual in his act of communion, and to conceive of it, as Dom Gregory Dix underscores in his great history,
The Shape of the Liturgy, "as something passive, as a reception."[4]
At the same time, the cosmological immensity of the imagery
embodies Marlowe's characteristic sense of the vastness of the
universe and, here, of the tremendousness of the God who rules it
and yet concerns himself with every life, stretching out his arm
and bending his ireful brows.

The piety of the late Middle Ages had dwelt on miracles
where a host dripped actual blood, and had depicted scenes where
blood streamed down directly from Christ's wounds into the
chalice on the altar. The Counter-Reformation, in its own way,

---

[4] Dom Gregory Dix, *The Shape of the Liturgy* (Westminster: 1945), p. 635.

pursued such physical imagery and literal conceptions, which remained viable for the Roman Catholic world as embodiments of Grace. A hunger for this kind of physical resource appears in the way that Faustus /95/ envisages Christ's blood, visibly streaming, in drops to be drunk. But for the Elizabethan church, such thinking about Communion was "but to dream of a gross carnal feeding," in the words of the homily "Of the worthy taking of the Sacraments."[5] We have good reason to think that Marlowe had encountered Catholic ceremony during his absences from Cambridge, when the reasonable assumption is that he was working at intervals as a secret agent among Catholic English exiles and students on the Continent. The letter from the Privy Council which secured him his degree is best explained on that hypothesis, since it denies a rumor that he is "determined" to have gone beyond the seas to Reims and there to remain" (as secret Catholics were doing after graduation) and speaks of his having been employed "in matters touching the benefit of his country."[6] To have acted the part of a possible student convert would have involved understanding the Catholic point of view. And we have Marlowe the Scorner's talk, filtered through Baines, "That if there be any god or any good religion, then it is in the Papists' because the service of god is performed with more ceremonies, as elevation of the mass, organs, singing men, shaven crowns, etc. . . . That all protestants are hypocritical asses. . . ."[7]

What concerns us here is the way *Doctor Faustus* reflects the tension involved in the Protestant world's denying itself miracle in a central area of experience. Things that had seemed supernatural events and were still felt as such in Reims, were superstition or magic from the standpoint of the new Protestant focus on individual experience. Thus the abusive Bishop Bale calls the Roman priests' consecration of the elements "such a charm of

---

[5] The homily was issued in the *Seconde Tome of Homilies*, sanctioned by the Convocation of Canterbury in 1563 and "appointed to be read in all churches." It is quoted by C. W. Dugmore in *The Mass and the English Reformers* (London: 1958), p. 233. I am greatly indebted to Professor Dugmore's book, and to Dom Gregory Dix's *The Shape of the Liturgy*, throughout this discussion. Professor Dugmore, in exploring in detail Tudor views of the real presence in the elements of the Lord's Supper, and their background, brings into focus exactly the tensions that are relevant to *Doctor Faustus.*

[6] John Bakeless, *The Tragical History of Christopher Marlowe*, Vol. I, p. 77.

[7] Bakeless, *op. cit.*, Vol. I, p. 111.

/96/ enchantment as may not be done but by an oiled officer of the pope's generation."[8] Yet the Anglican church kept the basic physical gestures of the Mass, with a service and words of administration which leave open the question of how Christ's body and blood are consumed. And Anglican divines, while occasionally going all the way to the Zwinglian view of the service as simply a memorial, characteristically maintained a real presence, insisting, in Bishop Jewell's words, that "We feed not the people of God with bare signs and figures."[9] Semantic tensions were involved in this position; the whole great controversy centered on fundamental issues about the nature of signs and acts, through which the age pursued its new sense of reality.

In the church of the Elizabethan settlement, there was still, along with the Reformation's insistence that "Christ's Gospel is not a ceremonial law . . . but it is a religion to serve God, not in bondage to the figure and shadow,"[10] an ingrained assumption that the crucial physical acts of worship had, or should have, independent meaning. This was supported by the doctrine of a real though not physical presence of Christ. But for many worshippers the physical elements themselves tended to keep a sacred or taboo quality in line with the old need for physical embodiment. We can, I think, connect the restriction of the impulse for physical embodiment in the new Protestant worship with a compensatory fascination in the drama with magical possibilities and the incarnation of meaning in physical gesture and ceremony: the drama carries on, for the most part in secular terms, the preoccupation with a kind of realization of meaning which had been curtailed but not eliminated in religion. In secular life, the cult of royalty, as for example Elizabeth's magical virginity, carried it on also—bulking of course far larger than the drama for the age itself if not for posterity. /97/

In *Doctor Faustus* we have the special case where religious ritual, and blasphemous substitutes for ritual, are central in a drama. The Prayer Book's admonition about the abuse of Holy

<hr>

[8] Dugmore, *op. cit.*, p. 234, from *Selected Works*, P. S., 197. An Order of Council under Warwick in 1549 characteristically refers to "their Latin service, their conjured bread and water, with such like vain and superstitious ceremonies." *Ibid.*, 142.

[9] Dugmore, *op. cit.*, p. 229.

[10] *The First and Second Prayer Books of Edward VI* (London: 1949 [Everyman's Library, No. 448]), p. 3.

Communion strikingly illuminates Marlowe's dramatization of blasphemy:

> Dearly beloved in the Lord: ye that mind to come to the holy Communion of the body and blood of our Saviour Christ, must consider what S. Paul writeth to the Corinthians, how he exhorteth all persons diligently to try and examine themselves, before they presume to eat of that bread, and drink of that cup: for as the benefit is great, if with a truly penitent heart and lively faith we receive that holy sacrament (for then we spiritually eat the flesh of Christ, and drink his blood, then we dwell in Christ and Christ in us, we be one with Christ, and Christ with us:) so is the danger great, if we receive the same unworthily. For then we be guilty of the body and blood of Christ our Saviour. We eat and drink our own damnation, not considering the Lord's body.[11]

To eat and drink damnation describes not only Faustus' attitude but the physical embodiment of it, as we shall see in considering the ramifications of gluttony in the play.

Blasphemy implies belief of some sort, as T. S. Eliot observed in pointing, in his seminal 1918 essay, to blasphemy as crucial in Marlowe's work; blasphemy involves also, consciously or unconsciously, the magical assumption that signs can be identified with what they signify. Ministers were warned by several rubrics in the Tudor Prayer Books against allowing parishioners to convey the bread of the sacrament secretly away, lest they "abuse it to superstition and wickedness."[12] Such abuse depends on believing, or feeling, that, regardless of its context, the bread is God, so that /98/ by appropriating it one can magically take advantage of God. Spelled out in this way, the magical thinking which identifies sign and significance seems so implausible as to be trivial. But for the sort of experience expressed in *Doctor Faustus*, the identifications and displacements that matter take place at the levels where everyone is ignorant, the regions where desire seeks

[11] *Liturgical Services . . . in the Reign of Queen Elizabeth*, Parker Society, Vol. XXX, ed. William K. Clay (Cambridge: 1847), p. 189.

[12] From a rubric of the first Prayer Book of Edward VI, where the danger of such theft is made an argument against allowing the communicants to take the bread in their own hands. (*The Two Liturgies, A.D. 1549, and A.D. 1552:* etc., Parker Society, Vol. XXIX, ed. Joseph Ketley [Cambridge: 1844], p. 97.) The Second Prayer Book of Edward and the Prayer Book of Elizabeth provided that "to take away the superstition which any person hath, or might have in the bread and wine, it shall suffice that the bread be such, as is usual to be eaten at the table . . ." and that "if any of the bread or wine remain, the Curate shall have it to his own use." (*Ibid.*, pp. 282–3, and Clay, *op. cit.*, p. 198.)

blindly to discover or recover its objects. Faustus repeatedly
moves through a circular pattern, from thinking of the joys of
heaven, through despairing of ever possessing them, to embracing magical dominion as a blasphemous substitute. The
blasphemous pleasures lead back, by an involuntary logic, to a
renewed sense of the lost heavenly joys for which blasphemy
comes to seem a hollow substitute—like a stolen Host found to be
only bread after all. And so the unsatisfied need starts his Ixion's
wheel on another cycle.

The irony which attends Faustus' use of religious language to
describe magic enforces an awareness of this circular dramatic
movement. "Divinity, adieu! / These . . . necromantic books are
heavenly" (76–77) [I, i, 49–51]. What seems to be a depar-
ture is betrayed by "heavenly" to be also an effort to return.
"Come," Faustus says to Valdes and Cornelius, "make me
blest by your sage conference" (126–127) [I, i, 99–100]. And
Valdes answers that their combined skill in magic will "make all
nations to canonize us" (149) [I, i, 121]. In repeatedly using
such expressions, which often "come naturally" in the colloquial
language of a Christian society, the rebels seem to stumble un-
cannily upon words which condemn them by the logic of a situation larger than they are. So Mephistophilis, when he wants to
praise the beauty of the courtesans whom he can give to Faustus,
falls into saying:

> As wise as Saba, or as beautiful
> As was bright Lucifer before his fall.
>   (589–590)   [II, i, 155–6]

The auditor experiences a qualm of awe in recognizing how
Mephistophilis has undercut himself by this allusion to Lucifer
when he was still the star of the morning, bright with an altitude
and innocence now lost.

The last and largest of these revolutions is the one that begins
with showing Helen to the students, moves through the Old
Man's effort to guide Faustus' steps "unto the way of life,"
(1274) [V, i, 42] and /99/ ends with Helen. In urging the
reality of Grace, the Old Man performs the role of Spenser's Una
in the Cave of Despair, but Faustus can only think "Hell calls
for right" (1287) [V, i, 57]. Mephistophilis, like Spenser's
Despair, is ready with a dagger for suicide; Marlowe at this point

is almost dramatizing Spenser. Faustus asks for "heavenly Helen," "To glut the longing of my heart's desire" and "extinguish clean / Those thoughts that do dissuade me from my vow" (1320–1324) [V, i, 93–5]. The speech to Helen is a wonderful poetic fusion of many elements, combining chivalric worship of a mistress with humanist intoxication over the project of recovering antiquity. In characteristic Renaissance fashion, Faustus proposes to relieve classical myth in a Medieval way: "I will be Paris . . . wear thy colors" (1335, 1338) [V, i, 106–9]. But these secular elements do not account for the peculiar power of the speech; the full awe and beauty of it depend on hoping to find the holy in the profane. The prose source can provide a useful contrast here; Helen is described there so as to emphasize a forthright sexual appeal:

> her hair hanged down as fair as the beaten gold, and of such length that it reached down to her hams, with amorous coal-black eyes, a sweet and pleasant face, her lips red as a cherry, her cheeks of rose all colour, her mouth small, her neck white as the swan, tall and slender of personage . . . she looked round about her with a rolling hawk's eye, a smiling and wanton countenance . . .

On the stage, of course, a full description was not necessary; but Marlowe in any case was after a different kind of meaning. He gives us nothing of the sort of enjoyment that the Faust book describes in saying that Helen was "so beautiful and delightful a piece" that Faustus "made her his common concubine and bedfellow" and "could not be one hour from her . . . and to his seeming, in time she was with child."[13] There is nothing sublime about this account, but it has its own kind of strength—an easy, open-eyed relishing which implies that sensual fulfillment is possible and satisfying in its place within a larger whole. The writer of the Faust book looked at Helen with his own eyes and his own assumption that the profane and the holy are separate. But for Marlowe—it was his great, transforming contribution to /100/ the Faust myth—the magical dominion and pleasures of Dr. Faustus ambiguously mingle the divine and the human, giving to the temporal world a wonder and excitement which is appropriated, daringly and precariously, from the supernatural.

The famous lines are so familiar, out of context, as an apoth-

---

[13] *The History of the Damnable Life and Deserved Death of Dr. John Faustus* (1592), ed. by William Rose, London, n.d., p. 179 and pp. 193–4.

eosis of love, that one needs to blink to see them as they fit
into the play's motion, with the play's ironies (Eartha Kitt, telling *Life* magazine about playing Helen opposite Orson Welles,
ignored all irony, saying simply "I made him immortal with a
kiss.") By contrast with the Helen of the source, who has legs,
Marlowe's Helen is described only in terms of her face and lips;
and her beauty is *power:*

> Was this the face that launch'd a thousand ships,
> And burnt the topless towers of Ilium?
>
> (1328–1329)   [V, i, 99–100]

The kiss which follows is a way of reaching this source of power;
it goes with a prayer "Make me immortal with a kiss," and the
action is like taking communion, promising, like communion, a
way to immortality. It leads immediately to an ecstacy in which
the soul seems to leave the body: "Her lips suck forth my soul:
see where it flies!" The speech ends with a series of worshipping
gestures expressing wonder, awe, and a yearning towards encoun-
tering a fatal power. It is striking that Helen comes to be compared to Jupiter, god of power, rather than to a goddess:

> O thou art fairer than the evening air
> Clad in the beauty of a thousand stars;
> Brighter art thou than flaming Jupiter
> When he appeared to hapless Semele;
> More lovely than the monarch of the sky
> In wanton Arethusa's azured arms;
> And none but thou shall be my paramour.
>
> (1341–1348)   [V, i, 112–8]

Upward gestures are suggested by "the evening air" and "the
monarch of the sky"; Faustus' attitude towards Helen is linked
to that of hapless Semele when Jupiter descended as a flame, and
to that of the fountain nymph Arethusa when she embraced Jupiter in her spraylike, watery, and sky-reflecting arms. Consummation with the power first described in Helen's face is envisaged as dissolution in fire or water. /101/

I can imagine a common-sense objection at this point to the
effect that after all Faustus' encounter with Helen is a sexual
rhapsody, and that all this talk about it does not alter the fact,
since after all a kiss is a kiss. Mistresses, it could be added, are
constantly compared to heaven and to gods, and lovers often feel,
without being blasphemers, that a kiss makes mortality cease to

matter. But it is just here that, at the risk of laboring the obvious, I want to insist that Marlowe's art gives the encounter meaning both as a particular kind of sexual experience *and* as blasphemy.

The stage directions of the 1604 text bring the Old Man back just at the moment when Faustus in so many words is making Helen into heaven:

> Here will I dwell, for heaven be in these lips
> And all is dross that is not Helena:
> > *Enter old man.*
> > (1333–1334)   [V, i, 104–5]

This figure of peity is a presence during the rest of the speech; his perspective is summarized after its close: "Accursed Faustus, miserable man, / That from thy soul exclud'st the grace of Heaven."

Another perspective comes from the earlier scenes in the play where the nature of heaven and the relation to it of man and devil is established in conversations between Mephistophilis and Faustus. For example, the large and final line in the later scene, "And all is dross that is not Helena," has almost exactly the same movement as an earlier line of Mephistophilis' which ends in "heaven."

> And, to be short, when all the world dissolves,
> And every creature shall be purified,
> All place shall be hell that is not heaven.
> > (556–559)   [II, i, 122–4]

One does not need to assume a conscious recognition by the audience of this parallel, wonderfully ironic as it is when we come to hear it as an echo.[14] What matters is the recurrence of similar gestures in language about heaven and its substitutes, so that a meaning of heaven, and postures towards it, are established. /102/

The most striking element in this poetic complex is a series of passages involving a face:

> Why, this is hell, nor am I out of it:
> Think'st thou that I, that saw the face of God,
> And tasted the eternal joys of heaven,

---

[14] The echo was fiirst pointed out to me by Professor James Alfred Martin, Jr. of Union Theological Seminary.

> Am not tormented with ten thousand hells,
> In being depriv'd of everlasting bliss?
>
> (312–316)   [I, iii, 76–80]

Just as Faustus' rapt look at Helen's face is followed by his kiss, so in the lines of Mephistophilis, "saw the face of God" is followed by "tasted the eternal joys of heaven."

Both face and taste are of course traditional religious imagery, as is motion upward and downward. Marlowe's shaping power composes traditional elements into a single complex gesture and imaginative situation which appears repeatedly. The face is always high, something above to look up to, reach or leap up to, or to be thrown down from:

Faustus. Was not that Lucifer an angel once?

Mephistophilis. Yes, Faustus, and most dearly lov'd of God.

Faustus. How comes it then that he is prince of devils?

Mephistophilis. Oh, by aspiring pride and insolence;
For which God threw him from the face of heaven.

> (300–304)   [I, iii, 65–9]

A leaping-up complementary to this throwing-down, with a related sense of guilt, is expressed in Faustus' lines as he enters at midnight, about to conjure and eagerly hoping to have "these joys in full possession":

> Now that the gloomy shadow of the night,
> Longing to view Orion's drizzling look,
> Leaps from th' antarctic world unto the sky,
> And dims the welkin with her pitchy breath,
> Faustus, begin thine incantations . . .
>
> (235–239)   [I, iii, 1–5]

Here the reaching upward in *leaps* is dramatized by the word's position as a heavy stress at the opening of the line. There is a guilty suggestion in *gloomy*—both discontented and dark—linked with *longing to view*. An open-mouthed panting is suggested by *pitchy breath,* again with dark associations of guilt which carry /103/ through to Faustus' own breath as he says his *incantations* (itself an open-throated word). The whole passage has a grotesque, contorted quality appropriate to the expression of an almost unutterable desire, at the same time that it magnificently affirms this desire by throwing its shadow up across the heavens.

A more benign vision appears in the preceding scene, where the magician Valdes promises Faustus that "serviceable spirits" will attend:

> Sometime like women, or unwedded maids,
> Shadowing more beauty in their airy brows
> Than has the white breasts of the queen of love.
>
> (156–158)   [I, i, 128–30]

Here we get an association of the breast with the face corresponding to the linkage elsewhere of tasting power and joy with seeing a face. The lines suggest by "airy brows" that the faces are high (as well as that the women are unsubstantial spirits).

The complex we have been following gets its fullest and most intense expression in a passage of Faustus' final speech, where the imagery of communion with which we began is one element. To present it in this fuller context, I quote again:

> The stars move still, time runs, the clock will strike,
> The devil will come, and Faustus must be damn'd.
> O I'll leap up to my God; who pulls me down?
> See, see, where Christ's blood streams in the firmament.
> One drop would save my soul, half a drop, ah, my Christ.
> Ah, rend not my heart for naming of my Christ,
> Yet will I call on him: O, spare me, Lucifer!
> Where is it now? 'tis gone: and see, where God
> Stretcheth out his arm, and bends his ireful brows:
>
> (1429–1437)   [V, ii, 140–8]

Here the leap is discovered to be unrealizable. Faustus' blasphemous vision of his own soul with Helen—"See, where it flies"—is matched now by "See, see, where Christ's blood streams." It is "in the firmament," as was Orion's drizzling look. A paroxysm of choking tension at once overtakes Faustus when he actually envisages drinking Christ's blood. And yet—"one drop would save my soul." Such communion is denied by the companion vision of the face, now dreadful, "ireful brows" instead of "airy brows," above and bending down in overwhelming anger. /104/

When we turn to consider the presentation of the underside of Faustus' motive, complementary to his exalted longings, the Prayer Book, again, can help us understand Marlowe. The Seventeenth of the Thirty-Nine Articles contains a warning remarkably applicable to Faustus:

As the godly consideration of Predestination, and our election in

Christ, is full of sweet, pleasant, and unspeakable comfort to godly
persons. . . . So, for curious and carnal persons, lacking the spirit of
Christ, to have continually before their eyes the sentence of God's
Predestination, is a most dangerous downfall, whereby the Devil doth
thrust them either into desperation, or into wretchlessness of most
unclean living, no less perilous than desperation.[15]

Faustus is certainly a "curious and carnal person," and he has
"the sentence of God's Predestination" continually before his
eyes, without "the spirit of Christ." The Article relates this characteristically Calvinist predicament to the effort to use the body
to escape despair: "wretchlessness" (for which the New English
Dictionary cites only this instance) seems to combine wretched-
ness and recklessness. The phrase "most unclean living" suggests
that the appetites become both inordinate and perverse.

The psychoanalytic understanding of the genesis of perversions
can help us to understand how, as the Article says, such unclean
living is spiritually motivated—like blasphemy, with which it is
closely associated. We have noticed how blashemy involves a
magical identification of action with meaning, of sign with
significance. A similar identification appears in perversion as
Freud has described it. Freud sees in perversions a continuation
of the secondary sexual satisfactions dominant in childhood. The
pervert, in this view, is attempting, by repeating a way of using
the body in relation to a certain limited sexual object, to recover
or continue in adult life the meaning of a relationship fixed on
this action and object in childhood. So, for example, the sucking
perversions may seek to establish a relationship of dependence by
eating someone more powerful. Faustus lives for twenty-four
years "in all voluptuousness," in "wretchlessness of most unclean
living": it is the meanings that he seeks in sensation that make
his pleasures unclean, violations of taboo. We have seen how
what /105/ he seeks from Orion or from Helen is an equivalent
for Christ's blood, how the voluptuousness which is born of his
despair is an effort to find in carnal satisfactions an incarnation.
Perversion can thus be equivalent to a striving for a blasphemous
communion. In the same period that T. S. Eliot wrote the essay
in which he pointed to the importance of Marlowe's blasphemy,
his poem *Gerontion* expressed a vision of people in the modern

[15] Clay, *op. cit.*, p. 189.

world reduced to seeking spiritual experience in perverse sensuality and aestheticism:

> In the juvescence of the year
> Came Christ the tiger
>
> In depraved May, dogwood and chestnut, flowering judas,
> To be eaten, to be divided, to be drunk
> Among whispers; by Mr. Silvero,
> With caressing hands, at Limoges
> Who walked all night in the next room;
> By Hakagawa, bowing among the Titians;
> Madame de Tornquist, in the dark room,
> Shifting the candles; Fräulein von Kulpe,
> Who turned in the hall, one hand on the door.

As I read the elusive chronology of Eliot's poem, Marlowe would have envisaged Helen in the luxuriance of a "depraved May" associated with the Renaissance, from which we come down, through a characteristically telescoped syntax, to the meaner modern versions of a black mass. What immediately concerns us here is the seeking of incarnation in carnal and aesthetic satisfactions. The perverse has an element of worship in it.

When we consider the imagery in *Doctor Faustus* in psychoanalytic terms, an oral emphasis is very marked, both in the expression of longings that reach towards the sublime and in the gluttony which pervades the play and tends towards the comic, the grotesque, and the terrible. It is perhaps not fanciful to link the recurrent need to leap up which we have seen with an infant's reaching upward to mother or breast, as this becomes fused in later life with desire for women as sources of intoxicating strength: the face as a source of power, to be obliviously kissed, "airy brows" linked to "the white breasts of the queen of love." The two parents seem to be confused or identified so that the need appears in fantasies of somehow eating the father, panting for Orion's /106/ drizzling look. This imagery neighbors directly religious images, Christ's streaming blood, the taste of heavenly joys.

It is because Faustus has the same fundamentally acquisitive attitude towards both secular and religious objects that the religious joys are unreachable. The ground of the attitude that sustenance must be gained by special knowledge or an illicit bargain with an ultimately hostile power is the deep conviction that sustenance will not be given freely, that life and power must come from a being who condemns and rejects Faustus. We can see his blasphemous need, in psychoanalytic terms, as fixation or regression to infantile objects and attitudes, verging towards perverse developments of the infantile pursued and avoided in obscure images of sexual degradation. But to keep the experience in the perspective with which Marlowe's culture saw it, we must recognize that Faustus' despair and obsessive hunger go with his inability to take part in Holy Communion. In Holy Communion, he would, in the words of the Prayer Book, "spiritually eat the flesh of Christ, and drink his blood . . . dwell in Christ . . . be one with Christ." In the Lord's Supper the very actions towards which the infantile, potentially disruptive motive tends are transformed, for the successful communicant, into a way of reconciliation with society and the ultimate source and sanction of society. But communion can only be reached by "a truly contrite heart" which recognizes human finitude, and with "a lively faith" in the possibility of God's love. Psychoanalytic interpretation can easily lead to the misconception that when we encounter infantile or potentially perverse imagery in a traditional culture it indicates, *a priori,* neurosis or degradation. Frequently, on the contrary, such imagery is enacted in ritual and used in art as a way of controlling what is potentially disruptive.[16] We are led by these considerations to difficult issues about the status and limits of psychoanalytic interpretation beyond the scope of this essay, and to ultimate issues about whether worship is necessary which each of us must settle as we can. /107/

But for our purposes here, the necessary point is the perspective which the possibility of Holy Communion gives within Marlowe's play. Tragedy involves a social perspective on individual experience; frequently this perspective is expressed by reference to ritual or ceremonial acts, acts whose social and moral meaning is felt immediately and spontaneously. The hero one way or another abuses the ritual because he is swept away by the currents of deep aberrant motives associated with it, motives which

---

[16] In an essay on "Magical Hair" (*Journal of the Royal Anthropological Institute,* V. 88, Pt. II, pp. 147–169) the anthropologist Edmund Leach has made this point in a most telling way in evaluating the psychoanalytic assumptions of the late Dr. Charles Berg in his book *The Unconscious Significance of Hair.*

it ordinarily serves to control. In *Doctor Faustus* this public, social ritual is Holy Communion. How deeply it is built into sensi-
bility appears, for example, when Faustus stabs his arm:

> My blood congeals, and I can write no more.
>
> .   .   .   .
>
> *Faustus gives thee his soul.* Ah, there it stayed.
> Why shouldst thou not? Is not they soul thy own?
>
> (494, 499–500)   [II, i, 61; 66–7]

This is the crucial moment of the black mass, for Faustus is imi-
tating Christ in sacrificing himself—but to Satan instead of to
God. A moment later he will repeat Christ's last words, "Con-
summatus est." His flesh cringes to close the self-inflicted wound,
so deeply is its meaning understood by his body.

The deep assumption that all strength must come from consuming another accounts not only for the desperate need to leap
up again to the source of life, but also for the moments of reckless elation in fantasy. Faustus uses the word "fantasy" in exactly
its modern psychological sense:

> . . . your words have won me at the last,
> To practice magic and concealed arts:
> Yet not your words only, but mine own fantasy,
> Which will receive no object, for my head
> But ruminates on necromantic skill.
>
> (129–133)   [I, i, 102–6]

Here "ruminates" carries on the imagery of gluttony. Moving
restlessly round the circle of his desires, Faustus wants more from
nature than nature can give, and gluttony is the form his "unclean living" characteristically takes. The verb "glut" recurs:
"How am I glutted with conceit of this!" "That heavenly Helen
. . . to glut the longing. . . ." The Prologue summarizes his career
in the /108/ same terms,[17] introducing like an overture the
theme of rising up by linking gluttony with a flight of Icarus:

> Till swoll'n with cunning, of a self conceit,
> His waxen wings did mount above his reach,

[17] I first became aware of this pattern of gluttonous imagery in teaching a co-
operative course at Amherst College in 1947—before I was conscious of the blasphemous complex of taste, face, etc. Professor R. A. Brower pointed to the prologue's
talk of glut and surfeit as a key to the way Faustus' career is presented by imagery
of eating. His remark proved an Open Sesame to the exploration of an "imaginative
design" comparable to those he exhibits so delicately and effectively in his book,
The Fields of Light (Oxford: 1951). This pattern later fell into place for me in
relation to the play's expression of the blasphemous motives which I am analyzing.

> And melting heavens conspir'd his overthrow.
> For falling to a devilish exercise,
> And glutted now with learnings golden gifts,
> He surfeits upon cursed Negromancy.
>
> (20–25)   [Prologue]

On the final night, when his fellow scholars try to cheer Faustus, one of them says, " 'Tis but a surfeit, never fear, man." He answers, "A surfeit of deadly sin, that hath damn'd both body and soul" (1364–7) [V, ii, 36–8]. How accurately this exchange defines the spiritual, blasphemous motivation of his hunger!

Grotesque and perverse versions of hunger appear in the comedy. Like much of Shakespeare's low comedy, the best clowning in *Doctor Faustus* spells out literally what is metaphorical in the poetry. No doubt some of the prose comedy, even in the 1604 Quarto, is not by Marlowe; but when the comic action is a burlesque that uses imaginative associations present in the poetry, its authenticity is hard to doubt. Commentators are often very patronizing about the scene with the Pope, for example; but it carries out the motive of gluttony in a delightful and appropriate way by presenting a Pope "whose *summum bonum* is in belly cheer" (855) [not in B-text], and by having Faustus snatch his meat and wine away and render his exorcism ludicrous, baffling magic with magic. Later Wagner tells of Faustus himself carousing and swilling amongst the students with "such belly-cheer/As Wagner in his life ne're saw the like" (1343–1344) [V, i, 7–8]. The presentation of the Seven Deadly Sins, though of course traditional, comes back to hunger /109/ again and again, in gross and obscene forms; after the show is over, Faustus exclaims "O, this feeds my soul!" One could go on and on.

Complementary to the active imagery of eating is imagery of being devoured. Such imagery was of course traditional, as for example in cathedral carvings of the Last Judgment and in the Hell's mouth of the stage. With being devoured goes the idea of giving blood, also traditional but handled, like all the imagery, in a way to bring together deep implications. To give blood is for Faustus a propitiatory substitute for being devoured or torn in pieces. The relation is made explicit when, near the end, Mephistophilis threatens that if he repents, "I'll in piece-meal tear thy flesh." Faustus collapses at once into propitiation, signalled poignantly by the epithet "sweet" which is always on his hungry lips:

> Sweet Mephistophilis, intreat thy Lord
> To pardon my unjust presumption,
> And with my blood again I will confirm
> My former vow I made to Lucifer.
>
> (1307–1310)   [V, i, 78–81]

By his pact Faustus agrees to be devoured later provided that he can do the devouring in the meantime. Before the signing, he speaks of paying by using other people's blood:

> The god thou servst is thine own appetite,
> Wherein is fix'd the love of Belsabub.
> To him I'll build an altar and a church,
> And offer luke warm blood of new born babes.
>
> (443–446)   [II, i, 11–4]

But it has to be his own blood. The identification of his blood with his soul (a very common traditional idea) is underscored by the fact that his blood congeals just as he writes "gives thee his soul," and by Mephistophilis' vampire-like exclamation, as the blood clears again under the influence of his ominous fire: "O what will I not do to obtain his soul."

Faustus' relation to the Devil here is expressed in a way that was characteristic of witchcraft—or perhaps one should say, of the fantasies of witchhunters about witchcraft. Witch lore often embodies the assumption that power can be conveyed by giving and taking the contents of the body, with which the soul is identified, /110/ especially the blood. To give blood to the devil—and to various animal familiars—was the ritual expression of submission, for which in return one got special powers. Witches could be detected by the "devil's mark" from which the blood was drawn. In stabbing his arm, Faustus is making a "devil's mark" or "witch's mark" on himself.[18]

The clown contributes to this theme in his role as a common-sense prose foil to the heroic, poetic action of the protagonist. Between the scene where Faustus proposes a pact to buy Mephistophilis' service and the scene of the signing, Wagner buys a ragged but shrewd old "clown" into his service. He counts on hunger:

[18] These notions, which are summarized in most accounts of witchcraft, are spelled out at length in M. A. Murray, *The Witch-Cult in Western Europe* (Oxford: 1921), pp. 86–96 and *passim*. One may have reservations as to how far what Miss Murray describes was acted out and how far it was fantasy; but the pattern is clear.

. . . the villain is bare, and out of service, and so hungry that I know
he would give his soul to the Devil for a shoulder of mutton, though
it were blood raw.

(358–361)   [I, iv, 6–9]

We have just heard Faustus exclaim:

> Had I as many souls as there be stars,
> I'd give them all for Mephistophilis.
>
> (338–339)   [I, iii, 102–3]

But the clown is not so gullibly willing to pay all:

How, my soul to the Devil for a shoulder of mutton, though 'twere
blood raw? Not so, good friend, by 'r lady I had need to have it well
roasted, and good sauce to it, if I pay so dear.

(362–365)   [I, iv, 10–1]

After making game of the sturdy old beggar's ignorance of Latin
tags, Wagner assumes the role of the all-powerful magician:

Bind yourself presently unto me for seven years, or I'll turn all the
lice about thee into familiars, and they shall tear thee in pieces.

(377–380)   [I, iv, 19–21]

But again the clown's feet are on the ground:

Do you hear sir? you may save that labour, they are too familiar with
me already. Swounds, they are as bold with my flesh, as if they paid
for me meat and drink. /111/

This scene has been referred to as irrelevant padding put in by
other hands to please the groundlings! Clearly the clown's independence, and the *detente* of his common man's wit which brings
things down to the physical, is designed to set off the folly of
Faustus' elation in his bargain. Mephistophilis, who is to become
the hero's "familiar spirit" (as the Emperor calls him later at line
1011) [not in B-text], "pays for" his meat and drink, and in
due course will "make bold" with his flesh. The old fellow understands such consequences, after his fashion, as the high-flown
hero does not.

One final, extraordinarily complex image of surfeit appears in
the last soliloquy, when Faustus, frantic to escape from his own
greedy identity, conceives of his whole body being swallowed up
by a cloud and then vomited away:

> Then will I headlong run into the earth:
> Earth gape. O no, it will not harbour me:

> You stars that reign'd at my nativity,
> Whose influence hath allotted death and hell,
> Now draw up Faustus like a foggy mist ·
> Into the entrails of yon labouring cloud,
> That when you vomit forth into the air,
> My limbs may issue from your smoky mouths,
> So that my soul may but ascend to heaven:
>
> (1441–1449)   [V, ii, 152–60]

Taken by themselves, these lines might seem to present a very far-fetched imagery. In relation to the imaginative design we have been tracing they express self-disgust in terms exactly appropriate to Faustus' earlier efforts at self-aggrandizement. The hero asks to be swallowed and disgorged, anticipating the fate his sin expects and attempting to elude damnation by separating body and soul. Yet the dreadful fact is that these lines envisage death in a way which makes it a consummation of desires expressed earlier. Thus in calling up to the "stars which reigned at my nativity," Faustus is still adopting a posture of helpless entreaty towards powers above. He assumes their influence to be hostile but nevertheless inescapable; he is still unable to believe in love. And he asks to be "drawn up," "like a foggy mist," as earlier the "gloomy shadow," with its "pitchy breath," sought to leap up. The whole plea is couched as an eat-or-be-eaten bargain: you may eat my body if you will save my soul. /112/

In the second half of the soliloquy Faustus keeps returning to this effort to distinguish body and soul. As the clock finally strikes, he asks for escape in physical dissolution:

> Now, body, turn to air,
> Or Lucifer will bear thee quick to hell:
> *Thunder and lightning.*
> Oh soul, be chang'd into little water-drops,
> And fall into the ocean, ne'er be found:
>
> (1470–1473)   [V, ii, 180–3]

It is striking that death here is envisaged in a way closely similar to the visions of sexual consummation in the Helen speech. The "body, turn to air," with the thunder and lightning, can be related to the consummation of hapless Semele with flaming Jupiter; the soul becoming little water-drops recalls the showery consummation of Arethusa. Of course the auditor need not notice these relations, which in part spring naturally from a pervasive

human tendency to equate sexual release with death. The auditor does feel, however, in these sublime and terrible entreaties,
that Faustus is still Faustus. Analysis brings out what we all feel
—that Faustus cannot repent. Despite the fact that his attitude
towards his motive has changed from exaltation to horror, he is
still dominated by the same motive—body and soul are one, as he
himself said in the previous scene: "hath damned both body and
soul." The final pleas themselves confirm his despair, shaped as
they are by the body's desires and the assumptions those desires
carry.

·   ·   ·   ·   ·

I said at the outset that because Marlowe dramatizes blasphemy as heroic endeavor, his play is irreducibly dramatic. But in
the analytical process of following out the themes of blasphemy
and gluttony, I have been largely ignoring the heroic side of the
protagonist, the "Renaissance" side of the play. It is high time to
emphasize that Marlowe was able to present blasphemy as he
did, and gluttony as he did, only because he was able to envisage
them as something more or something else: "his dominion that
exceeds in this / Stretcheth as far as doth the mind of man." We
have been considering how the play presents a shape of longing
and fear /113/ which might have lost itself in the fulfillment of
the Lord's Supper or become obscene and hateful in the perversions of a witches' sabbath. But in fact Faustus is neither a saint
nor a witch—he is Faustus, a particular man whose particular
fortunes are defined not by ritual but by drama.

When the Good Angel tells Faustus to "lay that damned book
aside . . . that is blasphemy," the Evil Angel can answer in terms
that are not moral but heroic:

> Go forward, Faustus, in that famous art
> Wherein all nature's treasury is contain'd:
> Be thou on earth as Jove is in the sky,
> Lord and commander of these elements.
> (102–105)   [II, i, 75–8]

It is because the alternatives are not simply good or evil that
Marlowe has not written a morality play but a tragedy: there is
the further, heroic alternative. In dealing with the blasphemy, I
have emphasized how the vision of magic joys invests earthly

things with divine attributes; but the heroic quality of the magic depends on fusing these divine suggestions with tangible values and resources of the secular world.

This ennobling fusion depends, of course, on the poetry, which brings into play an extraordinary range of contemporary life:

> From Venice shall they drag huge argosies
> And from America the golden fleece
> That yearly stuffs old Philip's treasury.
>
> (159–161)   [I, i, 131–3]

Here three lines draw in sixteenth-century classical studies, exploration and commercial adventure, national rivalries, and the stimulating disruptive influence of the new supply of gold bullion. Marlowe's poetry is sublime because it extends desire so as to envisage as objects of passion the larger life of society and nature: "Was this the face that . . ."—that did what? ". . . launched a thousand ships." "Clad in the beauty of . . ."—of what? ". . . a thousand stars." *Doctor Faustus* is a sublime play because Marlowe was able to occupy so much actual thought and life by following the form of Faustus' desire. At the same time, it is a remorselessly objective, ironic play, because it dramatizes the ground of the desire which /114/ needs to ransack the world for objects; and so it expresses the precariousness of the whole enterprise along with its magnificence.

Thus Faustus' gluttonous preoccupation with satisfactions of the mouth and throat is also a delight in the power and beauty of language: "I see there's virtue in my heavenly words." Physical hunger is also hunger for knowledge; his need to depend on others, and to show power by compelling others to depend on him, is also a passion for learning and teaching. Academic vices and weaknesses shadow luminous academic virtues: there is a fine, lonely, generous mastery about Faustus when he is with his colleagues and the students; and Mephistophilis too has a moving dignity in expounding unflinchingly the dreadful logic of damnation to Faustus as to a disciple. The inordinate fascination with secrets, with what cannot be named, as Mephistophilis cannot name God, includes the exploring, inquiring attitude of "Tell me, are there many heavens above the moon?" The need to leap up becomes such aspirations as the plan to "make a bridge through the moving air / To pass the ocean with a band of men." Here we have in germ that sense of man's destiny as a vector moving through open space which Spengler described as the Faustian soul form. Faustus' alienation, which we have discussed chiefly as it produces a need for blasphemy, also motivates the rejection of limitations, the readiness to alter and appropriate the created universe—make the moon drop or ocean rise—appropriating them for *man* instead of for the greater glory of God, because the heavens are "the book of Jove's high firmament," and one can hope for nothing from Jove. Perhaps most fundamental of all is the assumption that power is something outside oneself, something one does not become (as a child becomes a man); something beyond and stronger than oneself (as God remains stronger than man); *and yet* something one can capture and ride—by manipulating symbols.

Marlowe of course does not anticipate the kind of manipulation of symbols which actually has, in natural science, produced this sort of power; Mephistophilis answers Faustus with Ptolemy, not Copernicus—let alone the calculus. But Marlowe was able to exemplify the creative function of controlling symbols by the way the form of poetic drama which he developed uses poetry. He made poetic speech an integral part of drama by exhibiting it as a mode of action: Faustus can assert about himself, "This word /115/ damnation terrifies not him, / For he confounds hell in Elysium." The extraordinary pun in "confounds hell in Elysium" suggests that Faustus is able to change the world by the way he names it, to *destroy* or *baffle* hell by *equating* or *mixing* it with Elysium.[19]

Professor Scott Buchanan, in his discussion of tragedy in *Poetry and Mathematics,* suggested that we can see tragedy as an experiment where the protagonist tests reality by trying to live a hypothesis. Elizabethan tragedy, seen in this way, can be set beside the tentatively emerging science of the period. The ritualistic assumptions of alchemy were beginning to be replaced by ideas of observation; a clear-cut conception of the experimental testing of hypothesis had not developed, but Bacon was soon to

---

[19] In a commentary on the Virgilian and Averroist precedents for this line, in *English Studies,* XLI, No. 6 (Dec. 1960), pp. 365–368, Bernard Fabian argues for a sense of it consistent with my reading here.

speak of putting nature on the rack to make her yield up her secrets. Marlowe knew Thomas Harriot: Baines reports his saying
"That Moses was but a juggler, and that one Heriots being Sir
W. Raleigh's man can do more than he." Faustus' scientific questions and Mephistophilis' answers are disappointing; but the
hero's whole enterprise is an experiment, or "experience" as the
Elizabethans would have termed it. We watch as the author puts
him on the rack.

Faustus. Come, I think hell's a fable.

Mephistophilis. Ay, think so still, 'till
      experience change thy mind.

                              (559–560)   [II, i, 125–6]

In *Tamburlaine,* Marlowe had invented a hero who creates
himself out of nothing by naming himself a demigod. By contrast with the universe assumed in a play like *Everyman,* where
everything has its right name, *Tamburlaine* assumes an open situation where new right names are created by the hero's combination of powers: he conceives a God-like identity for himself, persuades others to accept his name by the "strong enchantments"
of an Orphic speech, and imposes his name on stubborn enemies
by the physical action of "his conquering sword." This self-creat-
ing process is dramatized by tensions between what is expressed
in words and what is conveyed by physical action on the stage:
the hero declares /116/ what is to happen, and we watch to see
whether words will become deeds—whether, in the case of Tamburlaine, man will become demigod.

The high poetry, the bombast, of Marlowe and kindred Elizabethans is not shaped to express what is, whether a passion or a
fact, but to make something happen or become—it is incantation,
a willful, self-made sort of liturgy. The verbs are typically future
and imperative, not present indicative. And the hero constantly
talks about himself as though from the outside, using his own
name so as to develop a self-consciousness which aggrandizes his
identity, or cherishes it, or grieves for it: "Settle thy studies,
Faustus, and begin . . ." (29) [I, i, 1]; "What shall become
of Faustus, being in hell forever?" (1382–1383) [V, ii, 50–1].
In the opening speech, Faustus uses his own name seven times in
trying on the selves provided by the various arts. In each unit of

the speech, the words are in tension with physical gestures. As Faustus "levels at the end of every art," he reaches for successive volumes; he is looking in books for a miracle. But the tension breaks as he puts each book aside because "Yet art thou still but Faustus and a man." When finally he takes up the necromantic works, there is a temporary consummation, a present-indicative simultaneity of words and gestures: "Ay, these are those that Faustus most desires." At this point, the actor can use gesture to express the new being which has been seized, standing up and spreading his arms as he speaks the tremendous future-tense affirmation: "All things that move between the quiet poles. / Shall be at my command. . . ." At the very end of the play Faustus' language is still demanding miracles, while the *absence* of corroborating physical actions make clear that the universe cannot be equated with his self: "Stand still, you ever-moving spheres of heaven. . . ." King Lear in the storm, at the summit of Elizabethan tragedy, is similarly trying (and failing) to realize a magical omnipotence of mind: ". . . all-shaking thunder, / Smite flat the thick rotundity of the world. . . ."

The double medium of poetic drama was peculiarly effective to express this sort of struggle for omnipotence and transcendent incarnation along with its tragic and comic failure. The dramatist of genius can do two things at once: Marlowe can "vaunt his heavenly verse," animating the reach of Faustus' motive—and putting into /117/ his hero much that, on the evidence of his other plays and of his life (beyond our scope here), was in himself. At the same time he is judge and executioner, bringing his hero remorselessly to his terrible conclusion. At the end of the text of *Doctor Faustus,* Marlowe wrote "*Terminat hora diem, Terminat Author opus.*" As my friend Professor John Moore has remarked, it is as though he finished the play at midnight! The final hour ends Faustus' day; but Marlowe is still alive. As the author, he has been in control: *he* has terminated the work and its hero. This is another kind of power from that of magical dominion, a power that depends on the resources of art, realized in alliance with the "patient judgements" in an audience. It has not been a drumhead trial and execution, moveover, based on arbitrary, public-safety law. Though the final Chorus pulls back, in relief, to such a position, we have seen in detail, notably in the final soliloquy, how the fate of the hero is integral with his motive. In *Tamburlaine,* it was the hero who said "I thus conceiving and subduing both. . . . Shall give the world to note for all my birth, / That Vertue solely is the sum of glorie." Fundamental artistic limitations resulted from the identification of Marlowe with his protagonist in that play. But now, at the end of *Doctor Faustus,* Marlowe has earned an identity apart from his hero's—he is the author. He has done so by at once conceiving and subduing the protagonist.

The analogy between tragedy and a scapegoat ritual is very clear here: Faustus the hero has carried off into death the evil of the motive he embodied, freeing from its sin, for the moment, the author-executioner and the participating audience. The crop of stories which grew up about one devil too many, a real one, among the actors shows how popular tendencies to project evil in demons were put to work (and controlled, so far as "patient judgements" were concerned) by Marlowe. Popular experience of public executions provided, as Mr. John Holloway has recently pointed out (and Wyndham Lewis before him).[20] another paradigm for tragedy. We can add that, in Marlowe's case at least, some of the taboo quality which tends to stick to an executioner attached to the tragedian, a sense of his contamination by the sin of the /118/ victim. He proudly claims, in classical terms, the prerogative of the author who terminates the work, has done with it. But in his own life what was working in the work caught up with him by the summons to appear before the Privy Council, and the subsequent death at Deptford—whether it was a consequence of his own tendency to give way to "sudden cruelty," or a successfully camouflaged murder to get rid of a scandalous client of Thomas Walsingham. Art, even such austere art as *Doctor Faustus,* did not save the man in the author. But the author did save, within the limits of art, and with art's permanence, much that was in the man, to become part of the evolving culture in which his own place was so precarious. /119/

[20] *The Story of the Night* (London: 1961); *The Lion and the Fox* (London: 1927).

Magic and Poetry in *Doctor Faustus*

D. J. PALMER

Magic is not only the subject of *Doctor Faustus,* it is the means by which the dramatic illusion generates power and conviction. As in *Tamburlaine,* Marlowe evidently conceives the stage as an area liberated from the limitations which nature imposes on the world around; the restraining conditions of probability here seem to be in abeyance, and Marlowe's stage affords scope to realise the gigantic fantasies of his heroes. In *Doctor Faustus* the stage assumes the properties of a magic circle, within which dramatic spectacle is transformed into enchanted vision, and poetry is endowed with the power of conjuring spirits. We do wrong to feel, as many critics have done, a kind of embarrassment, or even intellectual superiority towards the necromantic elements in the play, for it is precisely through the business of magic that Marlowe effects the heightening and tension necessary to the tragic experience. Few would claim that the play maintains its tragic intensity throughout, or that a sense of structure was one of Marlowe's strengths as a playwright. The farcical episodes which occupy the middle of the action do not have a very sophisticated appeal, and whoever actually wrote them, they remain Marlowe's responsibility as the chief architect of the play. However, the clowning with the Pope, Emperor and the rest, frivolous as it is, should not obscure from us the subtler effects which Marlowe obtains from stage-magic elsewhere in the tragedy. Theatrical trickery is certainly stuff to thrill the groundlings, but the same exploitation of Faustus' supernatural powers in terms of dramatic illusion also underlies those moments of poetic rapture and tragic grandeur that constitute Marlowe's supreme achievement. There was one controlling idea behind the dramatising of the Faust-Book: that the drama, particularly the poetic drama, is itself a kind of enchantment.

Reprinted from *Critical Quarterly,* VI (1964).

The notion of drama as the art of illusion is at least as ancient as the rival view that drama imitates life; the two concepts are not really contradictory, though they have their respective origins in the literary theories of Plato and Aristotle. Shakespeare, as we should expect, lent his support to both views: Hamlet's advice to the players restates the mimetic function of drama, "whose end, both at the first /56/ and now, was and is to hold, as 'twere, the mirror up to nature", while in *The Tempest* Prospero's speech at the conclusion of the masque pays memorable tribute to the imaginative power of illusion. But most of our critical terminology for discussing drama has come down to us through the Aristotelian tradition of mimesis, and in judging characterisation and action in all kinds of drama we almost inevitably look for probability and truth to nature. Sir Philip Sidney, surveying the popular drama of his day in *The Apologie for Poetry*, scorned it for the neglect of those unities of time and place which critical authority held to be the basis of credible dramatic action:

> . . . you shal have *Asia* of the one side, and *Affrick* of the other, and so many other under-kingdoms, that the Player, when he commeth in, must ever begin with telling where he is, or els the tale wil not be conceived. Now ye shal have three Ladies walke to gather flowers, and then we must beleeve the stage to be a Garden. By and by, we heare newes of shipwracke in the same place, and then wee are to blame if we accept it not for a Rock. Upon the backe of that, comes out a hidious Monster, with fire and smoke, and then the miserable beholders are bounde to take it for a Cave. While in the meantime two Armies flye in, represented with foure swords and bucklers, and then what harde heart will not receive it for a pitched fielde? Now, of time they are much more liberall, for ordinary it is that two young Princes fall in love. After many traverces, she is got with childe, delivered of a faire boy; he is lost, groweth a man, falls in love, and is ready to get another child; and all this in two hours space . . .

Sidney did not live to see Marlowe endow the popular stage with poetic genius, but whether his criteria would have been different if he had written during the 1590s, during the flourishing of the London theatres, is of less interest than the fact that Sidney's description here suits exactly the treatment of time and place which we find in *Doctor Faustus*. The action covers twenty-four years of Faustus' life, and ranges over most of Europe in presenting his adventures: far from trying to concentrate his plot in the manner of a Corneille or a Racine, by observing on his stage the same physical limitations which would govern it as a location in the real world, Marlowe exploits the stage as a world free from the laws of time and place. His stage is exciting precisely because it is not true to nature in the respects laid down by Sidney, and evidently in this disregard for probability he was perpetuating the habits of popular drama. No doubt Marlowe's play, like those of his predecessors, would have been better constructed if more attention had been paid to the unities, affording concentration and probability, and no doubt some tightening-up along these lines would have spared us from the low farce in the middle of the play (the episodes included in the 1616 Quarto but omitted from the 1604 Quarto suggest a play of potentially variable length: with twenty-four adventure-packed years to choose from in the source book there was no lack of material). But /57/ a neo-classical *Doctor Faustus* would be a radically different play, for the most successful effects of Marlowe's tragedy are also derived from his conception of dramatic illusion. Even his poetry is employed to convince us of the reality of impossibilities.

The methods with which Marlowe, Shakespeare and their contemporaries went to work make it easy to understand why the unities of time and place were never properly accepted in Elizabethan drama. It was essentially a narrative art, transposing for the stage stories from non-dramatic sources, and retaining that multiplicity of incident which was so much to Elizabethan taste, as we can also see in the *Faerie Queene* and the *Arcadia*. The chronicle play, with its seemingly intractable material drawn from the flux of history, was a characteristic Elizabethan invention. In dramatising these narratives playwrights found certain means of compressing or externalising action in the stage conventions surviving from the moralities and interludes. Thus, Marlowe uses the rather awkward device of the Good and Bad Angels to project the conflict over Faustus' soul as though he were the everyman of the older allegorical drama, and the counsel offered by the saintly Old Man is clearly derived from the same tradition. The conventions of the soliloquy permitted Marlowe to schematise and compress a train of thought, as in the opening scene of the play, where Faustus' review and rejection of each branch of learning is presented in formal terms that summarise and represent an interior process independent of time.

The physical shape of the projecting stage itself, in a theatre open to the sky, also assisted the playwright in freeing his scenes from any localised setting.

On a stage where the laws of material reality are suspended at will, Marlowe's disregard of probability is at one with Faustus' flouting of divine commandment, and Faustus' demonic power over nature is both image and source of the drama's hold upon its spectators. We are, as literally as possible, spellbound. As with Tamburlaine's astounding progress, the spectators collaborate readily in this vicarious experience of infinitely extended power, which affords a conscious exhilaration and sense of release. At its simplest level, the illusion enlists merely a kind of wish-fulfilment or indulged fantasy; the havoc which Faustus creates at the Pope's banquet, like Tamburlaine's treatment of captive kings, is an obvious appeal to our secret and anarchic fantasies, thinly veiled in good Protestant sentiment.

Few Elizabethan playwrights had any qualms about the spectacular, and in *Doctor Faustus* Marlowe seems to exult in the power of dramatic illusion: the first entrance of Mephostophilis, the pageant of the Seven Deadly Sins, the vision of Helen, each show Marlowe's love of strong visual appeal. But the pull of the magic stage is not dependent on spectacle alone, and what Marlowe cannot present in material form he conjures in lyrical, almost ecstatic poetry, so that we are caught up in Faustus' swelling aspirations of becoming a "demi-god": /58/

> How am I glutted with conceit of this!
> Shall I make spirits fetch me what I please,
> Resolve me of all ambiguities,
> Perform what desperate enterprise I will?
> I'll have them fly to India for gold,
> Ransack the ocean for orient pearl,
> And search all corners of the new-found world
> For pleasant fruits and princely delicates;
> I'll have them read me strange philosophy
> And tell the secrets of all foreign kings;
> I'll have them wall all Germany with brass
> And make swift Rhine circle fair Wittenberg . . .
>
> [I, i, 79–90]

In later scenes there is more in this vein, which recalls Tamburlaine's vaunting speeches, where the insistent future tense opens up vistas of fantastic splendour. The characteristic Marlovian

mode extends the boundaries of the drama far beyond the physical limits of the stage, and the elemental powers of the universe
seem to attend at the summons of this mighty rhetoric. Well
might Faustus say, "I see there's virtue in my heavenly words".
The visions which haunt the imaginations of Marlowe's ambitious heroes are as much a part of the action as the machinery of
spectacular showmanship, and expressed with the vividness and
brilliance which the Elizabethans termed *enargia*. Marlowe's poetry is an important vehicle of dramatic illusion; its purpose is to
make us feel as much aware of the visions described as though we
were seeing them with our own eyes:

> Learned Faustus,
> To find the secrets of astronomy,
> Graven in the book of Jove's high firmament,
> Did mount him up to scale Olympus' top,
> Where, sitting in a chariot burning bright
> Drawn by the strength of yoked dragons' necks,
> He views the clouds, the planets, and the stars,
> The tropics, zones, and quarters of the sky,
> From the bright circle of the horned moon
> Even to the height of *primum mobile;*
> And, whirling round with this circumference
> Within the concave compass of the pole,
> From east to west his dragons swiftly glide
> And in eight days did bring him home again.
>
> [III, Prologue, 1–14]

Here the verbal tense shifts from past to present to reinforce the
illusion, and under the spell of this poetry the invisible regions
are revealed before us, transcending the narrow confines of the
stage: the poetry partakes of that power with which language
calls forth the spirits of another world. Whatever else in Marlowe's play would have displeased Sir Philip Sidney, here indeed
is that "vigor of his owne invention" which Sidney attributed to
the true poet, in a passage that draws more upon Platonism than
upon the Aristotelian doctrine of mimesis: /59/

Nature can never set forth the earth in so rich tapistry as divers Poets
have done, neither with pleasant rivers, fruitful trees, sweet smelling
flowers, nor whatsoever els may make the too much loved earth more
lovely. Her world is brasen, the Poets only deliver a golden.

By creating a world more compelling in its imaginary vastness
and beauty than the actors' scaffold which, stripped of the illu-

sion, is all that actually exists, Marlowe's verse is performing the
tasks which Elizabethans assumed to constitute the art of poetry.
To move, to persuade, to convince, were the ends to which the
poet applied his mastery over language, while the rhetoricians
and figurists documented the means by which he was able to
sway those whom he addressed.

Yet the transforming spell which this rhetoric exerts upon the
drama never rests complete, for the tragedy will show that the
magic is a cheat, and that Faustus, who would be a "demi-god",
is "but a man condemn'd to die". The tragedy demands simultaneously the breathtaking sense of infinite time and space, the
persuasive vision of supernatural wealth and beauty, and also the
awareness that these are illusions, an underlying feeling of disen-
chantment. This sense of the emptiness of Faustus' ambitions,
however vast and splendid they are, is first apparent in his interrogation of Mephostophilis, through the revelation that the
demon has come of his own accord, not under the compulsion of
Faustus' conjuring. In fact the characterisation of Mephostophilis in his grave and melancholy replies to Faustus, invests him
and the infernal regions whence he came with a reality and dignity besides which the bravado of Faustus is now seen with critical detachment as a foolish deception we can no longer share:

> F. Tell me, what is that Lucifer thy lord?
> M. Arch-regent and commander of all spirits.
> F. Was not that Lucifer an angel once?
> M. Yes, Faustus, and most dearly lov'd of God.
> F. How comes it then that he is prince of devils?
> M. O, by aspiring pride and insolence,
> For which God threw him from the face of heaven.
> F. And what are you that live with Lucifer?
> M. Unhappy spirits that fell with Lucifer,
> Conspir'd against our God with Lucifer,
> And are for ever damn'd with Lucifer.
> F. Where are you damn'd?
> M.   In hell.
> F. How comes it then that thou art out of hell?
> M. Why, this is hell, nor am I out of it.
> Think'st thou that I, who saw the face of God
> And tasted the eternal joys of heaven,
> Am not tormented with ten thousand hells
> In being depriv'd of everlasting bliss?
> O Faustus, leave these frivolous demands,

> Which strike a terror to my fainting soul. /60/
> F. What, is great Mephostophilis so passionate
> For being deprived of the joys of heaven?
> Learn thou of Faustus manly fortitude
> And scorn those joys thou never shalt possess.
>
> [I, iii, 63–86]

In this first part of the play, the initiative seems to pass from Faustus to his attendant spirit: his disbelief in the pains of hell, his hubristic blindness, strike hollow against the measured affirmation of Mephostophilis that "Where we are is hell, / And where hell is, there must we ever be", and his magic powers dwindle to a mere means of diversion when Faustus dismisses the subject and asks to be given a wife. Later, he calls upon Christ, and with a terrifying stroke of irony, he is confronted instead by Beelzebub. It seems as though the satanic powers have assumed complete control. There is a shift in the dramatic illusion; the fantasies of magic lose their conviction in the face of Mephostophilis' passionate suffering, Faustus' hubris serves as a foil to heighten the awesome reality of hell, and the demon seems paradoxically more tragic and human than the man. Having at the outset enlisted our belief in a stage free from the limitations of natural probability, Marlowe now sets off those boundless visions of enchantment against the eternal tortures of the damned, an imprisonment infinitely more terrible than the circumscription of nature's law, and in the device of this new perspective which secures our acquiescence, it is an illusion of much more compelling reality. Sufficiently compelling, at least, to foster one or two strange stories about contemporary performances, such as the following:

Certain Players at Exeter, acting upon the stage the tragical storie of Dr. Faustus the Conjurer; as a certain nomber of Devels kept everie one his circle there, and as Faustus was busie in his magicall invocations, on a sudden they were all dasht, every one harkning other in the eare, for they were all perswaded, there was one devell too many amongst them; and so after a little pause desired the people to pardon them, they could go no further with this matter; the people also understanding the thing as it was, every man hastened to be first out of dores. The players (as I heard it) contrarye to their custome spending the night in reading and in prayer got them out of the town the next morning.

The scenes with Mephostophilis in the first half of the play are a remarkable piece of dramatic writing. The creation of dialogue does not seem to have come easily to Marlowe, who preferred wherever possible the direct impact upon the audience conveyed in set speeches, with their greater scope for the soaring rhetoric of his mighty line. Even the earliest of Shakespeare's plays have a fluency and genuine engagement between the characters in dialogue that are seldom found in Marlowe's work. The dialogue between Faustus and Mephostophilis is a catechism, a formal interrogation, in which the demon expounds theology and astronomy and explains the terms of the bond Faustus wishes to make. Yet Marlowe manages to transform this rather cramped framework into a vehicle of astonishing /61/ dramatic interest: Mephostophilis is characterised through his reluctance to dwell upon the suffering that Faustus cannot grasp as real, and through those baffling retorts which reveal his unsuspected independent volition:

> F. Did not he charge thee to appear to me?
> M. No, I came hither of mine own accord.
> F. Did not my conjuring speeches raise thee? Speak.
> M. That was the cause, but yet *per accidens*.
>
> [I, iii, 43–6]

The middle scenes of the play have been universally condemned. I do not believe they can be redeemed on the grounds that the descent to mere buffoonery and triviality is a deliberate stratagem to underline Faustus' self-deception or the Devil's fradulency. The play simply does not possess that kind of unity, and our uppermost impression, that this section lacks tragic intensity, is not to be argued away by over-sophisticated interpretation. Perhaps only Shakespeare at the height of his powers was able to sublimate clowning and farcical indignities to a level of high seriousness, as in *Hamlet, King Lear,* and *Antony and Cleopatra:* even here he did not discard the knockabout-horseplay which was so firmly rooted in the traditions of popular drama. However different in tone, and whoever actually wrote them, the middle scenes in *Doctor Faustus* were licensed by dramatic usage and authorised by the source-book. That does not make them any better than they are, but we should perhaps not so much think of them as letting down the rest of the play as rather marvel at the poetic heights to which Marlowe was able to lift other parts of his material. His sins were those of omission rather than commission, though it is doubtful whether this troubled Marlowe greatly in the business of transposing the Faust Book for the stage: certain moments and situations suggested opportunities for effects of grandeur and rapture, which Marlowe exploited according to his gifts. That he did not raise all the material to the same exalted level indicates the limited range of his genius, and the best that may be said of these scenes of low comedy is that however frivolous, they are not on that account altogether tedious. Much more instructive is the fact that the same exploitation of scenic illusion underlies the farcical episodes and the scenes of great tragic intensity alike.

The vision of Helen is remembered for the brilliance of Faustus' invocation. Yet this scene depends too upon the presentation of magic in terms of theatrical spectacle. From its context the rapturous hymn to beauty gains a richness of meaning and implication which eludes us if we read it as a detachable piece of lyric verse:

> Was this the face that launch'd a thousand ships
> And burnt the topless towers of Ilium?
> Sweet Helen, make me immortal with a kiss.
> Her lips suck forth my soul: see where it flies!
> Come, Helen, come, give me my soul again. /62/
> Here will I dwell, for heaven is in these lips,
> And all is dross that is not Helena.
> I will be Paris, and for love of thee
> Instead of Troy, shall Wittenberg be sack'd,
> And I will combat with weak Menelaus
> And wear thy colours on my plumed crest,
> Yea, I will wound Achilles in the heel
> And then return to Helen for a kiss.
> O, thou art fairer than the evening air
> Clad in the beauty of a thousand stars,
> Brighter art thou than flaming Jupiter
> When he appear'd to hapless Semele,
> More lovely than the monarch of the sky
> In wanton Arethusa's azur'd arms,
> And none but thou shalt be my paramour.

[V, i, 99–118]

The speech is wonderfully articulated in three sweeping movements, the second strophe beginning with that evocation of the heroic world which reaches a minor climax in returning "to

Helen for a kiss" before the final strophe takes flight to a yet more ecstatic pitch. Faustus commences, we notice, with a tribute to the power of beauty, as though he recognises in Helen's charms an enchantment akin to his own demonic powers. The properties of magic communicate themselves through the poetry, which in its imagery and rhythm first transforms Faustus and Wittenberg into Paris and Troy, and then metamorphoses Helen and her lover into gods. Here in the final part of the speech there is a curious reversal of rôles implied in the images: Helen's appearance before Faustus is compared to that of Jupiter to Semele, and that of Apollo to Arethusa. In each case the literal sense assets that Helen's beauty is figured in the male god, but the inclusion of Semele and "wanton Arethusa" assist the transposition which we naturally make, so that what we actually understand by these lines is that Faustus has himself assumed the majesty (and immortality) of the gods, while Helen really takes her place with the nymphs. It is a subtle effect, a species of enchantment that not only deifies but also suggests a sexual metamorphosis in the union with Helen.

Faustus' poetry invests Helen and himself with mythological splendour; it lifts them into another dimension of illusion, and clothes the nakedness of the stage. It is a kind of speech used on several occasions by Shakespeare, whenever the presence of a character was of itself insufficient to create the heightened awareness and romantic mood he required. So Romeo identifies the vision of Juliet at her balcony with the beauty of the stars, in a speech which simultaneously lends to Juliet an added loveliness and creates the necessary setting of night; Portia is transformed to a fabulous treasure in Bassanio's words, even before we have seen her,

> . . . the four winds blow in from every coast
> Renowned suitors, and her sunny locks /63/
> Hang on her temples like a golden fleece,
> Which makes her seat of Belmont Colchos' strand,
> And many Jasons come in quest of her . . .;

and, most magical of all, the silent Hermoine is at last restored to her husband, transformed to a statue, before she becomes alive indeed: a double metamorphosis. Faustus' verbal transfiguration of Helen may help to disguise the limitations of the boy actor,

but as the rhapsodic verse sweeps us from Bankside and Wittenberg to the Golden Age, we become aware of an undertone of
dramatic irony which runs counter to the soaring curve of his vision. His very urgency, while it impels our imaginative participa-
tion, yet betrays his desperation; there is no mistaking the an-
guished recollection of his bond in the cry,

> Sweet Helen, make me immortal with a kiss,

or the hint in the succeeding lines that Helen is a phantom, a
demonic spirit who would indeed suck forth his soul:

> Here will I dwell, for *heaven* is in these lips,
> And all is *dross* that is not Helena.

The ironies reveal a lurking horror even to those spectators who
failed to recall the *Metamorphoses* of Ovid, where Semele was
reduced to ashes by her heavenly visitor, and where the embrace
of Arethusa was unattainable, since she was transformed into rip-
pling water to evade the lustful clutches of Alpheus. The dramatic
excitement in the speech is generated entirely in terms of illusion: we are made to confess to both the glamour and the sham
of the vision, for each have a "reality" of their own. The tragic
insight depends upon this double awareness.

Marlowe skilfully manages the foreboding which now gathers
over the closing episodes of the play. Faustus' farewell to the
scholars is well placed as a subdued and elegiac prose prelude to
the catastrophe, that sustained soliloquy which by a staggering
tour de force keys the emotional pitch of the tragedy to almost
unendurable climax. In sheer virtuosity there was nothing in Elizabethan drama to match Faustus' last speech for several years to
come. The kind of advance in the technique of the soliloquy
which it represents can be measured by comparing it with the
soliloquy at the opening of the play. There Faustus' rejection of
legitimate studies is displayed in a schematised logical progres-
sion which summarises and crystallises the steps which led him to
necromancy. The speech is evidently contrived, and within its
conventions it does not require us to suppose that it represents
any particular moment in Faustus' psychological history. The
conception of the final soliloquy is radically different: it does
move in the plane of time, as the stark simplicity of the first mono-

ςyllables announces:

> Ah, Faustus,
> Now hast thou but one bare hour to live.   [V, ii, 130–1] /64/

The effects Marlowe is striving for here are those of spontaneity; the conception is much more inward, and dramatises the fleeting thoughts as though they were actually passing through Faustus' mind at the time. Instead of the predictable controlled development of the opening soliloquy, here are confusion and contradiction, the very process of the struggle to come to terms with the situation. Of course, the deliberate preconceived movement of the earlier speech befits our impression of the confident Faustus which the beginning of the play requires, and the action must open on a comparatively low emotional pitch, while at the catastrophe the situation demands a frantic and desperate Faustus, and high tension. But the soliloquies are not accounted for in terms of their contexts alone: there is an essential difference in their dramatic representation of inner processes. In the final speech, Marlowe created what was virtually a new vehicle for articulating with immediacy the flux and uncertainty of a mind under pressure. It is only the exaggeration of this vital difference to say that previous soliloquies demanded an orator, while this calls for an actor. As an attempt to turn the speech of distraction into poetry, Faustus' last soliloquy has affinities with Kyd's development of Senecan rhetoric, particularly in his invention of stage madness as an occasion for wild and whirling words.

The licence Marlowe boldly permits himself with metre here is the fundamental means of creating an impression of bursts of rapid speech punctuated by irregular pauses. Figures of repetition, like "Fair nature's eye, rise, rise again", "See, see, where Christ's blood . . .", "Mountains and hills, come, come", and climatic constructions, such as

> The stars move still, time runs, the clock will strike,
> The devil will come, and Faustus must be damn'd.
>
> [V, ii, 140–1]

allow the poetry to take wing, until the flight is sharply arrested often by means of a heavy caesura. A static delivery is impossible, and the strenuous vehemence carried by the disjointed verse insists upon the physical movements implied by the sense. It is impossible to give full weight to "O, I'll leap up to my God! Who pulls me down?" with the same gesture as in

> Then will I headlong run into the earth.
> Earth, gape! O, no, it will not harbour me.
> [V, ii, 152–3]

The chimes of the clock are a further cue for action, and this device illustrates how Marlowe succeeds in organically relating the speech to the stage, compared with the static and perhaps literally sedate character of the opening soliloquy. This final scene has returned to Faustus' study, where the play began; yet however localised, the swift transitions which the soliloquy makes in its verbal imagery, from the heavens and planets, to the earth with her mountains and thence to the ugly gaping of hell-mouth, seem to conjure the whole creation to witness the catastrophe. It is a magnificent recollection /65/ of the medieval stage which transforms Faustus' study into a microcosm.

This is the supreme example of Marlowe's ability to create dramatic illusion through his poetry. Faustus' flights into other magical realms, away from the here and now, have in earlier scenes been the dramatic occasions for extending the fixed "realities" of the stage into the imaginary dimensions of poetry. The resources of the dramatist have corresponded to those of the magician. Not elation but terror now inspires Faustus' vision of all that lies beyond the physical boundaries of the stage. He conjures the elements in vain, and even if Marlowe's groundlings failed to applaud the full brilliance of giving such a strange context to a line from Ovid, "O lente, lente currite, noctis equi" they would nevertheless recognise in the Latin another esoteric piece of sorcery, which it is. Faustus' magic is no longer of any help to him, but in the imagery of his lines we as spectators seem to become part of a cosmic audience attending his last hour. The theatre scarcely seems able to contain the scene, and yet, paradoxically, Faustus' utter helplessness conveys an almost claustrophobic awareness of confinement, as though the study is a cage from which he is frantically trying to escape.

One cannot say which is the more "real", the illusion of a vast scene embracing heaven, earth and hell, or the illusion of a stage that has shrunk to cramping dimensions. But both are mutually dependent. Faustus is at bay, trapped in a corner, and yet his end is a universal drama. The dramatic effect, perfectly accommodated to the physical conditions of the Elizabethan stage, is derived principally from Marlowe's solution to the problems of space and time, the same problems which neo-classicism solved in terms of the unities. The awareness of Faustus' existence in these two simultaneous illusions of space generates tremendous dramatic tension and corresponds to a similar duality in the plane of time, each equally illusory. Faustus is now trapped by the clock, and by a bold theatrical device time passes with unerring swiftness: the minutes have diminished to seconds, just as the stage seems to have contracted, and closed in upon the doomed man. Yet we are intensely aware too of timeless infinity, of the imminence of perpetual damnation. The whole tragic conflict is epitomised and crowded into this final scene, for these contrary tensions dramatise that antithesis between human and superhuman for which Marlowe saw no certain reconciliation.

Doctor Faustus in its own time considerably extended the range of dramatic techniques, and it is not surprising that the play had its imitators. The treatment of necromancy in Greene's *Friar Bacon and Friar Bungay,* and Shakespeare's *Henry VI Part 2* (where Margery Jourdain the witch is introduced), merely exploit the unsophisticated appeal of spectacular conjuring tricks, but Shakespeare also made an unsuccessful attempt to reproduce the effects of Faustus' last soliloquy in Richard the Third's speech on the eve of his defeat: /66/

> Have mercy, Jesu! Soft! I did but dream.
> O coward conscience, how thou dost afflict me!
> The lights burn blue. It is now dead midnight.
> Cold fearful drops stand on my trembling flesh.
> What do I fear? Myself? There's none else by.
> Richard loves Richard; that is, I am I.
> Is there a murderer here? No—yes, I am.
> Then fly. What, from myself? Great reason why—
> Lest I revenge. What, myself upon myself?
> Alack, I love myself. Wherefore? For any good
> That I myself have done unto myself?
> O no! Alas, I rather hate myself
> For hateful deeds committed by myself . . .

There is ample evidence that the popularity of *Doctor Faustus*

survived the turn of the century, and even Jonson's *Alchemist*
pays homage to Marlowe's play, reducing the theme to comic
terms by presenting the illusion of magic power as a series of delusions: Sir Epicure Mammon's luxurious fantasies are doubtless
meant to parody the rhapsodic poetry of Faustus. Ultimately,
however, it was Shakespeare who learned most from Marlowe's
exploitation of theatrical illusion, and he developed the dramatic ideas found in *Doctor Faustus* nowhere more effectively than
in *Macbeth* and *The Tempest*. The fear and guilt that haunt
Macbeth and his wife through their soliloquies and hallucina-
tions transform the stage to a nightmare world that supplants
"reality", "and nothing is but what is not". As Faustus was
shown the pageant of the Seven Deadly Sins, so the witches reveal the procession of phantom kings before Macbeth. In *The
Tempest,* however, the powers of magic are not satanic: Prospero's virtue is a condition of his art, which he employs in the
cause of merciful justice. The image of the stage itself as a magic
circle becomes explicit in the closing lines of Prospero's Epilogue,
and we may not be deceived if we catch an echo of that earlier magician in his words:

> Now I want
> Spirits to enforce, art to enchant;
> And my ending is despair
> Unless I be reliev'd by prayer,
> Which pierces so that it assaults
> Mercy itself, and frees all faults.
> As you from crimes would pardon'd be,
> Let your indulgence set me free.

The conceit is well-turned, for the spectators are here reminded
of the necessary part they themselves bear in working the enchantment. Shakespeare bade farewell to the theatre with a play
that celebrated his own art through the nobility and virtue of a
magician. What better tribute could be paid to Marlowe, whose
Faustus was damned, but whose genius redeemed the magic of
stage illusion from the censure that it lacked both dignity and
beauty. /67/

Selected Bibliography

Bevington, David M. *From Mankind to Marlowe: Growth of Structure in the Popular Drama of Tudor England.* Cambridge, Massachusetts, 1962, pp 245–62.

Brooke, Nicholas. "The Moral Tragedy of Doctor Faustus." *Cambridge Journal,* VII (1952), 662–87.

Campbell, Lily B. "Dr. Faustus: A Case of Conscience." *Publication of the Modern Language Association of America,* LXVII (1952), 219–39.

Cole, Douglas. *Suffering and Evil in the Plays of Christopher Marlowe.* Princeton, 1962, pp. 191–264.

Davidson, Clifford. "Doctor Faustus of Wittenberg." *Studies in Philology,* LIX (1962), 514–23.

Frye, R. M. "Marlowe's *Doctor Faustus:* The Repudiation of Humanity." *South Atlantic Quarterly,* LV (1956), 322–28.

Hunter, G. K. "Five Act Structure in *Doctor Faustus." Tulane Drama Review,* VIII (1964), 77–91.

Kaula, David. "Time and the Timeless in *Everyman* and *Doctor Faustus." College English,* XXII (1960), 9–14.

Kocher, Paul H. *Christopher Marlowe, a Study of His Thought, Learning and Character.* Chapel Hill, 1946.

Kocher, Paul H. "The Witchcraft Basis in Marlowe's *Faustus." Modern Philology,* XXXVIII (1940), 9–36.

McCloskey, John C. "The Theme of Despair in Marlowe's *Faustus." College English,* IV (1942), 110–13.

McCullen, Joseph T. "Dr. Faustus and Renaissance Learning." *Modern Language Review,* LI (1956), 6–16.

Mizener, Arthur. "The Tragedy of Marlowe's *Doctor Faustus." College English,* V (1943), 70–5.

Morris, Harry. "Marlowe's Poetry." *Tulane Drama Review,* VIII (1964), 134–54.

Ribner, Irving. "Marlowe and Shakespeare." *Shakespeare Quarterly,* XV (1964), 41–53.

Ribner, Irving. "Marlowe and the Critics." *Tulane Drama Review,* VIII (1964), 211–15.

Ribner, Irving. "Marlowe's 'Tragicke Glasse.' " in *Essays on Shakespeare and Elizabethan Drama in Honor of Hardin Craig.* Ed. R. M. Hosley. (Columbia, Missouri, 1962), pp. 91–114.

Sachs, Arieh. "The Religious Despair of Doctor Faustus." *Journal of English and Germanic Philology*, LXIII (1964), 625–47.

Smith, James. "Marlowe's *Dr. Faustus.*" *Scrutiny*, VIII (1930), pp. 36–55.

Steane, J. B. *Marlowe: A Critical Study*. Cambridge, 1964, pp. 117–65.

Westlund, Joseph. "The Orthodox Christian Framework of Marlowe's *Faustus.*" *Studies in English Literature*, III (1963), 191–205.

Wilson, F. P. *Marlowe and the Early Shakespeare*. Oxford, 1953, pp. 68–85.